Radio in the Global Age

For Henrietta

Radio in the
Global Age

David Hendy

Polity Press

First published in 2000 by Polity Press in association with Blackwell Publishers Ltd.

Editorial office:
Polity Press
65 Bridge Street
Cambridge CB2 1UR, UK

Marketing and production:
Blackwell Publishers Ltd
108 Cowley Road
Oxford OX4 1JF, UK

Published in the USA by
Blackwell Publishers Inc.
Commerce Place
350 Main Street
Malden, MA 02148, USA

Library of Congress Cataloging-in-Publication Data
Hendy, David.
    Radio in the global age / David Hendy.
       p.   cm.
    Includes bibliographical references and index.
    ISBN 0-7456-2068-X—ISBN 0-7456-2069-8 (paper)
    1. Radio broadcasting.   I. Title.
HE8694.H45   2000
384.54—dc21
Typeset in 10.5 on 12 pt Plantin
by Best-set Typesetter Ltd., Hong Kong
Printed in Great Britain by T.J. International Limited, Padstow, Cornwall

This book is printed on acid-free paper.

Contents

Figures

Tables

Boxes

Abbreviations

ABC	Australian Broadcasting Corporation
AOR	Adult (or Album) Orientated Rock
BBC	British Broadcasting Corporation
CBC	Canadian Broadcasting Corporation
CHR	Contemporary Hit Radio
CPBS	Central People's Broadcasting Station (China)
CRCA	Commercial Radio Companies Association
CRN	Canadian Radio Networks
DAB	Digital Audio Broadcasting
ENPS	Electronic News Production System
ENPSN	Electronic News Production System Newsletter
FCC	Federal Communications Commission
IRN	Independent Radio News
MCPS	Mechanical Copyright Protection Society
MOR	Middle of the Road
NAC	New Adult Contemporary
NERA	National Economic Research Associates
NPR	National Public Radio
ORF	Österreicher Rundfunk
OTH	Opportunities to Hear
PPL	Phonographic Performance Limited
PRS	Performing Rights Society
RAJAR	Radio Joint Audience Research
RSL	Radio Services Limited
RTLM	Radio Télévision Libre Milles Collines
SABC	South African Broadcasting Corporation
Soft AC	Soft Adult Contemporary
VOA	Voice of America

Acknowledgements

Very many friends and colleagues have helped me with this book at various stages. My first debt is to colleagues in the School of Communication, Design and Media at the University of Westminster – those who offered feedback on earlier drafts, who provided encouragement, or who simply enabled me to have the time off normal teaching duties in order to write it. Paddy Scannell and Peter Goodwin have my thanks in particular, but also Dave Laing, John Tulloch, Norton York, Jim Latham, Michael Dodd and Tim Carter. There is a growing sense of the importance of radio in academic study, perhaps illustrated most recently by the founding of the UK's 'Radio Studies Network': it provides a valuable source of ideas and help beyond the traditional walls of a single university department, and I have benefited directly from discussions with Peter Lewis, Tim Wall, Ken Garner, Eryl Price-Davies and Tim Crook in particular. I also owe thanks to my students over the past six years. They have taught me far more than they realize, and working with them has allowed me to test ideas, helped me change some of my assumptions and expand my horizons. I have been supported and helped, too, by all those at Polity Press – John Thompson, Gill Motley, Lynn Dunlop, Pamela Thomas and Debbie Seymour in particular – who have shown patience and professionalism throughout the process of putting this book together. I should also thank the anonymous Polity readers who made several valuable suggestions which have helped me to improve upon an earlier draft.

Though the book draws on much academic literature, it would have been impossible to write without the help, advice, discussions and interviews I have been able to have over the past year or two with

many people in the radio industry. In the BBC, this includes Chris
Lycett, Jeff Smith, Ian Parkinson, Wendy Pilmer, Matthew Bannister
and staff in the Corporate Press Office, BBC Radio International,
and BBC Digital Radio. Others who have helped me a great deal
include three producers in particular – Piers Plowright, Matt Thompson of Loftus Productions and Jefferson Graham, formerly of the
Independent Radio Group – as well as Samantha Moy from Somethin' Else, Wendy Marr from Ladbroke Productions, Sue Clarke,
Stewart Clark from Music Alliance, Susan Smith from Digital One,
Dr Gary Heller from Radio and Records Online in Los Angeles,
Mike Powell from UKRD and Julie Unsworth from WorldDAB
Forum.

All these people have helped in numerous ways, but my biggest
debt is to my family, who have put up with many months of me being
in a distracted and neglectful mood. So let me here thank Eloise and
Morgan – who are both young enough still to be mystified by the
voices coming from their father's radio sets – and, above all, Henrietta, who has been unstinting in her support and encouragement
from beginning to end. To her I dedicate this book in friendship and
love.

The author and publishers wish to thank the following for permission to use copyright material: National Economic Research
Associates for figure 1.1 from NERA 1998: *Report on UK Commercial Radio's Future: Final Report*, p. 18; Radio and Records and Dr
Gary Heller for figure 1.2 from 'National Format Shares' in *Radio
and Records Ratings Directory: Ratings, Industry Directory & Program
Supplier Guide*, vol. 2, Los Angeles: Radio and Records, p. 9 (Copyright © 1999 Radio and Records, Inc. reprinted by permission);
Taylor & Francis Group/ITPS Ltd for figure 1.3 from Wallis, R. and
Malm, K. 1993, From State Monopoly to Commercial Oligopoly:
European Broadcasting Policies and Popular Music Output Over the
Airwaves, in T. Bennett, S. Frith, L. Grossberg, J. Shephard, and G.
Turner (eds), *Rock and Popular Music: Politics, Policies, Institutions*,
London: Routledge, p. 165, and for box 4.1 and several other extracts
from Crisell, A. 1994, *Understanding Radio*, 2nd edn, London: Routledge, p. 50 and others; World DAB Forum for figure 1.4; Reed Educational and Professional Publishing Ltd., for figure 2.1 from
McLeish, R. 1994, Radio Production, 3rd edn, Focal Press, p. 159,
and for table 2.1 which draws upon data in Keith, M. C. 1997, *The
Radio Station*, 4th edn, Focal Press, pp. 70–83; BBC Radio for
extracts from their *Radio 4 Commissioning Guidelines 1997/8*, reproduced in figure 2.2 and box 3.1; SAGE Publications Ltd for box 4.2,
which includes extracts from Higgins, C. S. and Moss, P. D. 1984,
Radio Voices, in *Media, Culture & Society*, volume 6, pp. 353–75; Dr

Tim Wall of the University of Central England for box 4.3, which is extracted from *The Meanings of Black and Dance Music in Contemporary Music Radio*, a paper delivered to the Third Triennial British Musicological Societies' Conference, University of Surrey, Guildford, July 1999; *The Observer*, for box 5.2, which reproduces a news report, 'Rockers issue writ to regain status', by Michael Ellison in *The Guardian*, 1 March 1996, p. 2.

Parts of my discussion of radio, music and cultural change in chapter five are drawn from original research which is due to be published more extensively in the journal *Media, Culture & Society* in November 2000 in an article provisionally titled 'Pop music radio in the public service: BBC Radio 1 and new music in the 1990s'; similarly, parts of my discussion of digital broadcasting appear in more extensive form in the USA in the May 2000 edition of the *Journal of Radio Studies*.

Introduction

Radio in the social landscape

Marshall McLuhan famously described radio as a 'hot' medium. Calling some media 'hot' and others – like television – 'cool' was the sort of grand concept which helped make McLuhan's name in the 1960s. And nearly forty years on the idea remains striking in its originality. But not, I would say, entirely convincing. For a start, his classification now seems rather topsy-turvy. Take his definition of television. It is 'cool', he suggested, because it gives us a 'low definition' sense of the world: the information it provides is meagre, unclear, equivocal. It is, so to speak, like a cartoon compared with a photograph – a mere outline. Radio, however, is 'hot' because it is just like a fully-fledged photograph – it 'extends one single sense in "high definition"'. This all makes radio sound rather powerful. But that was not McLuhan's view. He saw the future belonging to 'cool' media like television. People in the late twentieth century, he suggested, *want* room in their lives for differences, ambiguities, alternative interpretations – and would therefore reject radio's over-heated certainties – certainties which set fire to all ambivalence. So McLuhan believed that radio's time would pass – it would gradually be displaced by the 'cool' media of the electronic revolution, media which do not privilege any voice or point of view (McLuhan 1994; Cashmore and Rojek 1999: 332–4).

Today, though, it appears to many observers that it is television which gives us the world in 'high-definition', with its vivid images overpowering us, casting us into a role as passive observers of the world. The rhetoric surrounding radio, however, is suffused with the language of McLuhan's cool ambiguity. We talk of radio's ability to 'stimulate the mind's eye' – that in giving us a sense of the world that is entirely lacking in any visual clues, it demands *more*, not less, audience participation (Crisell 1994; Shingler and Wieringa 1998). We talk of radio's ability to keep us company, even to draw us into new relationships, by building up a sense of intimacy with broadcasters and fellow listeners (Douglas 1999). We talk of its ability to be a wider window on the world, to mark out a discursive space where people's voices can be heard and a debate sustained in a way that makes the world and all the people in it somehow more tangible, more *real* (Scannell 1996). We even talk of its powers of emancipation – a cheap and technically easy medium to master, allowing people otherwise excluded from the mainstream media a voice and a role, a real chance of interpreting the world for themselves (O'Connor 1990; Lloréns 1991; Hochheimer 1993).

And radio does not seem to be facing extinction at the hands of television either. There is a lot of it around. Some 9,000 stations across Europe, another 11,000 or so in the USA, many thousands more in Latin America, and growing numbers in Asia, Africa and Australasia – perhaps somewhere in the region of 40,000 or more stations worldwide when various community stations and pirates are also taken into account. This is much, much higher than the number of television stations worldwide. And while television is an experience still fixed largely in the home, we listen to all this radio in more circumstances and in more places around the world: on a personal stereo as we walk or jog down the street, in the car when we travel to work, in the house while we prepare our meals. In the developing world, radio is a conveniently cheap and portable medium wherever poverty and the absence of an electricity supply places television beyond the reach of most people. It is also a conveniently oral medium wherever literacy is low. Unsurprisingly, then, the number of radio receivers owned in many parts of Africa and Asia is many, many times more than the number of television sets. Radio 'remains the world's most ubiquitous medium, certainly the one with the widest reach and greatest penetration' (Pease and Dennis 1993: xii).

Despite – or perhaps *because of* – this pervasive quality, radio is for those of us in the developed world a taken-for-granted part of our lives. We probably have four or five sets positioned around our homes, and most of us listen for about three hours each day – almost as much time as we spend watching television. We use it – and generally trust it – for news and information about the world, and in the USA talk-radio galvanizes public opinion and influences policy-makers. We talk *to* it, apparently finding it easier sometimes to call radio phone-ins and confide in an anonymous listening audience than in our own friends and family. Above all, perhaps, we listen to it – even sing along to it – in its role as the world's most ubiquitous transmitter of recorded pop music. Even as McLuhan first espoused his theory of 'hot' and 'cold' media in 1964, radio was reinventing itself as *the* medium for music and for teenagers, where the young could listen to *their* music on cheap portable transistors away from the rest of the family (Douglas 1999; Fornatale and Mills 1980; Barnard 1989). Nearly four decades on, the repertoire of pop music is infinitely bigger, and the explosion in the number of radio stations appears to offer all of us, from the very young to the very old, the chance to tune in to *our* music. In the constellation of radio services at the start of the new millennium, we cannot help but feel that there is something for everyone.

Yet we do not wonder in awe at this medium any more – why should we when it is simply there in the background, almost all the time? And we don't read or hear about the radio medium very much either – it rarely makes the front pages, rarely arouses the same sort of heated debates over say, violence or sex or sensationalism, that television seems to engender. It has its stars – the odd Chris Evans here or Howard Stern there – but it is mostly not an industry of big stars, or big money, or big corporate players. It is relatively prosperous – a fast-expanding area of advertising and a sector prone to frenzied take-overs – but in the media pond it is still an economic minnow, and in society as a whole it is largely ignored. In short, its profile in the social landscape is small and its *influence* large.

This introduction is not a manifesto for triumphalism, though. And the book as a whole is not a *celebration* of radio. Certainly, were McLuhan to be alive today he might be forced to admit that radio not only survives, it often thrives. But this, really, is beside the point. The critical question is, what *sort* of radio do we have nowadays? And what role does it play in contemporary society? Another Canadian, Jody Berland, writing almost exactly thirty years after her compatriot McLuhan, looked around her and was struck by the ubiquity, not so much of radio in general, but of one form of radio in particular, namely commercially funded and highly formatted music radio. This, she argues:

> place[s] together sound messages that are disparate in terms of their location of origin, their cultural purpose, and their form, in order to create a continuous enveloping rhythm of sound and information. The rhythm's 'reason' isn't about insight, originality, history, logic or emancipation. It's about the market. Since the continuous rhythm of sound is more powerful than any single item enveloped in its progression, the reception of particular items is substantially determined by the larger

discourse of radio programming, which teaches us addiction and for-getfulness. In commercial radio, the pleasures of location and identity, of specific recognitions or discoveries, are sacrificed to the (real) plea-sures of the media's 'boundless hospitality,' which defends itself against anarchy by being totalitarian in its mode of address and in its struc-turing of programme, genre, and rhythm. (1993b: 211)

There are interesting echoes here. What Berland sees as radio's 'totalitarian mode of address' conveys something of McLuhan's 'hot' media which extend 'one sense in "high-definition"' (1994: 22). Berland's listeners are overwhelmed, again much like McLuhan's are excluded by the complete lack of ambivalence in a medium's message. Berland's answer to the question, what sort of radio do we have nowadays, suggests that although we might have travelled a long way since 1964, we might have ended up somewhere close to where we began. The American author Susan Douglas puts it in similar, though perhaps more vividly personal terms:

Whether you're in Providence or Albuquerque, the music . . . is the same. . . . Formats allow us to seek out a monotone mood with only the tiniest surprises. . . . DJs differ in 'their sense of where things are headed. Some feel that the industry is so powerfully centralized and consolidated, so in the grip of [audience] research, consultants, and investment groups, that insurgencies are no longer possible. They are pessimistic that radio stations will ever again regard listeners as music lovers instead of niche markets. They note that those, especially young people, who are looking for community-building communication tech-nologies that allow for independent, unconventional expression, are deserting radio for the Internet. . . . But I, and millions like me, don't have a radio station to listen to anymore. (1999: 347, 354, 356)

Douglas surveys a media landscape changed almost beyond recog-nition since the early 1960s. Radio in America has always been run on commercial lines, of course, in contrast to the more pluralist mix of commercial, state-controlled and public-service stations across` Europe and elsewhere. But, as Blumler describes it, in using a term borrowed from the economist Joseph Schumpeter, there has been 'a gale of destruction' unleashed on electronic media systems through-out the advanced industrial world in the last three decades (1991: 194). A relatively stable pattern, in which a large number of small commercial local radio stations, perhaps co-existing with some national networks, and broadcasting a fairly wide range of program-ming to mass audiences, has been disturbed. State regulation has given way in leaps and starts to market regulation, and technologi-cal changes – satellite delivery systems, automation, computerization

and so on – have unleashed a quickening process of change in contemporary society as a whole. One recurring aspect of these changes
is the sense in which the world is 'rapidly being moulded into a shared
social space', and 'globalization' is the conveniently permeable term
often employed to encompass this process in all its aspects. Globalization, as many writers warn, is a term in danger of becoming the
cliche of our times, but it does perhaps 'capture some of the lived
experience of an epoch' – an experience characterized by 'the widen-
ing, deepening and speeding up of worldwide interconnectedness'
(Held et al. 1999: 1–2).

Radio, so long thought of as a predominantly local medium, would
appear at first to fit rather uneasily within this broader debate. But
if this book has a unifying theme it is this: that radio, though very
often local, and so very cheap and easy to set up for oneself, and with
so many qualities all of its own, is *nonetheless* a medium that is fully
part of the electronic mass-media environment. It may have different qualities to television – most obviously that it is a *sound*-based
medium, not a visual one – but it is similarly engaged in the task of
mass-producing something called 'broadcasting', a time-based activity, domestic in scale and rapid in turnover, pulling together news,
information, entertainment, music and so on day-after-day and year-
after-year. It may be television's poor relation, but there is still money
to be made in radio, and many of the same processes – the growth
of multinational corporations, the splitting of audiences into niche
markets, the drive to reduce costs and maximize profits – can, I think,
be used to explain many of its characteristics. It may evoke nostalgic
associations with the music of our youth or a harmless amateurism
characterized by radio 'hams', community stations and heroic pirates,
or even a spirit of experimentation and artistry in sound, but it is
first and foremost an industry – an industry that may bring pleasure
and contribute much to our cultural life, but an industry all the same,
and one with global dimensions and a global reach that gives it an
influential place in shaping our cultural lives. It is a medium I love
– a medium I know a little personally from the inside – but focussing
on its 'unique' qualities, even talking too much of a 'Golden Age' of
radio, as many aficionados are tempted to do, would be to do it a
disservice, I think: it would make it *too* special, *too* different, and as
a result keep it rather isolated from interesting contemporary debates.

Radio, then, needs to be reconnected with the mainstream of
media and communication studies. It is a medium through which
we can explore issues of policy, technology, identity, ideology and
culture, just as fruitfully as by studying the other media – television,
cinema or the press. Our efforts, though, must have one clear proviso.
We cannot jump from accepting radio's relevance in broader media

debates towards any attempt at a 'Grand Theory' of radio. Perhaps such an attempt would be dangerous enough for *any* of the mass-media, but for radio it is particularly unwise. First, the sheer *quantity* of radio around us presents an insurmountable empirical task: a lifetime's study would not allow us to listen to more than a fraction of output, so any analysis will end up being very partial. Secondly, the *range* of activity at any given time, too, is huge – tiny pirate and community stations, so-called 'micro'-radio stations, large national networks, multinational satellite services, syndicated chains and groups, a burgeoning number of Internet-only radio stations – all broadcasting almost anything from non-stop urban rap to business-news: these strikingly different phenomena cannot easily be grouped under the one heading of 'radio' and *explained* in the same way. Thirdly, radio can sometimes be an extraordinarily *dynamic* medium – changing too quickly to let us 'see' it properly. Douglas talks of radio's 'technical insurgency', of how, because 'corporate control is never complete' in such a do-it-yourself technology, it has reinvented itself so frequently:

> It was just at those moments when programming seemed so fixed – in the late 1940s and early 1950s, and again in the late 1960s and early 1970s – that off in the audio hinterlands programming insurgencies revolutionized what we heard on the air. When social movements and radio have intersected, previously forbidden and thus thrilling listening possibilities have emerged. (1999: 357)

Radio, then, is simultaneously more taken-for-granted than television and paradoxically a larger, more diverse, more changeable, field of study. I will not, then, offer a theory of radio here, nor even attempt anything approaching a comprehensive global survey.

What I *do* hope to achieve in the space of this book are two things. First, to sketch out some connections between the many tightly-focussed 'micro' studies of particular radio stations or programmes around the world with some of the 'macro' ideas contained in more general studies of media, communication and society. It sometimes involves a leap of faith to discuss in the same breath American and British radio, let alone aboriginal radio in Australia and pop music on the Internet. Nonetheless, to do so reminds us that some more systematic attempt at what Beck (1998) calls 'mid-level' study needs to be made of radio in the future. It also reminds us, perhaps, that not all radio is the radio that *we* listen to, or would even *like* to listen to. Secondly, despite the complexity with which I have characterized the radio landscape as a whole, I hope to draw out some of the central paradoxes of the medium. Recurring themes are discernible. One dichotomy which weaves itself through the chapters of this book, for example, is that between the 'unifying' powers of a medium like radio, and the ability it apparently has to pull us apart into separate audience 'niches'. Scannell has written extensively on radio's (and television's) ability to carve out a public sphere, not just in an austere political sense but also in terms of providing a space for *shared* fun and sociability (1991, 1996). As radio's technical reach around the globe has expanded, so too has the scope of this public sphere. Globalization makes the world a *smaller* place for those who produce radio – everywhere is within their reach; it simultaneously *expands* the horizons of listeners, who can 'experience' distant events and people and music in a way that previous generations could not. But there is something else happening too. There is a process in which more and more stations help divide the listening communities into a larger number of separate communities, defined it seems by ever narrower tastes in music or talk. We may still listen, Berland intimates, but we 'in fact *hear* less' (1993b: 211). The questions at hand, then, are these: how do such contradictory processes unfold? Does radio connect us with wider 'imagined' communities in a way that somehow frees us from the geography of where we live, or does it take away the 'shared experiences' once regarded as a central feature of broadcasting and that once seemed to bring us together? Does radio in the global age give us a larger window on the world, or expose us dreadfully to the homogenized and banal output of a few multinational media chains and record companies? Is radio as a whole defined by these conflicts, or are we talking of different kinds of radio? We may not be able to answer all these questions, but asking them is a start.

The structure of this book

In talking of 'recurring themes', I hope to suggest that no one aspect of radio can be fully understood without some reference to three interrelated aspects of the medium: first, the ways in which it is *produced*, secondly the form and content of its programming – what media analysis generally calls the medium's *texts* – and thirdly the interpretations and reactions of its consumers, the *listeners*. No discussion of the music played on radio, for example, can make much sense without some parallel discussion of the economic forces at play within the media and music industries. Or, for that matter, without some discussion of the way we listen to radio and extract some meaning from its programmes. In broad terms, then, this book adopts the same structure used by similar studies of popular music and of television (Longhurst 1995; Abercrombie 1996). Except, that is, in one minor respect: that I have preferred to discuss the 'consumption' of radio, the way listeners listen to it, *before* moving on to discuss more directly the meanings attached to its output and its wider cultural impacts. This is not an attempt to 'make a statement', merely to point out that, in radio at least, it appears to me that the listeners – whether as free and active citizens or as more passive members of a mass-audience 'market' – provide such a central perspective on all that follows, that to treat them as mere consumers and not as *in some sense* also the 'producers' of radio is to misunderstand the medium and, so to speak, put the cart before the horse.

Specifically, then, chapter 1 looks at the way radio is produced as an industry, and focuses on the changes taking place which affect production on a large and global scale. Chapter 2 narrows the focus to look at the way radio is produced on a day-to-day basis within stations and programme-teams – in particular, it looks at the way the freedom of radio producers is constrained by a range of aesthetic, financial and organizational factors. Chapter 3 discusses the listeners to radio – *how* we listen, and how the *way* we listen in turn shapes the production of programmes and the meanings they may convey. Chapter 4 attempts to explore some of the innate qualities and meanings that can be attached to various types of radio – and, in particular, to the talk and the music we find commonly broadcast; it also tries to draw together some of the threads of debate on radio's relationship with our sense of time and place in the age of 'modernity'. Finally, chapter 5 is an attempt to map out some of the cultural impacts the medium appears to have in contemporary society in three main areas – in democratic culture, in our sense of identity (whether defined linguistically, geographically or ethnically), and in its ability to shape our musical tastes.

Though the book as a whole has aspirations to be holistic in tone, it will have many omissions, for all the reasons I have discussed. Even so, the hope is that readers can test some of the specific or abstract ideas explored here against their own radio listening, and alongside the many thousands of programmes and stations I have never listened to, let alone written about.

1

Industry

This chapter aims to analyse the ways in which radio is organized as an industry. This must be a starting point for any analysis of radio as a medium, since the commercial, political and technological context within which radio is produced has a direct bearing on the form and content of the programming that we hear on our radio sets. The major difficulty is that any attempt to characterize the structure of a media industry is to aim at a fast-moving target, since radio, like television, is changing quickly in terms of how it is owned, produced, distributed and consumed. The chapter is therefore designed, not so much to establish the *existing* patterns of radio, but to establish the *dynamic* forces which are shaping the medium at the start of the twenty-first century. First, the chapter offers different ways in which the radio industry can be categorized in global terms. This includes an examination of the basic economics of radio and the way in which this helps define its public or commercial goals. Secondly, it identifies two main forces for change: commercialization and rapid technological development. Many media analyses of the television and film industries have taken ownership as a central issue, arguing that a *concentration* of control into the hands of an ever smaller number of ever larger multinational conglomerates has created *globalized* patterns of production, programming and viewing. Although there are clearly parallel processes at work in the radio industry, exaggerated by many of the technological developments, this chapter will argue that the outcomes are likely to be be somewhat different. The third part of the chapter therefore focusses on how the industry can be understood in terms of two apparently contradictory processes: on the one hand, the *consolidation* of ownership and programme formats into a few dominant 'brands', and on the other hand, the *fragmentation* of radio into what appears at least to be a larger number of stations and new players aiming specialized programming at ever smaller audiences. In so doing, the chapter aims to identify the relevance to radio of certain ideas raised by political economy and cultural theory.

The global structures of radio

The radio industry has always been a relatively small player within the media as a whole. Head and Sterling estimated that in the late 1980s, some 60,000 worked directly in radio in the USA, compared with about 168,000 in broadcast and cable television and more than 900,000 in a single corporation like General Motors (1990: 210–12); by the mid 1990s, the number working in radio had reached more than 100,000, but was also starting to fall again (Keith 1997: 31). In the UK, the number employed was put at about 3,800 in the early 1990s (Woolf and Holly 1994; Murroni et al. 1998) though this appears not to have included those working within the BBC who served both radio and television, nor those in commercial production houses and independent companies, and the real number is now probably nearer 10,000 – still low compared with an estimate of about 36–40,000 employed in the UK television industry (Goodwin 1998: 158–60). And the largest radio operators, if they are not subsumed within bigger broadcasting or media organizations, have significantly smaller turnovers of revenue than their television counterparts: the BBC spends about a quarter of its income on its domestic radio services – typical of similar organizations across Europe, and the sort of funding provided for National Public Radio by the USA's Corporation for Public Broadcasting (Ledbetter 1997: 121). Capital Radio, the UK's richest commercial radio company had an annual turnover of about £78 million in 1996 compared with Carlton Television's £1.67 *billion* (NERA 1998: 21; Carlton 1998: 1). The radio industry in Europe as a whole has an annual turnover of some $8.8 billion – in the USA it is now over $15 billion – though again, these figures are a fraction of the size of that for television (Tyler and Laing 1998: 5; RAB (US) 1999).

Yet, if the profits to be made from radio are relatively modest, the industry is much more pervasive than television. In the USA alone, where there are some 3,500 television services, there are well over 11,000 radio stations – in other words, about three times as many (FCC 1999). Even much smaller countries like Belgium, the Netherlands and Greece have some 500 or 600 radio stations each. There is a decisive economic basis for this profusion: at any level, radio is significantly cheaper to produce than television. One hour of network radio costs the BBC about one-twentieth of the outlay on an hour of network television (see table 1.1). A local commercial station, with smaller overheads, could broadcast 24 hours a day at an average cost of well under £1,000 per hour (Graham 1999). A 'micro-radio' or pirate operator could start transmitting radio with a one-off investment in equipment of little more than one thousand pounds. The radio industry as a whole, then, consumes a much smaller share of resources than the television industry, but produces more output through many, many more outlets.

Industrial sectors

Amid this bewildering array of activity, some general patterns are discernible. One broad distinction that can be drawn is between four overlapping activities in radio – regulation, servicing, broadcasting and production. The regulation of radio springs originally from the need to manage the relatively scarce resource of the world's electromagnetic spectrum so that at the very least there is little or no interference between the signals from different stations. Internationally, the spectrum is managed between countries by the International

Table 1.1 Cost per hour of 'originated' programmes on BBC services: a comparison between network radio and network TV, 1997–8

Radio network	Cost per hour of programming (£)
Radio 1	2,700
Radio 2	3,400
Radio 3	5,200
Radio 4	10,200
Radio 5 Live	5,300
Average	5,360

Television network	Cost per hour of programming (£)
BBC 1	120,000
BBC 2	80,000
Average	100,000

Source: BBC Annual Report and Statement of Accounts, 1997/8

Telecommunication Union, composed of member states. Other international bodies, such as the European Union, have developed telecommunications policies which encompass radio, though again, they are more concerned with controlling transmission than the details of content. Most regulation of radio, however, is by nation states, and it is at this level that the radio industry is shaped by the political and cultural values of governments. Legislation enforced by agencies like the Federal Communications Commission (FCC) in the USA, or the Radio Authority in the UK, controls not just the allocation of frequencies, but also the limits on ownership and rules over much of the content of what is broadcast, such as the amount of news or locally produced material it carries, or requirements for impartiality. This regulation can have a range of overtly political goals, such as reflecting the national culture, increasing choice or ensuring quality standards, but the underlying justification of control remains the notion that the spectrum is a public resource, and must therefore in some sense be made to serve public goals. The apparatus of regulation is small, but decisive, therefore. The radio services sector is much more diffuse, but encompasses radio advertising sales houses which help sell advertising slots, information providers (such as news agencies and travel-news suppliers), transmission and satellite services which lease and manage distribution networks for radio stations, marketing firms and specialist research companies which supply stations with details of listening figures and the lifestyles of their target listeners. Its size is difficult to gauge, but it is likely that wherever radio operators choose to 'slim down' their range of activities and cut support staff in order to concentrate on what they see as their 'core' business, a peripheral service sector will grow to support them.

The most easily defined activities in the radio industry are broadcasting and production. *Broadcasting* involves the control of radio schedules and the actual transmission process, effectively creating the *form* of programming – determining whether in broad terms it will be a general service of speech or music to a wide audience or a more targeted mix designed for a tightly defined group of listeners. It is usually based on a 'licence' to operate for a certain number of years on a specific frequency, from a set of transmitters reaching a clearly defined geographical area. *Production* activity, however, creates the actual audio *content* of these broadcasts, the various programmes themselves, from individual news bulletins and traffic updates to music shows and documentaries, phone-ins and the commercial breaks in-between. Often, these two activities are conducted within the same organization, which might range in size from a small independent local radio station to a large national corporation. But the two activities of broadcasting and production are sometimes quite separate, so that radio stations and national networks simply buy-in and relay 'content' produced elsewhere. Head and Sterling describe how commercial radio stations and networks in the USA see any programme production, not as a source of added revenue, but as an extra and unwanted expense; consequently the American industry is characterized by a clear distinction between the producers of programmes like Rush Limbaugh's or Howard Stern's talk-shows, which are distributed by satellite, and the receiving broadcasters, the so-called 'affiliate' stations, who mix the satellite feeds with local jingles and identifying 'call-signs' to produce a local – and individual – sounding product (1990: 183–250).

Much of the global radio industry employs a mix of these two models, with some production in-house and a variable proportion of content commissioned from outside independent producers. In the UK, a medium-sized independent production company can sell a half-hour programme to a BBC network for between about £2,000 and £7,000, and a syndicated feature across a chain of commercial stations for much the same. Similarly, news providers like the UK's Independent Radio News (IRN) or America's National Public Radio (NPR) receive a subscription fee from every station which takes its service. But in the UK and the rest of Europe the total *size* of this independent production sector is modest simply because the market in programme sales is much more limited in the radio industry than in the television industry. It remains limited geographically by the essentially language-based nature of the medium: whereas a television programme can be dubbed or subtitled for international consumption, a fully-completed radio programme can rarely be syndicated across national boundaries. The BBC's experience illustrates this graphically. It sells some £126 million of programme material overseas in one year, but more than £125 million of this is from the sale of *television* programmes, making it Europe's largest exporter of television programmes (BBC 1998; Mann 1999). BBC radio programmes are sold to more than 100 radio stations around the world, including ones in Latin America, Asia and Africa, as well as the USA, but the majority are minority English-language stations, many of whom are not rich, and the rights for rebroadcast are sold cheaply. Even *within* national markets, the relative ease and low cost of radio production has provided little incentive for broadcasters like the BBC – which represents the largest single part of the UK radio market – to put more than about 13 per cent of its radio programming out to independent production (Murroni et al. 1998: 20). The result of their low economic cost is that, apart from in the USA, most production and broadcasting activity has until now at least remained entwined within each radio station and network, as an *in-house* activity. This explains why independent *production* companies in the UK, like Ginger Media, are keen to secure a controlling interest in radio stations themselves, and are frequently involved in bids for several licences: such *vertical integration* of production and broadcasting activities allows such companies a share in what is still regarded as a radio operator's biggest single asset, namely the licence it holds to broadcast.

Funding and goals

We can, then, view the radio industry in terms of a series of different, but overlapping, sectors. A second way of categorizing the radio industry is to divide it according to the way it is funded and – related to its funding – how it is *motivated*. Motivation in this sense means discerning the goals of the broadcasters at an institutional level, goals which may be broadly economic, political or cultural in character. Here, five models can be identified:

- State radio;
- Underground radio;
- Community radio;
- Public-service radio;
- Commercial radio.

A decade or so ago, UNESCO calculated that state-controlled radio, where there is direct government finance and operational control of broadcasting systems, was the most common form of radio worldwide (Head and Sterling 1990: 492). Its dominance has been lost with the collapse of Soviet communism, but it remains in three guises. First, under existing authoritarian governments, and in parts of the developing world where widespread poverty means that licence fees or advertising revenue would be hard to raise; secondly, many transnational broadcasting services – ranging from operations like the BBC's World Service to underground revolutionary or counter-revolutionary stations – are either indirectly controlled or funded by governments, for cultural or political purposes; thirdly, although many state-run broadcasting monopolies have been privatized over the past few decades, the state still defines the regulatory framework for both private and public-service operators.

Much more widespread globally, though, are the panoply of underground radio stations. They are defined by their illegal status – they transmit without any licence – but their motives vary enormously. They sometimes operate from ships anchored offshore, transmitting from beyond the territorial limits of their target countries; often they are land-based, reaching highly localized urban audiences; more and more are using the Internet as their medium of transmission. Some are drawn by political or cultural goals into a form of so-called *free-radio*, where ignoring obligations to be fair or balanced, or flouting direct censorship is an expression of opposition. Sometimes, as with the French *radio libres* or the Italian 'Autonomia' movement of the late 1970s – this can create a remarkable efflorescence of radio styles and voices.

One of the most striking bursts of activity in recent years has been the appearance of 'micro-broadcasters' in the USA: small, sometimes one-person operations using very low power transmitters the size of a brick and costing perhaps no more than $1,000 to reach a handful of neighbourhoods (Sakolsky and Dunifer 1998: 185). Such stations have, in recent years, provided 'everything from Haitian music in Miami to tenants' rights discussions in Decatur, Illinois' (Croteau and Hoynes 2000: 78–80). When considered altogether, many of these stations have the features of a defined political movement: there is much talk of the principle of free speech as a touchstone; there are networks of support, regular gatherings, and publications which trace a direct lineage with the earliest radical stations, such as San Francisco's Radio Free Berkeley or Bologna's Radio Alice; micro-broadcasters tend to share a clear antipathy to regulators like the FCC and the culture of a commercial mainstream which 'seeks to impose programming . . . using marketing criteria' rather than 'liberating' the airwaves 'on behalf of the voiceless . . . and viewing those waves as treasures in themselves which have unjustly been confiscated and debased by the rich and mighty' (2000: 9). Micro-radio, in short, creates 'new spaces for freedom, self-management . . . and the immediate fulfillment of desire' (2000: 8). There is, then, a conscious projection of a collective identity. But micro-broadcasting can also be seen as a term of convenience which covers quite disparate forms of radio. Many in the 'movement' are quite comfortable with being classified as 'pirates' – it accords well with notions of anti-authoritarianism. Others less so: they are keen to point out that whereas pirates deliberately evade all regulation, micro-radio should be licensed by the FCC and become a legitimate form of community radio. Many, indeed, go to great lengths to ensure that their signals *don't* interfere with those of other legitimate broadcasters. The FCC has dithered in its response to such overtures, switching between outright rejection – some 320 'pirate' stations were closed down in 1997–8 alone (Douglas 1999: 357) – and contemplating the full-scale licensing of micro-power as a new tier of radio in the USA (*NewYork Times* 11 April 1999).

In the meantime, many of the micro-broadcasters in America are, in the eyes of the law at least, radio pirates pure and simple. And it is certainly the case that many micro-stations reflect, not a movement, but a relatively uncoordinated activity which evades regulation simply to ignore expensive licensing and copyright laws and make a little money for the individuals involved through slick and populist programming barely distinguishable from legitimate commercial operators.

Despite the frequent presence of commercial motives, however, pirates can be seen as an index of the success with which legitimate licensed stations are meeting audience demands. There are countless examples of times and places where pirate activity has proliferated in direct response to an overregulated environment. In Austria for example, where radio remained a monopoly of the state broadcaster Österreicher Rundfunk (ORF) until the mid 1990s, many private Austrian business people started a wave of pirate radio stations in neighbouring Hungary and the Czech and Slovak Republics and captured significant numbers of listeners and advertising revenue (Trappel 1997: 9). Here, though, just as with the broader swathe of micro-stations in the USA, the established radio industry is adept at absorbing pirate activity as fast as it appears – perhaps by legitimating its broadcasts through licensing, but just as often by appropriating its music, recruiting the best of its staff, and driving it off the air through tighter enforcement. Even so, a sudden upsurge in pirate activity is often a clear signal to legal operators that they have failed to keep up with consumer tastes – and the fact that this also happens in a highly deregulated radio environment like that in the USA is a clear indication that 'market failure' should not be associated only with state monopolies.

Like pirate radio, 'community' radio can often be seen as a direct response to the inability of mainstream operators to meet audience needs – though in this case, its status is legitimate. Indeed, it can be argued that community radio is merely micro-radio in a legal guise, though perhaps with more of a concern with *communal*, rather than *individual*, rights of expression. It is usually understood to have three characteristics:

■ Smaller in scale than mainstream 'local' radio, so that it can be seen to be 'closer' to its listening community than other forms of radio.
■ More 'participatory' than mainstream radio, staffed more by volunteers drawn from the listening community rather than full-time professionals.
■ Run for the benefit of the local community rather than specifically to make a profit for shareholders.

Again, community radio's democratic and communitarian functions are explored a little further in chapter 5. For now, though, it is useful to note that although community radio in the UK is limited to a few hundred small-scale and temporary licences commonly issued each year to students and hospitals, it is a relatively established part of the radio landscape in other parts of the world. In France, for example, there are now some 500 'associative' stations which are locally based and non-profit making (Tyler and Laing 1998: 67). In Sweden, a large number of 'neighbourhood' radio stations have been established since 1978, with various churches, youth groups and local political parties allocated licenses to broadcast. Though many of these have since faced stiff competition from commercial local stations, they have themselves raised advertising revenue and endured as a distinct sector (Gustafsson and Hultén 1997: 211–13). Again, as with pirate radio, the crucial factor in their survival is the extremely modest start-up costs and running costs, which allow stations to survive on a mixture of voluntary donations and relatively small advertising incomes. Indeed, while most community stations do just *survive*, rather than flourish, the possibility of the FCC licensing hundreds of micro-stations in the USA, and the Radio Authority's recent introduction of permanent 'restricted service' licenses in the UK represents a considerable boost to the sector as a whole, and has raised its public profile. One recent industry report in Britain even concluded that public broadcasting, long dominated by the BBC, should be redefined to specifically include a new layer of community-radio licensees (Murroni et al. 1998: 36).

The two remaining systems, public-service and commercial radio, are the most widespread forms around the world, and are the main focus of the rest of this chapter. Public-service radio differs from state radio in being institutionally insulated from *direct* government control, though still usually dependent on the state for most of its financing. It is most common in parliamentary democracies, such as the UK, western Europe, Australia, Canada, New Zealand and Japan, and its traditional sources of income are either a share in licence fees collected from the public or government grants. Occasionally, stations are funded by subventions from commercial stations, and many more beyond the UK also receive money from advertising.

In practical terms, public-service radio usually follows one of two approaches. Canada's Canadian Broadcasting Corporation (CBC), Japan's national broadcaster NHK and the BBC offer a very broad range of programming, combining popular light entertainment with minority-taste cultural and news programmes, targeted through different services which collectively reach the *whole* population of their countries in terms of age, class and geographical spread. Indeed, the BBC has long been regarded as the classic example of public-service radio: a chartered organization, publicly funded but independent from direct political control as well as commercial pressures. Its philosophy as expressed in its 1992 policy document *Extending Choice* has been to avoid what it describes as the 'cultural ghetto' approach, and reach 'as many people as possible' with output of 'distinction and quality', not with programmes attracting a large audience 'for its own sake' (BBC 1992). In this approach, the licence fee, which is effectively a tax on every household, is sustainable provided that the broadcaster provides 'quality' programmes to a large enough section of the whole population. Garnham (1994) suggests that a 30 per cent audience share is a feasible minimum – a percentage which clearly becomes progressively harder to maintain as the number of rival services expands. In any case, this sort of audience share can only be achieved through a diet which includes many more populist programmes, so public-service radio funded by licence fees has always had to perform a difficult balancing act of populism and elitism.

The alternative model of public-service radio seen in the USA shares with broadcasters like the BBC a commitment to non-commercial goals, defined not simply as the avoidance of profit, but also as embodying a certain civic duty. NPR's original mission statement, for example, spoke of the organization's aim to 'encourage a sense of active, constructive participation rather than apathetic helplessness' (Ledbetter 1997: 117). What makes the American model of public-service radio different, though, is that it is a much less costly service which dispenses with the most popular forms of programme on the basis that they are provided in any case by commercial operators. Instead, it concentrates solely on broadcasting the sort of cultural and information programmes which might otherwise be unavailable. This approach circumvents the criticism of commercial operators, who argue that public-service radio should not try to compete on their territory. But it does so at the price of serving only very small sections of the audience, and becoming marginal to a nation's broadcasting culture. The main challenge of big national corporations like the BBC is to ensure that they can sustain a big enough audience share to ensure they avoid this marginalization.

Our final model, commercial radio, is characterized by ownership being in private hands and stations being run to make a profit. Commercial radio has long been dominant in the USA and much of Latin America, but a combination of more than two decades of deregulation throughout the West and the collapse of the Soviet Union and Eastern bloc regimes has led to a dramatic increase in the proportion of commercially owned radio systems throughout much of the rest of the world. The global radio environment is now predominantly 'pluralist' , with public-service and commercial radio co-existing, though with the commercial sector steadily expanding its share.

All these commercial stations seek very simply to deliver sizable audiences of consumers to those advertisers and sponsors which provide its income. The typical commercial station raises about 15–20 per cent of its income from sponsorship and promotion, in which company brands are attached to programmes and individual features such as travel news and weather forecasts (NERA 1998: 19; 40). The remaining 80–5 per cent comes from advertising, through selling 30-second or 1-minute 'spot' air-time slots (NERA 1998; GWR 1998). Typically, advertisers regard high-spending 16–35 year olds as the most desirable audience, and programmes that appeal to them in large numbers will tend to command higher rates for the advertising slots they contain. A large metropolitan station, like Capital FM in London, could charge close to £1,000 at 1999 prices for a 30-second slot on its popular breakfast programme, and perhaps £166 for an off-peak slot during the night; a primetime slot on a much smaller rural station could bring in about £13 per 30-second slot (Arrow FM 1999). Unsurprisingly, then, commercial radio *as a whole* will tend to favour popular programmes over those which might appeal only to a minority, and it will tend to target heavily populated, rich markets rather than thinly populated poorer markets. This bias towards richer urban markets means, for example, that while each listener in London has access to at least fifteen commercial stations, someone living in or around York has access to just three (NERA 1998: 11).

Whereas public-service radio's reliance on licence fees exposes it to political vicissitudes, commercial radio's reliance on advertising inevitably exposes it to more purely economic ones. A review of the UK's commercial radio sector was made in 1998 by National Economic Research Associates (NERA) on behalf of the industry's trade body, the Commercial Radio Companies Association (CRCA). It confirmed that the fortunes of the commercial radio industry as a whole respond in an exaggerated form to any general economic downturn (see figure 1.1). Slumps tend to affect consumer spending, which in turn decreases the amount of money spent on advertising. A similar pattern emerges in the USA, and at many points since the late 1980s only about *half* the commercial radio stations in either the UK or the US have been making any profit at all. Many in the commercial radio sector frequently complain that this vulnerability to dramatic changes in revenue puts them at a disadvantage against the budgetary certainties enjoyed by public-service organizations. But despite these complaints, and despite undoubted exposure

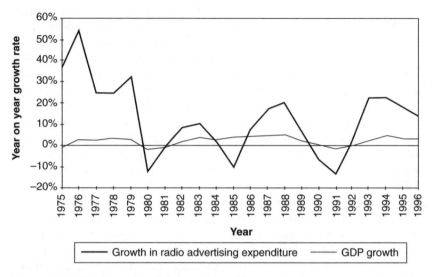

Figure 1.1   Radio advertising expenditure growth compared to GDP (Gross Domestic Product) growth in the UK, 1975–96
Sources: Advertising Statistics Yearbook, 1997, Economic Trends, Office of National Statistics, and reproduced in NERA 1998: 18

to larger cycles of boom and slump, the clear underlying trend is that in the UK and parts of western Europe, commercial radio's total revenues and its share of total advertising spending have both been steadily increasing. A concerted effort was made in the UK throughout the 1990s to raise the profile of radio advertising, against a prevailing view that radio adverts were less well made and less enjoyable than those on television (Barnett and Morrison 1989: 82–90), and radio was marketed as the least expensive and most targeted medium in which to 'publish' (Pease and Dennis 1993: xiii) . This effort clearly paid dividends, since radio was the fastest growing medium for advertising in the UK through most of the 1990s. The problem for the industry, though, is that much of this growth in revenue from advertising has been largely because of the big increase in the *overall* number of stations, and the appearance in particular of a *national* commercial sector in 1993 (NERA 1998: 7–42). The advertising revenue raised by the commercial sector as a whole, then, is being divided between a larger number of stations, and while the industry may look buoyant, profits are not necessarily being spread evenly throughout all operators.

These patterns of funding form an important backdrop for the changes in the industry which I explore later in this chapter, as well as for a broader understanding of the programming patterns and cultural impact of radio explored in later chapters. At this stage, though, we can conclude that commercial radio is funded in ways which are likely to lead to an uneven distribution of activity – with more stations in large cities, and many fewer in rural areas – and a competitive climate over relatively fixed sources of income which tends to lead to some companies going out of business and others consolidating a market lead. Public-service broadcasters may be less exposed to these pressures, but will often only be able to justify state funding from some form of 'taxation' by similarly competing for politically acceptable audience sizes.

Local, national and international dimensions

So far, I have looked at the radio industry in terms of separate processes, and in terms of different traditions of funding and motivation. A third approach to categorizing the radio industry, is *hierarchically* in terms of the size and geographical spread of target audience. Here, radio is strikingly paradoxical: perhaps the most local of the electronic mass-media, yet the first one to be distributed on a global scale. Television has only been able to broadcast internationally since the introduction of satellite technology, but radio's ability to use short-wave frequencies (which can be reflected from the ionosphere and thus travel long distances around the globe) made it an international medium as far back as the 1930s. At that time, it was the perceived power of the medium to influence public opinion that shaped the development of *international* broadcasting. The Nazis, who described radio as 'the most modern, the strongest and the most revolutionary weapon which we possess in the battle against an extinct world', sought to demoralize British listeners through William Joyce's 'Haw-Haw' broadcasts from Hamburg (Briggs 1995, vol. 3: 5, 128–45). In Britain, the BBC expanded upon earlier foreign language services for the Arab World and South America, and broadcast in German, Italian, and languages such as Polish, Norwegian, Danish and Dutch. The Cold War saw further expansion, and by the 1980s the USA and the Soviet Union dominated the field. Radio Moscow broadcast nearly 2,000 hours a week; the USA transmitted even more at Cuba and the Communist bloc in Europe and Asia on 'Voice of America', 'Radio Marti', 'Radio Free Europe', 'Radio Liberty' and 'Radio Free Asia' (Browne 1982). Nowadays, most countries with a state-controlled or public-service radio sector also run international broadcasts, invariably funded directly by governments or their security agencies. The BBC, for example, funds its World Service, not out of licence fee revenues, but from grants-in-aid from the government, which reflects its essentially *political* mission. There is, however, a broader range of goals at work here. Browne, in his definitive study of international broadcasting (1982), identified eight purposes to international broadcasting:

- As an instrument of foreign policy;
- As an advertisement for the national culture and civic values of the mother country;
- As a symbolic presence, for example as a symbol of a country's newly independent status;
- As a force for converting beliefs, for example on behalf of ideologically motivated regimes or religious movements;
- As a force for coercing or intimidating people, for example through threats of annihilation during wartime from clandestine stations;
- As educator;
- As entertainer;
- As a seller of goods and services, such as Bibles.

These definitions cover, not just the larger government-backed services such as Voice of America (VOA), the BBC World Service and Deutsche Welle, but stations run by religious organizations such as the Vatican and various fundamentalist sects.

In his study, Browne suggested that the majority of international broadcasting was in some sense ideologically motivated. But nowadays international radio is increasingly characterized by an array of much more purely *commercial* interests. Services such as those run by World Radio Network based in London or Bloomberg Business Radio based in New York use satellites such as Astra or Eutelsat rather than traditional short-wave frequencies to reach listeners directly or via 'rebroadcasting' through cable networks and affiliate stations. World Radio Network's English-language output is also used as a 'sustaining' service overnight by many national and community stations in North America, Australia and South Africa, and thus provides a global stratum of news for local audiences. Interestingly, it also provides an example of traditional public-service programming – in this case news and current-affairs – being broadcast for commercial ends by a private company.

The audience *size* for international broadcasts such as these is notoriously difficult to calculate. Browne estimated in the early 1980s that between a quarter and a half of the population of the Eastern European communist bloc were regular listeners, with major political crises seeing temporary jumps in numbers. In the industrialized democracies of the west, however, he calculated that fewer than one in twenty of the population tune in regularly to overseas services (1982: 330–1). The BBC, which describes itself as 'the world's leading international broadcaster', estimated its global listenership in 1997–8 to be 138 million people. This is a declining figure, which the BBC puts down to growing competition from television in parts of the developing world, but it also claims that its broadcasts are often particularly popular with highly educated and influential 'opinion formers' in many countries (BBC 1998: 28).

For most listeners most of the time, though, radio is not an international medium, but rather a national or, especially, a *local* one. In the USA, the size of the country, stretching across several time zones, has meant that radio has long been almost entirely local. There have, of course, been several generations of large national 'networks' since the 1920s and 1930s, when NBC, CBS and (a little later) ABC ran most stations, but no *single* national broadcasting operator of the scope of the BBC has emerged. Even within the 'networks', each 'affiliate' station remains associated clearly with the particular town and city in which it is located. In Europe, where there is a strong tradition of *national* broadcasting, the number of *local* stations is still several hundred times that of the number of national stations or networks (Tyler and Laing 1998: 8). The UK has only had a layer of local radio stations since the 1970s, but by 1999 they were capturing nearly 40 per cent of all radio listening between them, and a British radio listener was more likely to be tuned to a local commercial station than to any other single service (RAJAR 1999b). In part, of course, the localist nature of radio is based on the technology of transmission. AM signals can travel across the horizon, and reach listeners scattered across distances of several hundred miles – they could be seen as in some sense 'nation-building' in their power; FM signals, which have been much more widely adopted since the late 1960s because of their superior hi-fi sound-quality, cannot travel over the horizon, and are limited to a range of about 50 miles (Douglas 1999: 37–8). But, as with other aspects of the industry, the local character of radio is also a result of the costs of entry and running costs being low compared with television, which means that stations can survive with much smaller advertising revenues and can thus be satisfied with a smaller audience base. Whatever the precise reason for its local dimension, this aspect of radio is so central to its character, that I will return to it on several occasions later in this book.

The different layers of radio – from international broadcasting right through to highly localized community stations, are not separate and static entities, of course. Many local stations – as we shall see – carry network programmes and even international material, and

many are affiliated to – or owned by – larger companies or corporations. They also change character rapidly, perhaps changing format,
extending or shrinking their reach according to commercial or cultural needs and abilities. Our other definitions of global patterns in
radio, our categorization by 'sector', into production activity and
broadcasting activity for example, or our definitions of public-service
radio and commercial radio, must also be seen as complex, *evolving*
structures. Giddens (1984) reminds us that although such *structures*
are central to our understanding of the world, they are not fully
formed determining entities: structures may help define social life,
but they are also in turn reconstituted by it. And the agents of change
are indeed profound in radio. They can perhaps be grouped under
two broad headings: commercialization and technological change.
Only by exploring these in detail is it possible to begin to create a
dynamic picture of the radio industry.

Commercialization

Since the 1980s governments of both the right and the centre-left
across much of Europe and in the United States have applied the
principles of market capitalism to the broadcasting industries.
Curran and Seaton describe the underlying philosophy in the UK:

> The new, Thatcherite project was highly individualistic: it argued that
> public interest could only be secured by maximizing the capacity of
> individuals to choose; and that governments should seek to abandon
> controls, not exercise them. (1997: 209)

The precise reason for 'abandoning controls' was perhaps articulated
most explicitly by the American government's Federal Communications Commission in 1979. It identified two interrelated benefits
from 'deregulation':

> Producers of goods and services must be responsive to consumers'
> desires in order to compete successfully with rival producers. Con-
> sumers, by their choice of purchases, determine which producers will
> succeed. Moreover, not only does the competition among producers for
> consumers lead to the production of goods and services that consumers
> most want, the same competitive process forces producers continually
> to seek less costly ways of providing those goods and services. (FCC
> statement of 1979. Quoted in Head and Sterling 1990: 456)

Deregulation, in other words, is seen as leading the way to a competitive marketplace which, in turn, allows the emergence of *the most*

cost-effective delivery of the most 'wanted' radio services. Such market capitalism was a founding principle of American radio, and as such it has largely been viewed as uncontentious, but in Europe, legislative changes often served wider ends:

> Public service was seen as the inefficient self-serving camouflage of groups who wanted to protect their own interests from the correcting force of competition. Mrs Thatcher put the case inimitably in her memoirs: 'Broadcasting was one of those areas – the professions, such as teaching, medicine and the law were others – in which special pleading by powerful interest groups was disguised as high minded commitment to some common good'. (Curran and Seaton 1997: 210)

Deregulation has thus been part of a project to weaken the dominance and perceived cultural elitism of the public-service broadcasters – or at least force them into more responsiveness to audience desires as well as greater efficiencies in production (and so less call on the public purse).

But the most direct and intended effect of deregulation is first and foremost to increase the *total number* of radio services. Even in the USA, the FCC steadily loosened rules on ownership and programming obligations throughout the 1980s and 1990s, and saw the number of stations rise by over one thousand in just a few years. In the UK, the 1990 Broadcasting Act ended commercial radio's simulcasting on AM and FM to encourage separate services on each frequency, and it set up the Radio Authority to oversee the licensing of a welter of new local commercial stations as well as three national commercial stations. The Act marked the end of the BBC's monopoly on national radio services, and by 1995 commercial radio's share of the audience overtook BBC radio's for the first time (Crisell 1997: 227–33). The number of commercial stations had leaped from fewer than 50 in the mid 1980s to more than 150 by the mid 1990s, and by the middle of 1999 the number stood at 237, together with some 17 cable and 40 satellite services (Radio Authority 1999: 4). Across western Europe, the pattern has been much the same: an explosion in the number of local commercial stations combined with the ending of the quasi-monopoly of the public-service broadcasters at national level. In France and Italy deregulation was so complete in the 1980s that the number of new local stations reached well into the thousands. Elsewhere in Europe, the number of local stations now typically reaches into the hundreds, with perhaps between one and eight national commercial stations in each individual country. That deregulation has brought a huge *expansion* in radio activity seems beyond dispute. But the central question is whether it has in fact delivered the greater *choice* in radio-listening it promised. The question forces us to address two related issues. First, the issue of programme diversity, and what influences it. Secondly, the effects of large businesses consolidating control within the industry.

Diversity

I intend, shortly, to look in some detail at the issue of diversity in the British radio landscape. But since deregulation (and the subsequent proliferation of radio stations) happened earlier and more strongly in the USA, it might be useful to look first at what sort of diversity has actually been achieved there. In 1993, just one year after the FCC significantly relaxed ownership and programming rules, Stavitsky wrote admiringly of the American radio scene. He described examples of Alaskan native radio, Christian radio, children's radio, all-sports talk-radio, and country music radio, and argued that:

> Radio in America at the end of the 20th century is the electronic version of the Founding Fathers' vision of the free and open marketplace of expression. Then, as now, the quality of the message sometimes may be suspect, but its variety is proof of its vitality. (1993: 77)

In the same year, Ross asked the pertinent question of the American radio scene, 'does today's FM listener have choices that weren't available a decade ago?'. And he gave his answer:

> Sure. Seven years ago, the oldies format barely existed on FM and classic rock barely existed at all, but now most markets have at least one of each. You want diversity? In Los Angeles, the new No.1 station is an 8-month old FM specializing in 'banda', a polka-like Mexican subgenre that, despite being a century old, barely existed as a commercial radio entity until the last few years. (1993: 94)

This is a striking example of diversity, by any standards. But is it now somewhat out-of-date? Other American observers have noticed a significant *narrowing* of the range of programme output among radio stations in the years since 1993. Douglas, for example, writing in 1999, suggests that many of the differences between stations are exaggerated:

> There are currently something in the order of fifty officially listed formats, and the hairsplitting between them seems ridiculous to an outsider. What really is the difference between soft rock ('plays older, softer rock') and soft adult contemporary ('recurrents mixed with

some current music')? Classic hits features '70s and 80s hits from rock-based artists,' while classic rock features 'older rock cuts.' Country, whose AM audience . . . is primarily fifty-five and over, has gotten carved up into hot country or young country on the FM dial to attract younger listeners. (1999: 348)

In fact, many of the USA's eleven-thousand stations congregate around a relatively small number of formats: 'Adult Contemporary', Country and Talk have for some time been among the most popular, and between them account for about *half of all radio stations* (Keith 1997: 71; see figure 1.2). And Douglas makes a further point about diversity: that variety of programming *within* each station has been eroded in recent years:

In promotional ads listeners are assured, for example, that they won't ever have to hear heavy metal, rap or anything unexpected on their station. . . . So someone like me, who admittedly does not want to hear

National Format Shares – Spring 1999 (%)
(Fall 1998 shares in parenthesis)

Format	Share
News/Talk	**16.1** (15.3)
AC	**13.8** (14.4)
Oldies/Classic Rock	**13.0** (10.2)
CHR	**11.7** (10.6)
Country	**9.7** (9.7)
Urban	**8.5** (9.3)
Spanish-language	**6.5** (6.5)
Active Rock/Rock	**5.3** (5.3)
NAC/Smooth Jazz	**2.8** (3.2)
Nostalgia	**2.8** (3.4)
Classical	**1.6** (1.7)
Adult Alternative	**1.1** (1.3)

Figure 1.2 The most popular radio station formats in the USA in 1999
Source: Radio and Records 1999: 9 ('National Format Shares'). Copyright © 1999 Radio and Records, Inc. Reprinted by permission

Anthrax or Ice T if I can help it, also doesn't get to hear Beck, Arrested
Development, Salt-N-Pepa, or Ani Difranco on my 'classic rock' or
'contemporary hits' station. (1999: 348–9)

There are some interesting parallels here with the UK radio industry. British stations have noticeably less freedom to enact overnight
changes in format, because they are much more tightly bound than
their American counterparts by a so-called 'Promise of Performance'
agreed with the Radio Authority. Any change in the output of British
commercial radio stations is therefore incremental. Even so, some
changes have been real enough. Several of those stations launched
in the early 1990s with a promise to expand the range of output –
explicitly, in the words of the Radio Authority to increase diversity –
have themselves undergone quite radical programming changes. To
take just two examples in London: Kiss-FM has moved in stages from
a predominantly black and dance-music based station with an overtly
'pirate' style of presentation to a noticeably more polished format of
mainstream dance 'for young London'; Jazz-FM has moved gradually from a strict observance of its genre to a much wider interpretation, which includes broadcasting many mainstream acts with only
a vaguely discernible jazz sound. Such patterns tend to point in the
direction of the same process as in the USA: a steady *homogenization*
of radio output across large parts of the industry. Indeed, in the USA,
where the sort of regulations over programme content which are still
in force in the UK have largely disappeared, the process can be phen-
omenally quick. A station can reformat itself overnight – dropping or
increasing news coverage, moving from news to talk, perhaps from
more sports coverage to all-sports coverage, or from an eclectic mix
of 'indie' music to hard-rock, and maybe some months later moving
back again.

The critical question of course is, what lies *behind* this apparent
homogenization? Is it, for instance, a straightforward question of who
owns a station – that the concentration of more and more stations
into fewer hands is what is somehow narrowing the range of programmes? Or are there some more diffuse processes which also have
a role to play here – such as common approaches to targeting audiences, or shared assumptions about how to maximize profits and
reduce costs? Again, to explore this question, I will draw from experiences on both sides of the Atlantic, in the belief that any differences
in the *degree* of regulation between European and American radio are
on balance outweighed by what they share, operating as they do
within broadly market-led capitalist economies.

Let us start, then, with the question of ownership in the radio
industry. Certainly, there is evidence that as the number of radio sta-

tions has grown, many of them are indeed being steadily concentrated into the hands of a smaller number of big companies. In the USA, the 1996 Telecommunications Act abolished all restrictions on the number of stations a company could own nationally, though it limited it to eight in major markets like New York and other cities with forty-five or more commercial stations. The so-called 'antitrafficking' rule, which had stopped station owners from making quick profits by selling stations within three years of buying them, has also been abolished (Douglas 1999: 297). In the frenzy of buying and selling through much of the 1980s and 1990s, several conglomerates have emerged, to surpass the old networks in size and reach. By 1997, Capstar, Clear Channel and Jacor owned around two-to-three-hundred stations between them, and Infinity – which in turn has been swallowed up by Westinghouse/CBS – owns some 170 stations across the States, and dominates major cities like New York and San Fransisco. All these radio companies, though, are dwarfed by Chancellor Media Corporation, which controlled 463 stations by 1998 (1999: 297–8). There are behemoths in Europe too. In France, for example, Europe 1 and NRJ are two companies which own several national networks, and well over a hundred local stations; in Spain, over 430 stations are owned by – or affiliated to – SER (Tyler and Laing 1998: 68–70; de Mateo 1997: 203). The UK, of course, has many fewer stations in total, but here too there is a marked concentration of ownership. By 1998, GWR owned 31 stations (including the national station Classic-FM), making it the dominant operator across southern England. It employed about a thousand people, representing some 25 per cent of those working in the whole of UK commercial radio. In fact, the four largest groups in the UK – GWR, along with Capital Radio, EMAP Radio, and Scottish Radio Holdings – together owned 75 of the country's 220 commercial stations that were operating by the beginning of 1998 (see table 1.2).

There is, then, considerable evidence that more and more commercial radio stations are being bought by a small number of major companies in the industry. The question though is whether this 'concentration' has a direct bearing on diversity. The NERA report, which I mentioned earlier, was not so sure. It argued that takeovers may actually *help* diversity:

> Commercial radio services under single ownership will be deliberately different to each other, in order that audiences and revenues are maximized. It follows that the more services there are under single ownership, the greater the likelihood of diversity between them and the more opportunity there will be for the provision of well-resourced niche programming. (1998: 88–9)

Table 1.2 Key players in UK commercial radio industry and some of their other interests

Group	Number of stations under control June 1999	Brands	Other interests	Sales 1995–6 (£m)	Profits 1995–6 (£m)
Capital	15 (mostly south-east England)	Capital Gold Network, 'Sunny Day'	Restaurants, new media, Wildstar Records, news and advertising services	77.8	27.9
GWR	39 (mostly in southern England)	Classic Gold	Digital One, radio stations in Austria, Finland, Italy, Poland, the Netherlands and South Africa	63.8	12.0
EMAP	18 (mostly northern metropolitan cities and London)	Kiss, Magic	Part of EMAP publishing	55.8	17.5
Scottish Radio Holdings	15 (Scotland and borders area)	various	Radio stations in Ireland, poster sites, local newspapers	n/a	n/a

Source: Radio Authority Pocket Book, 1998, 1999, NERA 1998 and various company accounts 1998, 1999

There is some evidence to support this argument. Companies that operate more than one radio station in the same geographical area – or, to use commercial terminology, the same 'market' – do indeed seek to avoid competing against themselves. In London for instance, Capital Radio used the end of 'simulcasting' on its two frequencies in 1990 to split output between a more contemporary music service aimed at 16–35 year-olds on FM, and a 'Gold' service of classic hit records aimed at a slightly older audience on AM. In the USA, the ending of simulcasting has led to a proliferation of all-talk, all-business or all-sports formats on the AM dial, again, in contrast with the predominantly pop-and-rock music formats on FM.

Even so, such diversification can often be within a strikingly narrow range. In New York, for instance, Chancellor were running six stations in mid 1999 – two of them were Contemporary Hit Radio (one further described as 'Pop', the other 'Rhythmic'), two were Adult Contemporary, and the other two 'Oldies' and 'Classic Rock' (Radio and Records Online 1999): these were all formats duplicated several times over on other stations in New York run by other companies like Infinity – and in each case none could be described as particularly surprising or adventurous or in any significant sense *extending* the range of radio output beyond very well-tried formats. Commercial radio operators in the UK argue that the range of services they can offer is restricted by the much smaller amount of spectrum made available to them. If the Radio Authority, they say, only allows two or three commercial licences in any one town or county, then only the 'richest' markets will be served: this means services with only the broadest of appeal, and not true 'niche' radio. But if the evidence of recent American experience is anything to go by, even a city like New York, which is allowed many more stations than a British city like London, is nonetheless still dominated by a fairly small range of predictable mainstream formats offered by a few large companies.

On the face of it, this 'clustering' of stations around a few recurring formats is rather surprising, since there appears to be an economic imperative to identify new and ever more clearly defined niche audiences. It is, let us recall, the competition for *audiences* between operators which is the central activity of the deregulated radio marketplace. In fact, the *audience*, rather than the programme, can be viewed as the primary product, or commodity, of radio. In this analysis programmes are made simply to attract audiences; they are, as Mosco (1996) wryly observes, little more than the 'free lunch' that public houses once used to entice customers to drink. The idea of the audience-as-commodity has currency among those working in commercial broadcasting as a whole – though they would not quite put it in those terms – and it was advanced in academic literature by the American economist Dallas Smythe (1977). For him, as Mosco interprets, this '*commodification*' of the audience – the process by which listeners become a product to be bought and sold in the marketplace – brings media, audiences and advertisers together in a set of reciprocal relationships:

> Mass media programming is used to construct audiences; advertisers pay media companies for access to these audiences; audiences are thereby delivered to advertisers. Such an argument broadens the space within which media commodification takes place beyond the immediate process of media companies producing newspapers, radio broadcasts, television programmes, and films, to include advertisers or capital in general. The process of commodification thoroughly integrates the media industries into the capitalist economy not primarily by creating ideologically saturated products but by producing audiences, en masse and in specific demographically desirable forms for advertisers. (1996: 148–9)

The problem though for all radio operators in most of the western world, whether commercial or public service, is that the product over which they compete – the audience – is at best a static resource. There is virtually no growth in overall population, at least 86 per cent of the present British population already have and use radio sets – in the USA 99 per cent of households have more than five sets – and very few of these listeners show any signs of planning to listen for any longer than they already do (NERA 1998: 14; Keith 1997: 1). More stations competing for the attention of the same listeners simply means that the total audience is being divided between a larger number of operators. In the past two decades the obvious – and first – response within the commercial sector and the advertising industry has been to move away from the notion of chasing rather ill-defined mass audiences in order to target more specific ones: *narrow*casting, as opposed to *broad*casting. In this approach, a radio station refines the format of its programming in order to attract a very clear, tightly focussed group of listeners to be 'delivered' to an equally tightly focussed group of advertisers. The fact that a huge *mass* audience is not achieved is counterbalanced by securing the right *kind* of audience – the right 'niche' – for a particular set of advertisers.

So: given this incentive towards adopting 'niche' formats, why do so many operators seem to end up still favouring the same mainstream formats? There are, I would suggest, two factors which help explain this:

■ The manner of audience research;
■ A combination of inertia and fickleness within the radio industry itself.

First, the manner of audience research. A sizable sub-industry of
audience research organizations has grown to service the commercial stations' need to track the lifestyles and tastes of potential target
listeners: organizations like Arbitron in the United States or IPSOS-
RSL in the UK provide stations with regular information on
audience reaction to particular programmes and music output, and
the published audience *ratings* are regarded as a critical measure for
establishing advertising rates. One technique now approaching ubiquity is the music 'call-out', where a series of 5-second snatches of
new records are played down the phone-line to listeners, who are
then asked whether they would like to hear it on the radio: records
with a positive feedback will subsequently get played, others will not.
Another method, employed by several American and British stations
is the 'instant-response' survey, with target listeners gathered in an
auditorium: each 'listener' turns a dial on a handset, to give a second-
by-second response to output, ranging from highly negative to highly
positive. In this way, not just music, but news coverage, adverts and
speech output can be assessed to identify what Chrysalis Radio's Programming Director calls 'tune-out opportunities' (Radio Academy
1998: 6). But what precisely does all this audience research tell the
stations? They discover that much of the audience research, conducted in conditions of commercial secrecy and at great cost to individual stations and companies, leads to much the same conclusion:
pop music is more appealing to most than speech, and pop music
focussing on familiar, melodic hits is the most appealing of all.
     It has also been suggested that the *methodology* of the audience-
ratings industry, which relies on diary keeping, consistently underestimates the popularity of niche stations serving 'alternative' or
'indie' music to a young, transient population (see chapter 3). As a
result, the audience for such stations, although perhaps presenting a
potential niche market, is regarded as not quite large enough to attract
the quantity of advertising revenue needed for a station to become
profitable – in the jargon of the industry, the stations 'fail' to 'deliver
the demographics'. Take, for example, Stavitsky's description of what
happened to one indie station, KAVE-FM in Eugene, Oregon, following 'bad' audience figures:

> The Fall 1992 Arbitron ratings placed the station fifth in the market,
> with a 6.6 share. Station staffers argued that their listeners weren't the
> kind to fill out ratings books; one went as far as to write an op-ed

column for the local paper attacking Arbitron's methodology. Maybe, but no matter. With one week's notice, the owners told the staff they were abandoning the progressive format in favor of 'Z-Rock', a nationally syndicated, hard-rock music service. 'Z-Rock' is delivered by satellite, so there's no need for disc-jockeys, only salespeople. Eleven KAVE employees were laid off. In the calculus of contemporary radio, the move makes good business sense. The KAVE's owners cut their personnel costs considerably and, with the switch of another Eugene station from rock to country, now there's niche room. (1993: 84)

Significantly, KAVE-FM's change in programming did not come about as a result of a change in ownership: its existing owners merely acted in the same way as any other owner might have done. Most radio companies aiming to make a profit will share the same economic assumptions and the same cultural assumptions about their listeners' desires, and many will respond to the economic pull of a more mainstream, popular 'taste' – what Stavitsky calls the 'calculus of contemporary radio'. This means that even if more spectrum is made available for more radio stations in a particular region, and there is some diversification of output within companies in order to stop them from competing against themselves for the same listeners, most companies will replicate the same *package* of 'diversity', if only because they – and their audience researchers – will mostly identify the same range of tastes and demands.

This brings me to the second area which I have suggested contributes to a 'clustering' around the same few dominant formats: what I have referred to as inertia and 'fickleness' within the radio industry itself. Ross (1993), in his interpretation of the American radio environment, notes that many formats once pronounced dead in the early 1980s, such as hard-rock, have more recently made a comeback in popularity. This, he suggests is evidence of the *cyclical* nature of format use:

> If music radio were truly fragmented, Miami should still have an easy-listening station, Seattle should still have commercial jazz, and Detroit should still have an FM home for rhythm and blues (R&B) oldies. These are formats that make sense for their market demographics, but they're choices that have disappeared in those towns just since 1991. . . . There's no rule that the new FM stations have to go boldly where no other station has gone before, especially if it means serving anybody outside the prime 25–44 demographic that ad buyers desire most. For every broadcaster who fills an unmet need, there are three who will swarm into today's hot format, whether there's room or not, then head off somewhere else if they don't see immediate results. This boom-bust cycle is such a constant in radio that if you look at the last 14

years alone, you can already see it repeating itself in more than one format. (1993: 94–5)

There is, in other words, some sort of 'herd' instinct which overrides any ability to detect new and unserved audiences. This process of 'swarming' to certain formats has been noticed by Glasser. He points out that formats, though usually described as a means of minimizing competition for the same audiences, are *primarily* chosen for their expected ability to maximize profits – and that maximizing profits is not necessarily the same as avoiding competition:

A station will duplicate an existing format [within a market] rather than produce a unique format if its share of the audience for a duplicated format yields higher profits than the profits generated by the entire audience for a unique format. (1984: 129)

What, then, are formats for? According to Fornatale and Mills, a station's choice of format is dictated entirely by business rather than musical concerns:

Formats are not sought by radio stations to provide a diversity for its own sake. . . . Nor are they provided to satisfy listeners' demands. The purpose of . . . formats is to enable radio stations to deliver to advertisers a measured and defined group of consumers, known as a segment. (1980: 61)

Or, as McCourt and Rothenbuhler put it – 'the radio industry uses formats to institutionalize standardization and predictability' – to assure nervous advertisers, in other words, that their money is being well spent because they are consistently reaching their target audience (1987: 106). Berland observes the tendency towards duplication in Canada, and concludes that the refinement of research-based formats have:

contributed more to the expansion and rationalization of commercial revenues gained by the radio market as a whole than to the substantive diversity of tastes that is claimed to warrant such proliferation. . . . The organization of audiences by music format does rationalize the radio market, but this is not the same as diversifying or enriching radio programming. This would entail diversifying musical production itself, and diversifying the exposure of musics to specific audiences – the opposite of what has actually occurred in the evolution of music formats. (1993a: 108–9)

The publicly described format of each station or chain can be seen, then, as more of a tool for branding the station on crowded airwaves and for packaging audiences in a comprehensible way to advertisers than a guide to actual content.

All this suggests that the question of diversity in radio is not explained solely in terms of the concentration of ownership within the industry. It is better understood, perhaps, in terms of wider values within the market economy, and in particular the way that in a commodified culture particular audience 'segments' have to be packaged to the advertising industry in particular ways. Does this mean that ownership of stations is rather beside the point? Not quite. Ownership remains a central question to any discussion of diversity because the desire to *maximize audiences* which we have just seen is combined with another equally strong imperative, namely the desire to *minimize costs*. These costs are most readily reduced by achieving the 'economies of scale' wrought by the largest organizations. The *ownership* of more and more stations allows an operator to spread a limited amount of production effort across an expanding terrain: in so doing, the amount of money spent on each individual station is proportionately less – and, provided advertising revenue is buoyant, the margins for profit are proportionately greater.

How do these economies of scale unfold in radio? Or, to put it more specifically, what are the actual *costs* in radio that might be squeezed? All stations face certain 'overheads', which are relatively *fixed*. They include 'establishment' costs (such as the rent or maintenance bills for studio and office buildings), transmission costs (which include the cost of engineering staff and fees to transmitter operators), management and administration costs and marketing costs. Marketing costs can vary hugely across stations, but the growth in the overall number of commercial stations is encouraging most to spend more each year on promotional activities in order to brand their output more clearly and establish their place in the market. As a result marketing can account for as much as a quarter of total operating costs. Stations in the commercial sector also face considerable advertising sales costs: either the salaries and commissions for an 'in-house' sales team – which could be the largest part of a station's workforce – or payments to external sales 'houses' which sell airtime on their behalf. Since sales commissions are often set as a percentage of revenues, these particular costs can vary from year to year. Beyond these operating overheads, commercial operators in the UK might also need to make cash bids as part of their application for a licence to run a station, and pay various business taxes to the Treasury. All these operating costs have to be borne by a station regardless of the sort of programmes being broadcast.

Costs related to actual *programme production*, however, vary dramatically between different stations and networks. Figures for the commercial sector are sometimes difficult to gather because of issues of confidentiality, but figures from the BBC can suggest the broad patterns that apply across the industry in the UK (see table 1.3). They reveal that programmes on Radio 1 (dominated by pop music and with only a small proportion of news, sport and entertainment) cost an average of £2,700 per hour over the year, compared with programmes on Radio 4 (with virtually no music, but a large percentage of news and news-related programmes, drama and arts

Table 1.3 The impact of genres on programme-making costs for two BBC network radio services, 1997–8

Network	Genre	Hours of output per year	Percentage of output per year
Radio 1	Music	8,218	93.8
	News	389	4.4
	Presentation and trailing	64	0.73
	Sport	38	0.43
	Comedy/light ent.	27	0.31
	Leisure	10	0.11
	Knowledge building	6	0.07
	National debate	4	0.05
	Schools	4	0.05
	Total:	8,760	
	Average cost per hour:	£2,700	
Radio 4	News	2,281	29.6
	Knowledge building	1,782	23.2
	Drama	1,048	13.6
	Arts	629	8.2
	National debate	555	7.2
	Sport	469	6.1
	Comedy/light ent.	318	4.1
	Religion	228	3.0
	Presentation and trailing	122	1.6
	Leisure	120	1.6
	Schools	72	0.93
	Open University	66	0.86
	Multicultural	6	0.08
	Music	1	0.01
	Total:	7,697	
	Average cost per hour:	£10,200	

Source: BBC Annual Report and Statement of Accounts, 1997/8

productions) costing an average of £10,200 per hour. Since staff salaries alone can account for nearly two-thirds of a station's total running costs, the difference is largely a matter of how labour intensive each type of programming can be. News and current affairs involves a large web of production, employing staff to research story ideas, to gather information on the ground in costly bureaux across the globe, and yet more staff to select, edit and present the various bulletins and programmes in complex live studio operations. Pop music, however, is often – though not always – simply a matter of a single presenter playing recorded music in a studio. Music radio is generally cheap radio and, as Berland observes, the cumulative success of commercial radio would have been 'inconceivable' without music (1993a: 105).

Other factors complicate this binary spectrum, so that it cannot be argued that costs relate *simply* to the proportion of speech or of music. The average cost of programming on BBC Radio 5 Live, while double that of Radio 1, is still only about half that of Radio 4, despite output being even more dominated by news. What makes it cheaper than Radio 4 is the heavy use of *live* reportage, as opposed to the heavily 'packaged' treatment of news and current affairs on Radio 4 which inevitably demands more staff and resources, more *production*, in terms of editing and processing. An even cheaper form of speech programming is the phone-in, where again the live nature of the format means very little processing of material is required and where much of the speech is 'produced' virtually free of charge by listeners. Again, then, there is an economic basis for the popularity of 'talk' formats, which can be even cheaper than music formats. Music programming, in fact, has some hidden costs that mean it is not a universally cheap genre. A significant commitment to broadcasting live concerts and specially recorded live 'sessions', inflates costs considerably. Music radio also demands the payment of significant copyright and performance fees, and some radio services pay significantly more than others. In the UK, the Performing Rights Society (PRS) collects fees for song writers, while the Mechanical Copyright Protection Society (MCPS) and Phonographic Performance Limited (PPL) collect on behalf of record companies and publishers. They each calculate their charges to radio stations loosely on the basis of audience size or advertising revenues. Playing a 3-minute single on Radio 1, with its national audience of some 11 million listeners, involves a payment of about £50 to the person who wrote the song; playing the same record on Capital FM, which is the largest commercial station in the country's richest market, involves a payment of just £16. Overall, the BBC's five network radio services paid over £16 million to PRS in 1998 – compared with some £14 million in total for the UK's 200 or so local commercial stations, or about £70,000 per station on average (Performing Rights Society 1999). Overall, it has been calculated that spending on copyright fees by commercial radio amounts to around 10 per cent of the revenues of a station (NERA 1998: 40).

One interesting difference has emerged between the British and American experiences in the face of these costs. In the United States, the recording industry always perceived radio to be a useful means of advertising its products, and was reluctant to extract fees; in the UK, record companies made an early assumption that pop-music radio represented competition to record sales while musicians worried about the threat to live performances, and this led to 'needle-time' agreements that limited output severely: when Radio 1 began broadcasting in 1967, for example, it was allowed just seven hours of needle-time each day, to be shared with Radio 2 (Barnard 1989: 53). While this budgetary constraint undoubtedly encouraged the use of live music and specially recorded sessions, the other by-product was the encouragement of lengthy chat by presenters in order to fill airtime. The infamous patter of radio disc jockeys has its roots in raw economics as much as in the demands of the medium for intimacy and personality. Of course, personality – or to use the industry's own phrase, 'talent' – is itself a commodity that carries a price. Presenters who can attract an audience also command a high fee, and the overall growth in the number of stations has created a competitive bidding war in which talent costs have been increasing at many times the growth rate for average earnings (NERA 1998: 40). One estimate now puts the cost of talent at 40 per cent of total labour costs in the commercial sector.

Yet, despite these relatively fixed 'up front' costs, the average operating costs of commercial radio in the UK are steadily being brought *down* in relation to revenues, and are even predicted to fall in real terms for some over the next decade (NERA 1998: 40). This is precisely because the creation of whole chains of commercial stations under a single operator allows the sharing of programmes and in some cases staff, marketing costs, audience-research costs and advertising sales teams. Talent costs, for example, might be rising, but owning a chain of say ten stations allows a company to broadcast the efforts of one expensive presenter on all ten stations, rather than the work of ten different presenters and production teams at each site. Similarly, each individual station may have local news and local jingles inserted into its output to maintain a sense of localness to the listener, but much of the programming will actually be produced elsewhere and shared between the many stations within the group. Berland has described the Canadian radio environment at the end of the 1980s, where over one hundred stations relayed rock or country music programmes by satellite from St Catherine in Ontario, produced by Canadian Radio Networks (CRN): 'the programmes are live, DJ-hosted, delivered cheaply and all night long, from what is often the other side of the country' (1993a: 113).

Beyond the syndication of individual programmes to stations across a network, there is often also the 'rolling-out' of a single *brand* of programming. In Europe, for instance, NRJ brands some of its stations as a youthful high-energy form of Contemporary Hit Radio (CHR), and its separate 'Nostalgie' network as 'Gold'. In the UK, GWR's FM stations all broadcast 'today's better music mix', while all its AM stations consistently offer 'good times, great oldies'. What this means in practice is that even where GWR's individual stations have their own presenters, they often adopt identical slogans in their presentational links, and respond to centralized decisions about which records to play. Of course, the GWR stations are actually offering broadly the same CHR and Gold output as most other commercial chains, but they are *branded* differently in order to portray the output as somehow unique – and simultaneously raise the profile as a whole of the GWR name.

The creation of a quasi-national dimension to local stations gathered under one owner and sharing one brand of output also enables companies to tap into two separate strands of advertising revenue at once – a local strand *and* a national one – even though it may have one *unified* sales team:

> Let's take the North West, for example: EMAP now owns stations that cover an area comparable with Granada TV – so it can go along to a national advertiser like Proctor and Gamble or whoever, and say to them, 'you can buy the whole north-west so there's no benefit to you in going to just one stand-alone station'. It's tapped into national levels of advertising revenue. At the same time, a company can say to another more *local* advertiser that if they don't want to pay to cover the whole region, they can pay a fraction of the cost to reach just one town, or one particular age-group, as opposed to a wider spread of listeners or television viewers, where much of the effort will be wasted. And that's how local radio still makes its money from local companies. (Graham 1999)

Given this ability to capture both local and national advertising sales, by, on the one hand, pulling stations together into whole chains for *some* ad-campaigns and, on the other hand, 'decoupling' them into separate stations, each with their own tailor-made ad-breaks for quite different campaigns, it should be no surprise that the four biggest commercial radio groups in the UK took over 70 per cent of the total revenues for the sector in 1996 – up from just 39 per cent only three years earlier – despite owning little more than a third of the total number of stations. And as the largest companies' share in turnover has grown, so too has their profitability – with profit now standing at 29 per cent of their revenues. The smaller groups and those stations that remain independent, however, have fared less well: of the sixteen small radio groups listed in NERA's 1998 survey, six had made outright losses, all the others had done little more than break even (1999: 22–3). So, while the trend within the commercial radio industry as a whole is for greater profitability, much of this economic success is becoming concentrated disproportionately in the hands of a few big operators.

What, then, can we conclude about the issue of diversity in the radio industry? Two things, I suggest. First, that instead of a *fragmentation* of the traditional mass audience into an infinite variety of separate niches – the 'promise' of diversity implicit in the deregulation of the 1980s and early 1990s – most of us are now being 'packaged' into slightly more widely defined categories: a process of *market segmentation*. Wallis and Malm describe this as part of the same chronological process which occurs in many countries after deregulation. Their model of change is shown in figure 1.3. There is an initial increase in available programming, followed by the exclusion of some fragments and the bundling of others into segments, leading to a concentration of formats, and accompanied by networking which produces more and more concentration of ownership: 'this brings us back more or less to square one. The monolithic, monopoly corporation has been replaced by a new, small group of commercial owners' (1993: 164–7).

Represented in this way, ownership is clearly an integral part of the equation of diversity. Secondly, though, we can say that concentration of ownership merely enables companies to act more *efficiently* in operating what is *in any case* the assumed 'calculus of radio': namely, that in the context of a market economy and accountability to shareholders, *all* commercial operators will tend to be drawn to the few most profitable formats and will be tempted to streamline programming costs wherever possible – with a consequent reduction in overall programme range. Even small independent stations work on this basis – they are just not quite in the same position as the large chains to put this 'calculus' into effect.

Consolidation and control

The commercial radio industry, then, is not *de*regulated so much as *market* regulated. And this is a process that appears to be

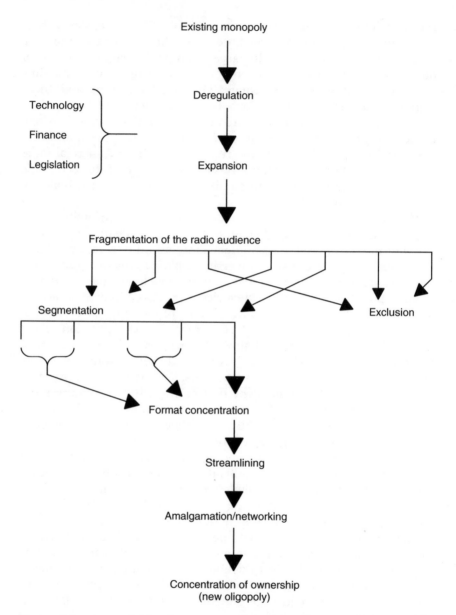

Figure 1.3 A model for the process by which deregulation of existing monopolies can eventually lead to new forms of ownership/format concentration
Source: Wallis and Malm 1993: 165

accompanied by a trend towards cheaper forms of programming *and* a steady consolidation of control over broadcasting by a small number of large players. Even so, companies and governments both recognize that the legislative power of the state can and does set the limits to commercialization. As Curran and Seaton observe in relation to postwar television in the UK:

> If financial pressures were the only influence, the programme-makers' aim would always be simply to reach the largest possible audience for the smallest amount of money. In practice this would have meant a diet of American soap opera, variety shows, filmed series, quizzes, and chat shows, based on proven formulae, endlessly repeated. . . . Current affairs would have been confined to news bulletins, and advertising spots would have been longer, more frequent and more intrusive. . . . Commercial broadcasting did not develop all these features in Britain, because of the framework of public regulations within which it was obliged to operate. (1997: 182)

But where will the balance of regulation lie in the future? With the market, or the state? Unsurprisingly, commercial radio operators, who clearly wish to maximize profits through acquisitions and mergers, argue that the 'deregulation' of the 1980s and 1990s has not gone far enough. Take the issue of so-called 'behavioural controls', imposed by regulators such as the Radio Authority and the Broadcasting Standards Commission in the UK, and by the FCC in America. Behavioural controls define acceptable programme content, such as the amount of news, local content – general 'public-service' elements – and many of these are laid down either in general law, industry codes of practice or in individual licensing agreements. In the USA, though, the FCC has spent much of the 1980s and 1990s relinquishing many of its behavioural controls, including the requirement for stations to offer 'community service' items, upper limits on the amount of airtime given over to advertising, and any obligation to treat controversial issues in a fair and balanced way (Fairchild 1999: 555–6). Even in the more tightly regulated UK, commercial operators argue that in the future they should be freed further from what they describe as the continued 'micro-management' of their programming: a format should be something that can be changed without lengthy renegotiation with the Radio Authority in direct response to perceived changes in audience demands. GWR's Chief Executive Ralph Bernard has put their case: 'Audience tastes shift, and it is the stations that know best what their audiences want.' (Speech to Radio Academy Conference, Birmingham, July 1998).

In determining the shape of the radio industry overall, however, it is the 'structural' controls that are key. These controls limit both the number of stations a particular company can own and the degree of cross-media ownership within the industry – a clear recognition that plurality of ownership is still regarded as some guarantor of diversity.

In the UK, for example, structural controls in the 1990 and 1996 Broadcasting Acts, and a 1995 rule change, restrict ownership on the basis of a 'points' system, measured by a station's *potential* audience size (which effectively is the same as saying the adult population of the geographical area its transmissions cover). It means that:

- No single company can hold more than 15 per cent of the 'points' across the country as a whole and no more than three station licences in a single local area.
- Holding licences in areas with overlapping potential audiences is subject to 'public interest' tests.
- No single company can provide a regional television service and a local radio service in the same area.
- Newspapers with more than a certain share of the local or national market may not own stations, or at least need to pass another public-interest test.

Larger radio companies like GWR – which was near the UK's ceiling of the 15 per cent share of points by 1998 – argue that a different measure of ownership is now required, such as one based on *actual* audience share, or 'share of voice', rather than *potential* audience size. Since the BBC stations, which fall outside the remit of the Radio Authority, take a share of the audience in any given area of the country, a measure of share rather than size would invariably produce lower headline figures and a stronger impression that no single commercial operator dominates a market. GWR itself, for instance, would account for only 9.5 per cent of actual audience share, rather than the 14.2 per cent of potential audience size which it currently accounts for in the points system. If the ceiling is then raised to 20 per cent or even 25 per cent – another demand of the commercial sector – even the largest of the radio groups would be able to more than double in size (NERA 1998: 85–90).

In the USA, this degree of deregulation has largely been accepted as government policy. The 1996 Telecommunications Act removed all national restrictions on ownership within the radio industry (other than those covered by more general competition policy), and relaxed considerably the limits on local ownership. The NERA report suggests that in the USA and New Zealand (where controls have been similarly relaxed), there have been no 'adverse consequences' to this further structural deregulation. But the evidence can just as easily be read as pointing in the direction of a quickening homogenization of output. Indeed, Fairchild points out that in allowing the largest radio groups to consolidate their hold over an expanding number of stations in the USA, deregulation is *directly* responsible for 'greatly reducing the number of voices' and rationalizing local news 'almost out of existence' (1999: 557–8).

Even in Europe, a second front is being fought between commercial operators and regulators over the issues of networking and syndication, which are precisely what lies behind the homogenization that Fairchild detects in the USA. Many European countries have sought to stem the tide: Denmark has long been insistent on the need for local content, and its government all but forbade the networking of syndicated radio programmes completely up until 1997; Greece restricts stations to no more than 5 hours a day of syndicated programming. Overall, though, many countries have been legislatively ill-prepared for fighting the trend towards networking, and enforcement has been quite ineffective: Tyler and Laing note that there has been much activity in the British and European radio that has been 'against the spirit of the broadcasting legislation' (1998: 9).

Overall, though, we can still say this: that for the time being at least the ability of radio companies to grow steadily in size faces legislative limits of some form or another in many individual countries – especially in western and northern Europe, though markedly less so in the USA. Faced with what they see as unnecessary limits on their freedom to buy stations and change formats in their domestic market, while simultaneously recognizing the advantages of economies of scale, some British companies have turned in the last decade to acquiring interests abroad. The UK-based GWR group, for example, has invested in radio stations in Austria, Finland, Italy, Poland, the Netherlands and South Africa, and made bids for stations in New Zealand. Several of these overseas stations carry its Classic-FM brand, launched first in London, and all of them are managed from the UK. But few of the other leading UK radio groups are as active abroad as GWR, and even GWR's overseas interests account for only a small proportion of its total annual turnover (GWR 1998). Conversely, the only significant overseas investor in UK radio so far has been the CLT-UFA group, which part owned the national commercial station Talk Radio and two London stations (RTL Country 1035 AM and Xfm), though it has since sold much of its interest. The American radio audience-research organization Arbitron has bought a UK research firm, but a bid to take over the contract for nationwide audience research on behalf of Radio Joint Audience Research (RAJAR) was unsuccessful, and the contract remains with Radio Services Limited (RSL), a subsidiary of the French company IPSOS.

In fact, *transnational* ownership is a more common phenomenon beyond the UK. The French-based radio chain NRJ, for instance, operates stations in Belgium, Switzerland, Germany and across Scandinavia, all broadcasting a popular CHR format. NRJ is also a majority shareholder in another French group, Nostalgie, which has in turn invested in 20 countries, mostly in Francophone Africa. American companies, though, are notable for their absence – so far at least – from *western* Europe: they have sought investment in stations further east operating in a radio landscape as deregulated as their own domestic market. Metromedia International, for instance, has bought shares in 11 stations in Hungary, the Czech Republic, Russia, Georgia and the Baltic States, and has planned to invest in Turkey, Belarus, Romania, Kazakhstan and Uzbekistan (Tyler and Laing 1998: 18–19). Since the other significant American overseas radio investor, the Texas-based Clear Channel Communications company, has mostly targeted New Zealand radio – where again, deregulation has gone further than in many countries – their criterion for expansion seems clear: to invest wherever the regulatory regime is at its loosest, so that quality and public-service programming requirements do not exist as a cap on profit margins.

In the absence of heavy American involvement in western European radio, the most powerful transnational radio company of all is CLT-UFA, which accounts for about 10 per cent of the total European radio advertising turnover (1998: 17). It owns stations in twelve countries. But unlike GWR, which describes itself as a 'pure radio' group, CLT-UFA is more than just transnational in scale: it is also *cross-media* in character. It is formed out of Europe's oldest private broadcaster, CLT Multi Media of Luxembourg (which ran, among other stations, Radio Luxembourg), and the German company Bertelsmann, which has vast and sprawling interests in newspaper and magazine publishing, record companies, market research, film production and television. One of its rivals, News Corporation, has recently taken an interest in radio, investing in Talk Radio in the UK. To conglomerates like Bertelsmann and News Corporation, acquisition in industrial sectors outside their immediate fields of interest (which in Bertelsmann's case was book publishing) is the fastest way to grow in size and to achieve the economies of scale that are so profitable. Diversification also gives them a share in the rewards of new markets while spreading the risks of lossmaking in declining markets. There is nothing inherently new in companies from outside the radio industry investing in the medium: newspaper publishers in particular have had a controlling interest in radio stations since the earliest days of sound broadcasting. But for much of the 1990s the global radio industry has been part of a much wider and faster process of *cross-media integration*, with television, publishing, information, music and retailing interests all active in buying shares in stations or whole networks. In recent years in the UK, for example, there has been heavy investment in radio by publishing groups such as EMAP, Associated Newspapers and the Guardian Media Group. There are some interesting recent examples of radio companies now large enough to reverse the trend, and become the active *buyers* in the marketplace. Capital Radio, for instance, has acquired interests in restaurants and new media in the UK. Radio chains like Capital, NRJ, Kiss and Fun, have a 'brand value': they have each built up a particular lifestyle statement which can be applied profitably to other aspects of their listeners' daily lives, from the clothes they wear to the meals they eat.

The expansion in activity by radio companies themselves has been welcomed by some within the industry as a sign of confidence and strength. Nevertheless, greater activity in the marketplace has clear risks. Even the largest radio groups are small in comparison with the giants of the media industry, like News Corporation and Bertelsmann, and the interests of these conglomerates lie *primarily* in the economically more powerful fields of television and film. When CLT-UFA sold its stake in the UK national station Talk Radio in 1998, despite growing audiences, it did so in order to raise cash for investment in digital *television* in Germany. On balance then, the economic pull of cross-media activity is more likely to see radio becoming, not a big player on the international scene and in control of its own destiny, but a *subordinate* sector within a larger industry.

The way in which radio is regulated is likely to reflect the trend for convergence within the media industries. Since 1990, commercial radio in the UK has been regulated by the Radio Authority, but the government is contemplating a single regulator to oversee the whole of broadcasting and telecommunications (Green Paper 1998). At a European level too, the EU Commission is busy producing a 'Convergence Action Plan', which lumps together radio, television and the Internet in developing its new policies. Commercial operators and the current Radio Authority are wary about the impact of radio losing a separate regulatory framework, that the price paid would be for 'television solutions' to be applied to 'radio problems'. This, though, might be the endgame of a decade of steady consolidation in the radio industry – a process in which major players are not just holding greater sway over radio broadcasting, but undergoing wider processes of horizontal and vertical integration, and cross-media ownership, processes, in short, which bring radio's future to a greater extent in line with that of the other mass media.

Technology

Broadcasting relies on hardware – transmitters, computers, studios and the like – so the *technological* dimensions of radio are part and parcel of what gives it its identity. Given this, we have to assume that rapid and significant technological developments are central to reshaping the global structures and economic bases of the radio industry – even if they do not actually *create* them. All technology undergoes gradual change, with occasional leaps in progress here and there. But we certainly appear to be in the grip of what is sometimes being described in terms of a second industrial revolution, this time around 'information technology' – an industrial sector in which the broadcasting media are firmly placed. Amid the excitement generated by this technological 'revolution', it is possible to identify three core processes at work: *digitalization, convergence* and *interactivity*. In this section, I will attempt to show how the specific technologies of digital production and digital distribution are unleashing these forces – though with two additional aims: to suggest that they are deeply intertwined, and to argue that these developments may unfold in complex and contradictory ways. The critical question, though, is this: to what extent do these technological pressures negate or enhance those processes of commercialization that we have already described?

First, then, let us look at the digitalization of production. This process has been underway in the radio industry since the early 1990s. Until then, the raw ingredients of radio had been recorded, edited, mixed, stored and played back on analogue equipment: it used magnetic tape which needed to be physically cut in the process of editing and laboriously copied onto further tapes in order to be assembled and mixed in studios into finished items for broadcast. Digital technology replaces this with computer files to be manipulated via a series of commands followed on-screen. At an industry-wide level, this technology has two notable effects. First, although the price of computers is relatively low compared with much specialized analogue broadcasting equipment, digitalization requires a heavy initial investment and staff-retraining costs. Some of these costs have been recovered by staff cuts and a restructuring of the workforce: specialized studio staff have been laid off as production work has become concentrated into smaller numbers of computer-operating, 'multi-skilled' producers. The total workforce in radio has therefore declined and those remaining are expected to encompass a wider range of work. Secondly, since all computer systems share the same underlying digital binary code – with sound, pictures and text all ultimately composed of 'bits' of information encoded into files – digitalization produces a vastly increased inherent potential for the technical convergence of media production platforms. The BBC, for instance, has introduced a single 'Electronic News Production System' (ENPS) across its various network and local and regional newsrooms. ENPS incorporates news agency wires, in-house scripts, archives and video and audio files within a computer network accessible by desktop computers across the organization. The system is designed to integrate different sound- and picture-editing software within a single unifying interface (BBC ENPSN 1997). The adoption of the computer as *the* standard production tool of the broadcasting industries means the merging of television and radio production processes – begun for a number of organizational and financial reasons – now has a real *technological* basis.

The computer's binary code is also the essential feature of the digitalization of *distribution* in radio. The electromagnetic spectrum available for new analogue programme services on AM and FM had long been regarded as a scarce resource suffering congestion and prone to variable sound quality by the time digital audio transmissions began in the mid 1990s. Digital Audio Broadcasting (DAB), which breaks a signal down into a stream of individual energy pulses assigned a binary code, overcomes this shortage of space: *several* programme services are bundled together within a *single* frequency channel or 'multiplex'. This means its most direct effect has already been to increase significantly the number of radio services available to listeners. In the UK, the 1996 Broadcasting Act allows for one national multiplex to be operated by the BBC, and one other by commercial radio broadcasters. There is also provision for at least 26 local and regional multiplexes to be licensed across the country, starting in the major cities, with two or three multiplexes (each capable of carrying between approximately seven and sixteen programme services) covering each area (Radio Authority 1998: 5–6; NERA 1998: 45). The BBC has so far used its national multiplex to offer two new national services (providing sports commentary and parliamentary coverage) to add to its five existing ones. Others are promised. Digital One, a consortium including the GWR radio group and the transmission company NTL, operate the single national commercial multiplex. It offers seven new services, in addition to the three national commercial stations carried on analogue frequencies (UKDRFN 1998). Overall, a conservative estimate is that in the UK alone, 196 DAB services will be operational soon after the year 2000, to add to the 260 or so stations already broadcasting in analogue (NERA 1998: 45). DAB radio services are also starting in most western European countries, as well as some eastern European countries, such as Hungary, Poland and Slovenia. Germany had 120 pilot DAB radio services by 1998, with plans to become fully operational in 1999. Elsewhere, significant numbers of licences for DAB radio services have been awarded in Australia and Canada. Developing countries tended to be still at the experimental stage by the end of 1999, with test transmissions but no fully operational services in China and Hong Kong, India, Malaysia, Mexico, Singapore, South Korea, South Africa and Turkey. Figure 1.4 shows the extent of digital services worldwide by 1999.

Two notable areas of slower development in digital audio broadcasting are the USA and Japan. In the USA, the radio industry has been sceptical about the so-called 'Eureka-147' standard on which most DAB technological development is based. Existing operators are concerned over the new competition that DAB would introduce, and are seeking alternative digital standards which might create even more spectrum and avoid the need to share transmitters. The Japanese government meanwhile has been watching what happens in America. Globally, it is the large national *public-service* broadcasters, with their strategic ability to invest in long-term research and without the need to deliver an immediate return of large audiences to advertisers, that have been central to the early development of DAB. And it is the relative weakness of this sector in the USA which appears to have inhibited the move to digital radio there.

Of course, what matters most to the world's radio industry – and particularly the commercial sector – is the number of people who are actually likely to *listen* to digital services. Potentially, at least, coverage is widespread, though biased towards urban conurbations. By the beginning of 1999, 60 per cent of the British population were covered, and across Europe as a whole digital signals could reach 100 million people (BBC DRRF 1998); the Canadian Broadcasting Corporation aims to bring DAB to 75 per cent of the population by 2003, and the German regional governments have set a target of 100 per cent coverage by 2008 (World DAB Forum 1998). Even so, digital radio services can only be heard by listeners who have bought entirely new digital radio sets. And, given the large sums of money required to buy the first, expensive, digital receivers, take-up is likely to be slow for the next few years.

Without the guarantee of mass audiences – and with it the promise of raising advertising revenues – the commercial radio sector has remained cautious about digital broadcasting. Some analyses, though, believe there is a viable demand for digital sets. A survey

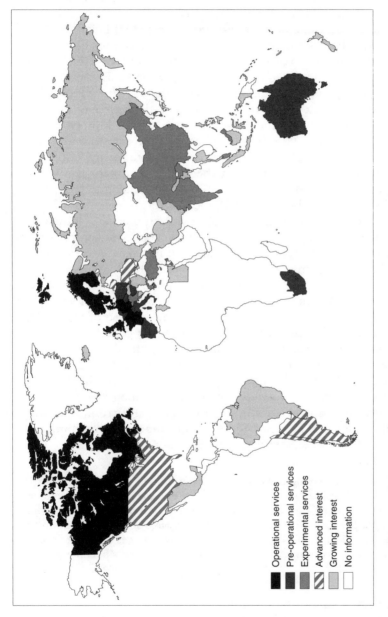

Figure 1.4 World map showing extent of digital audio broadcasting in 1999
Source: World DAB Forum website (http://worlddab.org/mapworld.htm)

Operational services
Pre-operational services
Experimental services
Advanced interest
Growing interest
No information

across six western European countries in 1997 suggested that 37 per cent of households would be 'very interested' in buying digital radios, and would be prepared to pay up to 50 per cent more than the price of an analogue set for a new digital car-radio and around twice as much for a new digital portable-radio (World DAB Forum 1998: 53). In the UK, the BBC argues that 'digital radio has mass market appeal if sets are sold at a reasonable price' (BBC DRRF 1998). The car radio has been identified as the first target for DAB. One-fifth of all radio listening takes place in the car and drivers, who stand to benefit from no longer needing to retune their radios as they travel from region to region, prove the most receptive 'early adopters' in market research. A more widespread audience, however, may depend on decisions by national governments to fix a date for the ending of all analogue transmissions. Though the UK government has indicated it might move towards a switch-off date for analogue television, no decision has so far been reached about radio.

The full impact of digital broadcasting on the radio industry as a whole is unlikely to be clear for several years. Even so, three particular trends already appear likely: first, an initial increase in segmentation of programming – and therefore also of audiences – into smaller special-interest markets; secondly, the concentration of digital broadcasting activity into a relatively small number of larger industrial groupings; and thirdly, an increasing use of the multimedia and interactive potential of digital radio to generate new sources of revenue for those operators who do enter the digital domain. Let us turn to exploring these trends in a little more detail.

On the face of it, the simple fact that digital broadcasting brings a dramatic leap in the *number* of potential outlets would appear to make greater niche programming a certainty. Murroni et al. suggest digital multiplexes now provide *the* main hope of overcoming radio's habitual desire to cluster around a few lucrative formats:

> [This] effect may hold when there are a limited number of competitors, but is less convincing when there are many alternative suppliers. There is a point after which it must be more rational to pitch services to a market niche than to intensify the already hot competition in the middle. . . . In the future, with 10–20 radio services available in each area, the opportunities for niche channelling clearly become greater. (1998: 14–15)

But diversity cannot be taken for granted. Let us, for instance, take a closer look at the programming on Digital One, which is running the UK's national commercial multiplex. Three of its ten radio channels are actually taken by existing analogue services, rather than entirely new ones. The remaining seven include a 'classic gold rock station', a 'rolling news and information' service, a sports channel, a 'soft adult contemporary station', a 'teenage music station', a night-time 'dance' channel and a drama channel (Digital One 1998). None of the music services could be described as anything other than main-stream; and the sport and news channels are formats which, in slightly different form, are already provided by the BBC. The choice of formats made by Digital One makes perfect (and predictable) *commercial* sense: we are in a world of expanded spectrum availabil-ity, but not yet in a world of *infinite* spectrum availability, and in these circumstances, operators are still compelled to concentrate on the most lucrative markets.

Nevertheless, if diversity is not guaranteed, sheer multiplicity of services is, and this has its own effects. For a start, the number of outlets is growing more quickly than either the quantity of staff or programme material that is available to service them. As Crisell observed: 'Digitization will probably mark the first time in broad-casting that there will be more channels available than content to fill them.' (1997: 251) In these circumstances – and bearing in mind digital technology's powers of instantaneous and cost-free duplica-tion – profit margins will be best protected by the efficient recycling of programme material rather than taking on the costs of original production. A second effect of expanded output is that more crowded airwaves are heightening the competition for existing audiences. Indeed, over time there may be a sufficient fragmentation of the mass audience to have a *negative* impact on traditions of high-quality public-service broadcasting:

> lower audiences imply either lower revenue or higher prices. This is in direct conflict with the desire for high quality programmes accessible to all. High quality programmes require high fixed costs, but the cost per viewer can still be very low provided that there are large audiences. The trouble is that, within the market, there is no incentive to recog-nize this. Everyone thinks they can 'free ride', migrating away to their special interest programmes without this having any effect on the core programmes. It is just as if, in a club, members want to buy each of the facilities, but are not willing to contribute to the cost of the build-ing. Of course in a full free market some high quality programmes would be made, but many of these would only be available at high prices. What is more in a commercial world that is looking for short-term returns, even these would be likely to be dominated by the incumbency of existing tastes. (Graham 1998: 37)

Without firm regulation, in other words, digitalization may split mass audiences *just enough* to threaten the funding of high-quality public-service broadcasting, but *at the same time fail to do enough* to compensate for this in the way of radically improved choice. This is merely a reflection of one flaw in market regulation – that left to its own devices the market, in order to allocate goods and services, merely aggregates individual preferences. 'As a result', Graham observes, 'by definition, it does not take account of the value of events that have intrinsic value from being shared, from people being part of a community and from doing things together' (1998: 36).

The battle in the digital arena, then, will be over audience *retention* rather than over audience *gain*. The traditional design of radio receiving sets – with manual retuning – has meant that until now most consumers have not been as 'promiscuous' when listening to radio as they have been when watching television: we might zap from TV channel to TV channel via our remote controls, but once our radios are set to a particular station we have tended to stay with it out of simple inertia. The development of push-button digital radio sets with instant retuning enables much more station-promiscuity, and indeed one senior figure in the development of DAB for the BBC has predicted what he calls 'scary' flows in audiences once digital sets are being bought widely (Mulholland 1998: 17). One technical response to this promiscuity has been to try to develop receivers which can be programmed to 'vector' between services *within the same radio chain* as a car moves around the country (UKDRFN 1998). If this proves possible, stations will have a clear incentive to create even more audible 'branding' of output, so that each service will have a distinctive 'sound' quickly identifiable by a listener when tuning in.

What are the likely effects of the start-up cost of moving to digital broadcasting? It involves expensive investment in new transmitter technology, as well as at least some programming and marketing. In the UK the transmission costs alone were estimated in 1998 to be £35 million for the commercial sector – representing 'a significant cost burden that most [smaller stations] will not be able to afford' (NERA 1998: 57). Unsurprisingly, therefore, Digital One was the *only* bidder for the UK's single national multiplex for commercial radio advertised in 1998. Its majority shareholder was the GWR radio group, one of the country's biggest radio operators, but one which nevertheless evidently saw the economic need for two other partners (the transmission company NTL, and the national commercial station Talk Radio) before making its bid. Regional multiplexes have attracted more interest, though again usually in the form of alliances between large operators: one bid, for example, involved Talk Radio, the Ginger Media Group (which owned Virgin Radio and various television production interests and which has since seen a take-over bid itself by Scottish Media Group) and the advertising company Clear Channel (Barrie 1999). The involvement of Clear Channel is significant: not only does it indicates the sheer weight of investment that is seen as necessary to enter the digital domain, it also represents the first wholesale effort by an American company to break into the UK's domestic radio market. GWR's Chief Executive, Ralph Bernard, has described the investment required by digital broadcasting as a 'threat' to the finances of commercial radio in the UK, and argues that the costs of digital broadcasting provide further evidence of the need to allow radio companies to grow in size and wealth. The sort of consortia formed by GWR, Ginger Media and Clear Channel are a way of achieving this growth within the owner-ship limits set by regulators. So: while digital broadcasting is often described by existing operators as a destabilising force, it is actually just as likely to help *consolidate* the market lead of the very largest operators – those able both to make the investments required and to bear a period of several years with listening figures well below the threshold usually demanded by advertisers or licence fee payers. It may also expose domestic markets to new levels of transnational activity.

Yet, if digital audio broadcasting is a domain only affordable by the largest radio operators in the market, it is possible that those who *do* cross the threshold to broadcast digitally can add new and poten-tially lucrative streams of revenue to their existing income. What lies behind these possibilities is the digital audio signal's use of the binary code, the common language of computers and television in the digital age: it enables not only an expansion in the number of programme channels, but the transmission of additional text, picture and infor-mation services attached to each radio programme. Digital radio sets receive this multimedia content in the form of scrolling text and pic-tures, perhaps providing information on the music being played, traffic updates and news headlines. This technology can, for instance, enable advertisers to market goods more directly at listeners, with scrolling text giving further details of goods advertised – or even of records being played – and inviting a 'direct response' in terms of buying its wares. There are indeed efforts to enhance the *interactive* ability of the listener by developing DAB 'transceivers', which use cellular phone technology to enable a much faster direct response to certain adverts (UKDRFN 1998: 8). A second potential revenue source comes through the use of so-called 'conditional access' tech-nology. This allows the broadcaster to control the receiver's ability to decode a particular signal, enabling an operator to charge the listener for certain 'premium' services (BBC CDR 1997). Digital One, for instance, has already been testing what it calls 'high value, real time stock market information which tracks share trading and currency price movements' (Digital One 1998). And it is because the provision of this type of service would seem to offer the best hope of creating new revenue streams – the sort of charges which have long been levied by satellite and cable television operators for pay-per-view – that radio operators in the UK argue that the restriction of 'additional data services' to just 10 per cent of a multiplex's capacity should be relaxed (NERA 1998: 58). Of course, if the amount of space within each multiplex currently devoted to subscription-only data services *is* increased, this would entail a consequent *reduction* in the space for more traditional audio services – a further blow for programme diversity. Whatever the eventual outcome, it is clear that the introduction of conditional access technology into radio means that some of the 'new' media content carried by digital radio will almost certainly be available *only for a specific fee* for each listener, rather than as a free (or at least cheap) public good, as in conventional broadcasting.

Digital broadcasting not only creates the conditions for an expansion in the number of radio channels, it also moves the industry *technologically* towards the multimedia future demanded by commercial imperatives. Radio will be produced and distributed by organizations with interests in other media, but also *consumed* by listeners using domestic technology that rolls together picture, data and audio services. This process of convergence is seen most strikingly in the steady expansion of 'Internet radio'. In simple technical terms, this involves live radio output being distributed over the Internet for people to listen to on their desk-top computers. Such 'webcasting' can entail the circulation of *video* images in real-time as well as audio, but whereas current technical standards mean most images remain jerky and prone to net congestion because of their file size, the standard of web *audio* is already at CD quality, and is readily accessible and readily *created* using quite simple software and hardware. One survey indicated that as early as 1996 there were over 1,200 radio station sites from 150 countries with web pages (Tyler and Laing 1998: 30). This is now a gross underestimate of the number of Internet radio services: by September 1997, the National Association of Broadcasters counted 4,178 stations with web sites in the USA alone. These figures exclude the many short-term webcasts by student radio stations and community groups. Indeed, since the Internet remains a largely unregulated environment without the tight policing of copyright faced by terrestrial broadcasters, many 'micro'-broadcasters now see the Internet as their natural home.

Radio's presence *within* the Internet creates new dimensions for the industry itself. First, the audience for any station on the Internet, whether it is originally conceived for a highly local audience or not, is truly global in reach even if the total number of global listeners is small: this offers radio companies the chance to establish a worldwide presence, and in some cases perhaps even a global brand. Second, radio stations may gain commercial advantages from the interactive capabilities of the Internet. Large commercial stations in the UK, like Capital Radio or Virgin, encourage listeners to use their station's web sites to hear exclusive interviews, commentary or live events that are not being broadcast on the main output; once there, listeners are encouraged to 'chat' online, join discussion groups – to become *interactive*; they are then exposed to further advertising and direct marketing, where they might order records and other goods. As with digital broadcasting, Internet radio also presents opportunities for introducing pay-per-listen charges for certain web site features; perhaps, for example, where users are charged to take advantage of so-called 'audio on demand' services where they can access a CD database to construct their own schedule of music. Radio stations are also using Internet services as a new programming tool, with user surveys helping to build databases on listeners' tastes and interests, to be used by the station or sold on to third parties.

Public-service broadcasters see Internet radio as a means of enhancing several of their non-commercial functions. Of the 18 million 'visits' per month to BBC Online by 1998, nearly half were from people in the workplace, and one-fifth from students. Since the average listener to a BBC speech-based network like Radio 4 is fifty-three, the BBC has some right to claim that online activity is broadening the Corporation's appeal to 'under-served audiences'. The BBC also uses the technology to alert office users by e-mail to what is available of interest to them or to provide continuous news headlines on-screen, 'on a personalised self-selection basis' (BBC 1998). Such an interactive approach to presenting information could see a change feeding *back* into the nature of conventional radio broadcasting. Dick Harris, who helped establish the 'rolling-news' radio format in the USA in the 1960s, has described the Internet as the natural home for analysis, with conventional radio news becoming shorter, acting more as a 'shopfront' (Harris 1997). What remains to be seen is whether public-service operators will be tempted to *charge* for such 'premium' services in order to supplement their traditional forms of income. Certainly, the dividing line between public and commercial funding has already been blurred by the use of advertising revenue for one part of the BBC's online activity, the more entertainment-based 'beeb@BBC'.

Many radio stations then, see an Internet service as an integral – though still secondary – part of their operations. The largest radio services produce their Internet radio in-house, or at least within wholly owned subsidiaries. Capital Radio's 'Interactive' division employs about 25 staff – roughly the size of a modest local commercial station (Hardy 1997). Other broadcasters contract separate 'new-media' production companies to build and manage their radio web site. In this way a new layer of radio production has opened up, with several businesses integrating radio within their broader portfolios of *new-media* activity. One of the largest areas of activity is in establishing 'gateways' or 'portal' sites which give access to countless other radio sites and services, sometimes arranged in 'channels' of special-interest genres or music formats – a virtual replication of the largest network broadcasters themselves. In the UK, BBC Online has expressed its ambition to become the gateway for mainstream UK audiences onto the Internet (White 1998). As part of this strategy it signed a deal with Microsoft in 1997 which saw a BBC button prominently positioned on the Microsoft web browser Internet Explorer 4.0 sold with the majority of PCs in Britain. The BBC, in turn, recently made some of its radio services available through the web site of the Dallas-based company 'broadcast.com' (which has since been taken-over by Yahoo and absorbed into 'Yahoo! Broadcast'). The company claimed then to be the largest 'aggregator and broadcaster of streaming media programming on the Web', relaying the broadcasts of several hundred radio stations and networks, in addition to several TV stations, audio-books and on-demand music; it also provided each site with tailored advertising and direct-marketing services in order to help generate revenues. The market position of 'broadcast.com' and its successor 'Yahoo! Broadcast' has been achieved through signing deals with other media interests like CNN International, software companies Microsoft and Progressive Networks, and even sports events such as the PGA golf tournament – deals which involve either exclusive rights or some form of co-promotion (*http://www.broadcast.com* 1999). The advantage to each radio station of an arrangement with companies like 'Yahoo! Broadcast' is that a single station's presence on the vast and bewildering World Wide Web is more noticeable and more accessible. The gatekeepers – and this applies to digital multiplex operators as much as Internet portal sites – understand, therefore, that their own value depends almost entirely on establishing an absolute pre-eminence:

> No-one will want to join a network or a standard that looks like a loser. . . . The firm that will win in a network battle is therefore the one that manages to acquire the critical mass. In the economics of networks there are no second prizes. The winner takes all. (Graham 1998: 32)

We can say this, then: that digitalization – in all its aspects – is leading the radio industry into new, and often unfamiliar, territory. Some changes are extremely difficult to chart: the way in which listening to radio might remain an activity in its own right, for example. Arbitron's survey of the use of the Internet in American homes suggests radio listening goes down as online activity goes up. A different survey of households in the UK revealed that the Internet was often being used as an alternative to TV viewing, but that radio listening increased (see chapter 3). And early trials of new digital radio receivers in the UK discovered that in many cases listening to the radio became preferable to listening to prerecorded music on cassette or CD (BBC DRFF 1998; Mulholland 1998). Whatever the precise trend, digitalization certainly brings with it a pattern of listening in which individuals take more control over how, when and where they use the medium. The outlook for radio *consumption*, then, is not altogether bleak, though it is somewhat unpredictable.

We can be a little more certain in summarizing how digitalization in radio is restructuring the industry as a whole. It increases the number of radio services available, but it is not necessarily leading to a huge explosion in programme diversity; it embeds radio more firmly within the multimedia world, but simultaneously reduces its status as a medium and as an industry in its own right; above all, perhaps, it is already leading to new battles for dominance in the industry – battles in which the market position of the largest players is likely to be strengthened, rather than weakened. Indeed, as Winston observes of the media industries as a whole, economic and social interests are driving technological change, rather than the other way round. Various technical prototypes or inventions can be inhibited or pushed forwards, he suggests, *depending on the balance of social forces for change*. The 'inexorable' operation of the 'law of the suppression of radical potential' means that technology which might radically disrupt pre-existing social relations is stifled, while that which benefits existing players is nurtured (1998: 336–42). Digital radio, I would suggest, is similarly only developing *at all* – and only developing *in certain ways* – because of what Winston would call certain 'supervening necessities'. In the sphere of digital radio these supervening necessities appear to be overwhelmingly the political and economic interests of the largest radio operators. This is not to say that digitalization will not produce real and exciting cultural shifts in the production and consumption of radio, or indeed produce what Crisell describes as 'a shoal of independent operators' (1997: 252). It is just that these will be *incidental* to the process, and *less far-reaching* than we might imagine.

A global or a local industry?

The combination of steady commercialization and rapid technological change in the global radio industries creates two apparently contradictory trends. On the one hand, the growth in the sheer number
of radio stations and services is splitting what might previously be
called the 'mass audience' into a larger number of separate audiences,
each listening to a station which more or less matches their tastes.
Technological change takes this further, with the use of radio on the
Internet, push-button retuning on digital radio sets and the ability to
select audio 'on demand', all conspiring to produce a more 'interactive audience', in which the listener is faced with becoming his or her
own scheduler of radio in the home. On the other hand, this listener
will very possibly be choosing radio programmes that have been
produced, not locally, but in some more distant production centre
by a small number of multiskilled producers employed by a large
multimedia company whose interest in radio is perhaps marginal to
television and film. Much of the radio will sound reassuringly local
and familiar, particularly the jingles and parts of the news and some
of the chat, but if it is a music station very many of the same records
will be being played on thousands of other stations and many of the
features might well have been carried around the globe by satellite.
How do we explain these apparent contradictions? Is the radio industry becoming a localized, fragmented industry, or a homogenized,
consolidated, global one? One tool adopted by media theorists to
help explain these apparent contradictions is to explore the concept
of 'globalization' itself more directly. Here I propose simply to touch
upon the idea in its more purely *economic* aspects, to see if it helps
explain some of these trends in radio.

It is, as Abercrombie observes in his work on television, a commonplace of contemporary debate that people's lives are becoming
more affected by events taking place very great distances away (1996:
93). Harvey (1989) writes of the phenomenon of 'time-space com-
pression', Giddens (1984) of 'time-space distanciation', and Cairncross (1997) seeks to alert us to 'the death of distance'. What all these
ideas share is the notion of worldwide *interconnectedness* – an interconnectedness which is somehow transforming our sense of distance
and of time. Marxist political economy suggests an economic basis
to this experience, arguing that capitalist industry uses improved
global transportation and communication to shrink the time and
effort needed to move goods, people and messages over distances,
and so reduce the constraints on profitability that space represents.
The media industry is a natural focus for this change: communica-

tion technology is central to helping the globalizing process in the wider economy, and globalization, in turn, seems particularly significant in an industry concerned with communication.

Abercrombie describes how television has become internationalized in five main respects: through its global content, its global reception, its transnational ownership of production and distribution, the overseas trade in programmes and the internationalized processes of production. Does the same hold true for the radio industry? In two respects, radio's experience is strikingly *different*. The huge costs of television production often force companies into international coproductions in order to share these costs and expand the market for programme sales; the much lower costs in radio favour indigenous development. The contrast is strongest in the poorer countries of the world, which often need to import cheap, and very often *American*, programmes to fill their domestic television schedules, but which can establish their own *radio* production base without too much burden. Similarly, the international *trade* in completed radio programmes is also negligible compared with that for the television industry. Radio programmes cannot of course be dubbed or subtitled, so the essentially language-based character of the radio medium sets its own very firm limits to imports and exports. German talk programmes may be happily consumed in Austria, but the market there for French or Italian radio programmes will be virtually nonexistent. The worldwide English-language market is potentially huge, but again the low costs in radio production remove any *economic* motive for significant levels of imports and exports between, say the UK and the USA. This makes any discussion of Americanization, or cultural imperialism more generally, much less appropriate for the global radio industry than it may be for television, in strictly economic terms at least.

Of course television also conducts a trade in *formats*, as well as in finished programmes. In radio, format means something slightly different: not a unique concept for a particular programme, but a more generalized type of programming like 'Contemporary Hit Radio' which has no intellectual copyright attached. Instead it is *brands* – like Kiss, Classic or NRJ – which are spread across national frontiers. This happens, though, not through any *market* in 'brands' as such but more as a direct result of commercial companies buying a controlling interest in foreign stations, just as they do within national boundaries. As more and more radio companies extend their ownership across national boundaries, so big-name brands also move beyond regional and national boundaries to encompass the global domain. Such transnational ownership has been small so far, but any large-scale take-over of radio companies by bigger conglomerates like News Corporation and Bertelsmann will probably see more global, as distinct from merely national, homogenization. In this sense the concentration of ownership we discussed earlier does indeed become a factor in globalizing the radio industry. But we also need to remember our earlier point: that ownership itself is less important than the shared market conditions in which different companies operate. Just as this explains why different radio companies within a country like the UK converge on the same formats and are driven to achieve the same economies of scale, the globalized hegemony of market-led economics leads to the same programming solutions – cheap, mass-appeal pop music or cheap phone-ins, both wrapped in well-defined brands – being adopted worldwide.

In any case, what makes programme sales and international coproductions largely redundant in the radio industry is the long-standing ability of broadcasters to transmit radio beyond national borders. Audiences clearly exist, both for direct reception of foreign broadcasts over long distances on AM and short wave, and for the more recent direct-to-home satellite radio services such as K-Rock. But, as we have noted, these audiences are relatively small. More significant is the use of international material received by local stations and then *rebroadcast* to the public within a *locally packaged* service. The relative ease with which radio can produce news reports from distant locations – a phoneline is all that is needed – has long made its news bulletins better able to convey remote foreign events than television, with its need to establish more complex satellite facilities. But the creation of satellite-distributed news services for radio like those of the World Radio Network, adds another layer to this dimension, with the same package of 'global news' delivered to subscribing local stations across the world, and rebroadcast to listeners tuned in to their *local* station. In this way, radio stations can and do contribute towards what Gurevitch (1996) sees as a global public opinion shaped by television. Indeed, radio's impact through the developing world is greater in this respect than television's, simply because radio sets are cheaper and more widely used. To take just one example: in Zimbabwe the national broadcaster ZBC reaches just 10 per cent of the country's population with its main television channel, but 96 per cent with its two leading radio services (Scannell 1997). To many people in Africa at least, radio is the *only* means of experiencing global events.

Most radio *content* is, of course, not news but *music* radio. And its main component, recorded pop music, has itself become an internationalized commodity. Globally, mergers are leading to the overwhelming dominance of a very small handful of huge conglomerates, such as Warner EMI Music (which is in turn part of the America Online/Time Warner group created early in 2000). Even by the early 1990s, Negus observed that the six conglomerates then in existence

– EMI Music, Polygram, Sony Music Entertainment, Warner Music International, BMG Music Group and MCA – were between them already producing over 70 per cent of the world's recorded pop music (1992: 1). This music is recorded, produced, marketed, seen and *heard* globally, and pervasively. Scannell, for example, examined the influence of foreign music broadcast on Zimbabwean radio (1997). ZBC's pop music station Radio 3 is supposed to fill a third of its schedule with local music, but the airwaves are almost entirely dominated instead by western music – rap and ragga were particularly popular in 1996 – and consequently almost all the copyright payments paid by ZBC go into the pockets of leading American and British bands.

Of course, it can be argued that while this clearly does not help support local musicians, it does allow many of the Zimbabwean listeners to regard their station as a 'window to the world at large'. In a similar way, the BBC's regional networking of many of its local stations during evening 'minority' programmes, though clearly designed to achieve economies of scale, has the virtue of spreading to a wider audience marginal musics and cultures – Italian football, Bhangra music, Caribbean news – which might otherwise be overlooked. It recalls the BBC's earliest efforts in the 1920s and 1930s to broadcast regional music to a national audience (Scannell and Cardiff 1991), or white American teenagers' first taste of black rhythm and blues records in the 1950s (Chapple and Garofalo 1977), or – more recently – Public Radio International's syndication of a daily news bulletin of Native American issues to some 145 public stations across the USA (Ledbetter 1997: 136). Radio networking, then, is not always and everywhere intrinsically a force for destroying difference and variety.

Nevertheless, the global *effect* of radio's close engagement with music is complex. 'Local' music, as Scannell (1997) reminds us in the context of Africa, is no longer the same as 'traditional' music: nowadays, whether recorded locally or not, it means a fusion in varying degrees of African and European musical instruments and styles. Wallis and Malm have described the process of 'cultural exchange' in the music industry in which 'two or more cultures or subcultures interact and exchange features under fairly loose forms and more or less on equal terms' (1990: 173), and Collins (1992) argues that the forms of 'western' music which are influential in South Africa have been developed from sounds previously exported *from* Africa in the days of slavery. If, as Garofalo argues (1992: 6), millions of people around the world buy Michael Jackson's records, not because they have been duped by imperialist power but because his music resonates 'with the cultural sensibilities of a broad international audience', it is the radio industry, as part of the international marketplace for music, which has played a central role in fostering this global resonance.

Of course these international records, just like the international news reports, are treated differently on different radio stations around the world. They are blended with a variety of other records and voices, by different presenters who use different jingles interspersed with mostly local adverts. In short, they create a different style of programme out of much the same raw material. Does this mean that listeners are tuning in to something local or not? Berland argues that radio presents itself through its rhetoric as *the* local medium, but is in fact becoming the localizer of more distant content (1993a: 106). The networked programmes she describes sustain an *illusion* of localness by presenters avoiding any mention of their location and offering geographically unspecific toll-free phonelines, but in reality a uniform diet of rock is being delivered simultaneously by satellite to over a hundred 'local' stations. In this way, she argues, commercialized radio 'restructures' time and space in a rather paradoxical way:

> Radio was developed to transmit across space, to overcome physical barriers and to make transitory messages broadly available; in this respect, it is a space-binding medium, ensuring the rapid, broad distribution of changing texts without restriction to an originary space or a cultural elite. On the other hand, it is aural, vernacular, immediate, transitory; its composite stream of music and speech, including local (if usually one-way) communication, has the capacity to nourish local identity and oral history, and to render these dynamic through contact with other spaces and cultures. This capacity for mediating the local with the new defines its styles of talk and construction of station identity. But format radio is thoroughly industrialized both in its temporal language and in its relations of production, which are increasingly technologically rationalized, and less and less local in origin or scale. This paradox allows format-based music radio to be omnisciently 'local' without arising from or contributing to local cultures. (1993a: 111–12)

The global and the local are, then, intertwined by radio. And this spatial relationship explains Raymond Williams' assertion as far back as 1983 that 'the nation state, in its classical European form, is at once too large and too small for the range of real social purposes' (1983: 197): the local and the global are encompassed at one and the same time by radio – as they are by other media too – leaving the nation state by-passed and redundant. This 'disaggregation' of locality and identity also points the way to a restructuring of radio audiences in which listeners are not defined geographically, tied en masse to one particular location, but in communities of interest linked around the globe by the technology which casts wide to get its catch.

Yet despite all this, the radio industry itself speaks increasingly not of global scales and mass audiences but of *individuals*. We have seen how 'niche' stations claim to identify and feed the tastes of ever narrower sections of the audience, and also how technology claims to offer the prospect of listeners becoming the creators of their own personal radio experience through interactivity. This echoes Poulantzas' notion of a steady 'individuation' in capitalist society (1978). People, he argues, may be intrinsically social actors – they are shaped after all by class, race, gender, nationality and so on – but they are increasingly being defined by the state and by industrial power as individual subjects whose value is connected to individual rights of expression and consumption, and they are consequently becoming more and more isolated from each other.

How, then, can a radio industry that is moving towards globalized patterns of production and programming serve such fragmented, individual desires? Let me attempt an answer by bringing into the equation the now rather unfashionable ideas of Adorno. He suggested (1991; originally 1941) that the way in which popular music feeds public taste is by assuming a variety of outward forms despite an essentially standard structure: variations are only superficial and interchangeable details, and do not alter the basic structure of a work. Each new piece of popular music would make the listener feel he or she was hearing something for the first time, but at heart it was a *standardized* experience. This process, which Adorno labelled *'pseudo-individualization'*, can just as well be applied, I believe, to much of the current radio industry's mediation of music, or indeed of speech. Each station, or brand of stations, will present itself as unique, through its particular arrangement of records, jingles, speech, weather reports and news bulletins in a set running order that differs from rival stations. But the basic ingredients will remain the same: the same records, the same presenter idioms, the same sources of news, arranged slightly differently but with broadly the same concern for pace and flow and the rhythms of daily life – news on the hour, traffic updates every 20 minutes, and so on. Even the jingles, which inevitably use a different melodic hook and catchphrase, will probably adopt the same production 'feel' – after all, they will probably have been produced at the same jingle 'factory' in Texas. In this view, interactivity and personal choice in the radio stations we select become rather meaningless concepts, since there is little that is *fundamentally* different to choose *from*.

Some critical theorists detect a countervailing force to such standardization, at least in the music industry. Small, independent record
companies counteract the concentration of the big record companies
by detecting and feeding previously unmet public demand for different sounds – and, it is argued, these small, intimate independents
facilitate a creative breaking-free from the standardized products of
the majors (Gillet 1988; Guralnick 1991). In the radio industry,
micro-broadcasters, pirates, small 'alternative' stations, and the independent production companies, similarly lay claim to creative intimacy and a quick-witted response to audience desires unmet by the
licensed broadcasters, since they are 'unburdened' by the corporate
control of a large management superstructure, like that of the BBC
or a big group like GWR or NRJ. But Negus reminds us that a polar
distinction between the small, innovative independents and the large
conservative conglomerates is misleading, as the recording industry
is actually 'a web of major and minor companies':

> These organizational webs, of units within a company and connections
> to smaller companies, enable entertainment corporations to gain
> access to material and artists, and to operate a co-ordinating, moni-
> toring and surveillance operation rather than just centralized control.
> The corporation can still shape the nature of these webs through the
> use and distribution of investment. But it is a tight-loose approach,
> rather than a rigid hierarchical form of organization; tight enough to
> ensure a degree of predictability and stability in dealing with collabo-
> rators, but loose enough to manoeuvre, redirect or even reverse
> company activity. (1992: 19)

This 'tight-loose' pattern has been characterized by the term 'post-
Fordist'. It describes a move away from the *mass* production, organization and promotion of utterly standard products for *mass*
consumption (like the original Ford-T car, a big record-label international artist, or for that matter a mainstream, mass audience CHR
pop music radio service), towards what has been called *'flexible specialization'*. Companies develop flexible structures – smaller teams of
multiskilled staff using adaptable computer technology, and short-
term contracts and alliances with outside bodies – so that they can
take on new forms rapidly to meet changing demands in a 'fragmented' consumer market of many different tastes and desires. In the
radio industry we see commercial operators spreading their risks
through minority shareholdings in stations outside their main group,
and buying and selling these stakes at a very fast rate. The BBC is
restructuring itself away from large in-house departments tied to particular radio network services and towards smaller 'commissioning'
departments which can issue contracts twice a year to buy pro-

grammes from any number of small specialist in-house programme teams or from any number of small independent production companies. Significantly, this commissioning process draws a distinction between 'open' and 'selected' commissioning, with proposals only invited from a select number of companies in the case of the latter process (BBC Radio 4 1998).

This is not a vertical *dis*-integration of the industry, but a more complex and subtle pattern of influence in which ownership is of less consequence than the less-formal networks of connections among the different sectors of the industry. Nor is flexible specialization proof that the radio markets are now irredeemably fragmented, as Hesmondhalgh usefully reminds us in his study of the music industry:

> The fact that marketing departments aim to sell their goods to specific target audiences is no evidence in itself of the end of mass markets: it merely means that marketeers are becoming more sophisticated in exploiting the mass market. (1996: 482)

We have already noted that the proliferation of music formats in radio can be seen to be more apparent than real, and that there is a tendency for radio groups to converge on certain formats in a cyclical fashion. Hesmondhalgh goes further, and argues that all we are really witnessing in musical genres is a process in which dominant forms are continually being broken up and reconstituted: fragmentation of music markets – and for that matter radio markets – is merely 'a strong term for what might better be described as cyclical changes in the nature of the mainstream' (1996: 483–4).

And it is the term 'mainstream' which is crucial here, for the nature of radio still allows for at least some renewal and diversity in the margins of the industry. Leaving aside digital transmission, the costs of entry to the radio industry remain minimal compared with television. New stations, both legal and illegal, are coming on stream faster than ever, and many remain – so far at least – beyond the reach of large operators. There is a small but thriving avant-garde radio scene which reaches a wider public on small short-term experimental city stations and in the margins of the schedules of the bigger public-service corporations. And public-service radio, particularly in the UK and Europe, still sees the work of highly individual programme makers – something that may be unique, surprising and even difficult to comprehend – as useful proof of their public-service identity, providing something different to that of the commercial operators. Taking in the radio industry as a whole, however, it is clear that such innovation is marginal. The mainstream of radio – commercial *and* public service – is deeply commercialized. It will tend towards max-

imizing audiences and minimizing costs. And much of its output –
though marketed as an array of different and unique brands – will
be a familiar blend of popular music and speech, claiming a local
identity but often representing a more distant production process and
a global appeal. Of course, the actual content of radio will always be
a product, not just of the economic and institutional framework, but
of the actions of individuals and teams on the ground – actions where
the industry might establish boundaries but cannot hope to determine completely the final shape of the radio product, or indeed how
exactly it is listened to. We therefore need to look beyond the industry at a macro level and focus on how radio is produced within individual stations and production teams. That is the aim of the next
chapter.

2

Production

Having examined broad trends within the radio industry as a whole, we need now to focus on the ways in which radio is actually produced *within* organizations. Although the most basic unit of production is usually seen to be the individual radio *station*, many of the changes in the industry we discussed in the last chapter, such as networking, syndication, cross-media activity, and internal markets, have all blurred the boundaries of activity. A single radio station may, for instance, broadcast programmes or news bulletins produced by entirely independent external production companies, or may hire technical facilities from specialist engineering firms, and even, in turn, offer some of its own programme material to larger networks. In many ways this mirrors the 'fragmentation of the work process' seen almost everywhere in the production of manufactured goods – a parallel which Abercrombie notes in respect of television production:

> It is a very complex process with a high degree of division of labour; the production process is broken up into a large number of stages, some of which may be subcontracted. A considerable degree of standardization is involved. . . . Each stage is carried out by skilled people who specialize in that activity. (1996: 109)

Radio, though, is a *much less* technically complex process than television, and it consequently involves much less division of labour and many fewer stages of separate activity. The roles of researcher, director, producer, editor, sound recordist, and very often studio operator and presenter, are almost always pulled together into the single role of the multiskilled radio producer. In this sense, radio is even more of a 'producer's' medium than television, and perhaps, therefore, it is more useful to start our discussion by thinking of the producer, rather than the station, as its basic 'unit' of production.

The radio producer will never have total artistic control over his or her programme, though, for two fundamental reasons. First, the station or network which broadcasts the programme will, as we know, want to attract an audience of one size and type or another: it is assumed that most listeners are drawn to a particular station by the clear promise of a certain package and style of talk or music, and their expectations must therefore generally be fulfilled. In practice, this means a radio programme invariably has to conform to some degree or another to an overall *station format* as well as its own *programme format*. It also has to fit in some way or another with a particular station's *schedule* of programmes over the course of each day, or week or year. Secondly, the sheer magnitude of broadcast output, twenty-four hours a day for 365 days a year, creates a demand for programmes which in the long term can only be sustained by the use of some form of production *template*, simply in order to avoid the uneconomical use of time, resources and mental energy. Most radio production is therefore 'serial' and 'routinized', not just in order to establish a reassuringly familiar sound or 'feel' to a programme over time, but for simple reasons of cost and time efficiency.

Production, then, has to be understood as a delicate balance of contradictory forces. On the one hand, radio involves the extraordinary technical possibility of individual producers making whole programmes from beginning to end with virtually no recourse to external help; on the other hand the medium seeks to retain audiences and manage its resources through the use of formats and schedules which can strongly inhibit the producer's scope for free expression. Sometimes these forces create real and open tension between creatively inclined producers or presenters and their station managers. But, as we shall also see, an intuitive understanding of the central importance of the audience and of the very real pressures of time pervades all levels of radio production. As a result, producers more often claim to be able to 'internalize' their own beliefs and tastes in order to reconcile them with the wider aims of the institutions which employ them. So: although I intend to look at producers, at formats, and at scheduling under *separate* headings in the rest of this chapter, they should not be taken as intrinsically *oppositional* aspects of the production process. Indeed, it is precisely through the combination of these elements at each stage and within each programme that many of these real tensions are dissipated and the 'production culture' of radio is formed.

Producers

Producers are the all-encompassing *programme makers* of radio. They generate and research ideas, plan running orders, record and edit material, and very often direct studio operations during transmission. 'First and foremost', McLeish asserts, they must have ideas – 'ideas for programmes, or items, people to interview, pieces of music or subjects for discussion' (1994: 249). McLeish, whose concern is primarily the training of producers, is clear about the tasks demanded of the role:

> Ideas are not the product of routine, they need fresh inputs to the mind. The producer therefore must not stay simply within the confines of his world of broadcasting, but must involve himself physically and mentally in the community he is attempting to serve. . . . Ideas for programmes must be rooted firmly in the needs and language of the audience they serve; the producer's job is to assess, reflect and anticipate those needs through a close contact with his potential listeners. . . . And if he cannot think of new ideas himself, he must act as a catalyst for others, stimulating and being receptive to their thoughts and at least recognize an idea when he sees one. (1994: 249)

The central need for radio producers to 'have ideas' is a recurring theme when producers speak for themselves. Yet these ideas, though central, are not usually seen as personal visions coming from nowhere other than the fertile minds of an isolated intellectual cadre, but rather as a product of the *interpretation and anticipation of their audiences' needs*. Some feature-makers and radio documentarists, of course, eschew the perceived tastes of listeners to offer highly personal and challenging programmes, both in form and content; others take an equal pride in making programmes which give no more and no less than precisely what most listeners are already known to want. Take, for example, the following striking contrast between two approaches to the producer's role:

> If there is a dip in RAJAR figures, we have to question what we're doing. . . . If it is a local station, then it should be appealing to local people, and playing the sort of music that they want to hear and that competitors are not playing, or playing a better mix of what that competitor's playing. Whether we're talking about a DJ's time-check or even a weather check, it can be done in a way that is appropriate to some people and not others, and the secret is to make a programme appropriate to more people more of the time. . . . How to increase your audience is the be-all and end-all. (Graham 1999)

For me, it's always been about an idea that becomes a personal passion and is carried through by me. I never say 'to hell with the audience', but I don't particularly think of an audience: I just think of following-up an interesting personal situation or place and making a piece about it, and fashioning it in a way I like, or feel works, often bouncing it off people and then saying 'this is it, take it or leave it'. In any case, I don't see how you can know your audience exactly, and you might wish to surprise yourself and the audience by producing something that wasn't expected. . . . Lord Reith said in 1924, 'It is occasionally represented to us [the BBC] that we are apparently setting out to give the public what we think they need and not what they want, but few know what they want and very few what they need.' I've always felt that was true. . . . I believe you don't have to be highbrow to take the same view. (Plowright 1999)

The difference in these two producers' visions goes to the heart of more fundamental debates about the mass media's relationship with their audience. If a producer talks of anticipating listeners' unspoken needs – anticipating what they-really-want-but-don't-yet-know-they-want – by, say, presenting a novel argument or adopting novel radio forms with which to express it, it is a line consistent with wider claims often made by public-service organizations such as the BBC: that broadcasters should have a notion of the audience member as a citizen, who needs to be informed and educated, not just entertained. Production in commercial broadcasting is clearly somewhat differently motivated. It tends to cast the audience member as a consumer – an individual whose existing needs should be satisfied, rather than questioned or changed (Abercrombie 1996: 127; Garnham 1986). In this sense, audience research can be a touchstone of the temperamental difference between commercial radio and public-service radio staff. Ledbetter noted, for example, that in the USA:

> employees of public radio have long had a passionate hatred for the use of ratings and market research. 'The reason commercial radio is a stinkhole is because of ratings,' said Larry Josephson, former station manager of Pacifica's WBAI station and host of the NPR program Bridges, at a 1979 conference. A manager of WPBX in Spokane expressed the same sentiment: 'The moment we ask research to answer metaphysical questions, and help us find cultural integrity, that is the moment I believe we become commercial broadcasters.' (1997: 122)

In reality, of course, and given the steady commercialization of public-service radio, this distinction is never as clear cut as that. NPR dropped its resistance to in-depth market research in 1980; the BBC has been undertaking systematic audience research for over half a century. Indeed, *all* producers of radio, whether working in the com-

mercial or public-sector spheres, will nowadays make their programmes with an audience *of some kind* in mind, and they may place
great importance on maximizing that audience. When a station
manager or network controller is persuaded into accepting the idea
of a demanding and challenging programme – one which will almost
certainly adversely affect listening figures – it is invariably with some
other institutional goal in mind which may serve the organization
equally well in the longer term: impressing regulators and opinion
formers with the commitment to 'quality' programming, or staking
out clear differences in style and content between rival services and
operators, for example, or even simply targetting a specific segment
of the available audience. Producing programmes in these circumstances is no less institutionally motivated – institutionally *constrained*
some would say – than pushing for a large audience and then
indulging it. As McLeish concludes, in persuading managers to commission an idea, 'the producer is involved in marketing his product
and normal consumer principles apply whether or not his radio
service is commercially financed' (1994: 250).

Ideas, then, are never entirely divorced from the perceived interests of the radio audience or the broadcasting institutions. They are,
though, only the starting point of the production process. Ideas will
need distilling in order to take on a workable form – and specifically,
that means translating the idea into what is understood to be 'good
radio'. Defining 'good radio' is a difficult task. Producers, like journalists, are notoriously reluctant to explain their craft: many regard
it as in one sense simply unteachable because they see it, not as a
science of clearly enunciated rules, but as an intuitive *art* born of long
experience leading to the creation of some unspoken set of 'professional' standards, implicitly understood as common sense by those
involved. Yet the producer's notions of what constitutes 'good radio'
demand unpacking, not least because we can detect several areas of
disagreement over both the form and substance of radio, alongside
the many practices in common. This unpacking can be done through
a brief exploration of what I suggest are three defining tasks in radio
production: first, the need to find voices and sounds – what is commonly referred to loosely as 'actuality'; secondly, the requirement to
structure material into some form of narrative; and thirdly, the recurring desire to achieve 'liveness', or at least topicality.

Producing 'actuality'

First, then, the need to produce actual sound. Just as television
requires ideas to be represented visually – in other words, for the

process to *capture* physically images that convey meaning – radio requires its producers to embody their ideas through sounds. Ideas need to find their *voice* – and it is the producers who have to find it. Very often these producers look to the real world and its 'raw' sound, and seek to let this sound 'speak for itself'. In so doing, they owe something to the pioneers of the 'realist' documentary film movement of the 1930s who first argued that more should be made of the film-camera's ability 'for getting around, for observing and selecting from life itself' (Grierson c. 1934–6, 1996: 97). Such emphasis on capturing actuality was much more than a concern with stretching cinema's technological capabilities, however: it could perform a social educative purpose, even constitute an art form, and – above all – it was founded on the belief that there are 'more complex and astonishing happenings in the real world than the studio mind can conjure up or the studio technician recreate' (1996: 97).

Some in the documentary movement, such as Ruby Grierson and Alberto Cavalcanti, were as gripped by the possibilities of sound caught by microphones as they were by the images captured on camera, and they experimented with truck-mounted sound-recording equipment in order to be able to interview people in their own homes: in Grierson's own words to her older brother John, to 'tell the bastards exactly what it is like to live in slums' (MacDonald and Cousins 1996: 122–3). Her challenge was taken up by early radio documentarists like Olive Shapley, who made several features for the BBC Northern Region in the late 1930s, in which the voices of working-class people 'formed the substance' of her programmes with 'linking commentary' kept to a minimum (Shapley 1996: 49–50). As with the film documentarists, Shapley's concern was avowedly to avoid merely 'recording the surface' of issues by offering instead a deeper reality through the sustained use of unmediated actuality (1996: 62–3). In the USA too, CBS pioneered the use of actuality in news reportage – a style embodied in Edward Murrow's subsequent war reporting, in which he once laid his microphone on the ground so that listeners could hear advancing tanks (Douglas 1999: 286).

Since then – and especially since the development (and continual miniaturization) of portable sound recorders – actuality has been seen by radio producers as an almost unremarkable device for making the aural experience of the listener more vivid, more three-dimensional, more *colourful*. NPR, for example, included in its founding mission statement its intention to 'provide listeners with an aural aesthetic experience which enriches and gives meaning to the human spirit' (Ledbetter 1997: 116–17). It proved exactly what it meant by this during its very first edition of *All Things Considered* in May 1971,

which coincided with anti-Vietnam war demonstrations throughout
Washington DC. The show's presenter told his listeners simply that:

> Rather than pulling in reports from all over town, we thought we might
> try to take you to the event, the feel and texture of the day, through a
> mix of sounds and events. (Robert Conley. Quoted in Ledbetter 1997:
> 117)

And, sure enough, what followed was a lengthy collage of recorded
interviews and sounds in which listeners could hear demonstrators
clapping, chanting, shouting slogans, being arrested and the din of
surveillance helicopters overhead (1997: 117–18). A similar effort to
conjure a sense of place through actuality is noticed by Donovan
(1997) in his more recent study of the *Today* programme on BBC
Radio 4. There is no lengthy collage of sound in the entire course
of the programme, but each three-minute recorded feature (or
'package') contains, in addition to the reporters' own voices and
those of their interviewees, several purely aural features introduced
to evoke place and mood – dogs barking, children playing, bagpipes,
and so on (1997: 186–8).

The crucial importance of this actuality, Douglas suggests, is that
in creating powerful mental images it offers a form of radio at once
more playful and less literal than tightly scripted and studio-bound
talking heads. Such playfulness, of course, is not confined to the
aesthetic uplands of the radio documentary-feature. Douglas, for
example, sees aural playfulness in the vocal performances of talk-
show hosts like Don Imus or Howard Stern: they often have ensem-
ble casts of characters supporting them, use sound effects, voice
impersonations, graphic descriptions of what is going on in their
studios; Rush Limbaugh imitates the sound of a dolphin when trash-
ing animal rights activists, and shuffles his newspaper cuttings in
front of his microphone (1999: 286). Radio actuality needs to be
understood in its widest sense, then: consisting not just of the raw
sounds of the outside world but of the full panoply of aural tricks
available to the producer. A music show, for example, which has as
its idea the creation of a 'sense of fun' will involve not just the col-
lation of certain upbeat records and the use of energetic jingles but
also a presenter or guests whose tone of voice and choice of words
helps create a total aural experience of 'fun'. 'Zoo' radio seeks to
employ a virtual cacophony of overlapping voices in the studio, in
which no single sound is as important as the total effect of them all
combined. Spontaneity is in large part the result of concerted effort
by a producer, working with a presenter, to achieve particular sounds
in a particular array.

In radio news and talk-shows, the task is both more mundane and more specific. The question each producer asks is not just 'What am I going to say?' but '*How* am I going to say it?': if a reporter or the host of a show is to retain any impression of impartiality, he or she has to find interviewees willing to express opinions which, no matter how moderate or uncontroversial, are regarded as unsayable by the broadcasters themselves. If these interviewees can express these opinions in highly articulate and perhaps even dramatic ways, so much the better. Much production in factual radio is therefore about finding people who will speak into a microphone on demand. Or, as one producer puts it: 'ninety-nine per cent of getting radio right is about *casting* a programme properly' (Thompson 1999). The 'casting' process applies to broadcasting as a whole, of course, not just radio. This is vividly illustrated in Silverstone's account of the making of a science documentary for television:

> As a film-maker [the producer] will need scientists with dramatically strong personalities . . . Concerned with how to present the material in filmic terms [the producer's] aim is to find sympathetic people to display it. (1985: 1, 12)

In television, though, producers can always 'fill' with images, where people fail to provide a good interview; in radio, despite the resources of music, 'effects' or atmospheric location sound to draw upon, the primary 'code' (as we shall see in chapter 4) is usually *verbal*. In practice, this means the radio producer is spending much of the time during the production schedule for a programme doing little other than researching possible interviewees. 'Good radio', here at least, is about giving ideas a voice through the audible display of *voices*. In this search for voices, a general concern for impartiality – or at least a reasonably accurate reflection of the views and voices contained within the community a given station serves – tries to ensure that no viewpoints or voices are systematically excluded. This is not always an easy task to achieve: for a whole number of practical, perhaps even ideological reasons, imbalances in the range of voices and ideas on offer can emerge – a subject to which we return in the section on radio and democracy in chapter 5.

The search for voices can, in any case, take a producer along differing routes. Traditional notions of 'reportage', with its emphasis on showing us the world *as it is*, tend to suggest the producer's role is first of all to help gather whatever pre-existing 'actuality' – voices, sounds, locations, events, facts – there is to be found, and only to ask questions of it later: to offer the world in all its bewildering and *unpredictable* manifestations. Radio documentaries and features as a whole, even when not specifically journalistic, share this concern to investigate subject matter which is often not reducible to scientific analysis:

> I would hate to think that I was setting out to prove a theory when I make a programme – I want to be continually surprised. . . . Stories develop as you go along and go off in strange directions. If I throw a stone in a pond there are ripples, and maybe a fish will pop up, maybe someone will drown. We don't know quite what, but *something* will be revealed as a result of this stone being thrown. Of course I think programmes should mean things, but I love the accidental, slightly curling, way that they can reveal things – and I don't like formulae. (Plowright 1999)

An alternative strategy, however, is implicit in the former BBC Director-General John Birt's influential concept of journalism's 'mission to explain'. The idea, first outlined in a series of lengthy articles in *The Times* newspaper written together with Peter Jay in the mid 1970s before Birt joined the Corporation, is based on the assumption that there is a 'bias against understanding' in much broadcast journalism. News stories, they argued, consisted of too many 'innumerable nuggets of self-contained fact' displayed simplistically in their attention-grabbing immediacy without being placed in their wider context so that viewers could reach a real understanding of issues (Barnett and Curry 1994: 78). The prescribed model for the production of news, as eventually introduced in the BBC, is summed up by Barnett and Curry: a 'method', in which there was 'a thorough process of research and telephone calls to work out precisely what the story was, and a series of draft scripts *before* any filming started' (1994: 80; my italics). Barnett identifies several weaknesses in this approach, not the least of which was that:

> taken to its extremes . . . interviewees were doing little more than playing walk-on roles in a predetermined script. This sometimes meant coaching them in what they were supposed to be saying, even if – as could happen – they had changed their minds, wanted to elaborate or wanted to express themselves differently. (1994: 80)

Although the focus of Birt's original critique was the way in which, specifically, *television* news was produced, radio news and current affairs producers were caught up in the prescription, at least within the BBC, where they soon came to be placed institutionally within a single bi-media directorate of 'News and Current Affairs'. Given the journalistic underpinning of much general radio programming, and Birt's eventual control over the whole of the BBC, 'Birtism' extended its influence beyond straight news and current affairs, and the debate over a mission to explain carried over to many other aspects of the British media (Barnett 1994).

In practice, though, the two production strategies – intuitive reportage on the one hand, and 'Birtist' meticulous analysis on the other – do not stand in mutually exclusive opposition to each other. The reality of everyday radio production is an ongoing and utilitarian mix of the two approaches: some initial research and plotting of argument, say, followed by revision in the face of the complex and unstructured 'actuality' found through interviews and location recording. In this respect, then, Silverstone's interpretation of the production process of the television science documentary stands for the mainstream of factual programming in radio too:

> Research consists in the continuing negotiation and renegotiation of an argument, which even in its final form may bear little or no relationship to the argument of the completed film. That argument will only emerge finally during editing when the fantasies about, and the reality of, the particular sequences which were shot to express it come into dramatic conflict. (1985: 45)

Whatever the precise strategies used by radio producers to capture the 'actuality' needed to illustrate ideas and arguments, it seems they soon face a second issue – how to pull this material together in a way that gives intelligible meaning to what could be a disparate and inchoate mass of sounds. Or, as Silverstone puts it, how to resolve the conflict between 'fantasy' (the idea) and 'reality' (the actuality, in all its unpredictable contradictions):

> All of it somehow has to be ordered and framed. The disorder and contradictions of an observed reality have to be transformed into an ordered coherent, plausible, vision of reality. (1985: 44)

This transformation is produced in broadcasting largely through the creation of narratives. Silverstone, for example, notes how, in order to give the television documentary as a whole a coherent point of view, the producer seeks, not just voices, but also *a* voice – a narrator. And this search for narrative structure is an essential part of the producer's job in radio too.

Producing narratives

Radio narratives are produced in both 'hierarchical' and 'linear' ways: hierarchical, in the sense that at any given point in a radio programme some voices and sounds are given dominance over others – indeed are used to 'frame' the others; linear, in the sense that over the course of time in which a radio programme unfolds on air, these same voices and sounds are juxtaposed in ways which create 'stories' in more or less subtle ways for the listener.

How, then, are the 'hierarchical' dimensions of radio narratives created? Hartley draws a distinction in broadcast news between 'institutional' voices – those that reflect the position and status of the broadcasting organization – and 'accessed' voices – those from the 'outside' world, perhaps from specific organizations or simply sample representatives of the general public (1982: 109). Fiske sees this as more than mere differentiation: there is a *hierarchy* at work in which the accessed voices are brought under the 'discursive control' of newsreaders, who simultaneously distance themselves from – and 'anchor' – everything around them by their introductory and closing remarks; reporters occupy some form of middle ground, lower than the newsreaders but still with 'institutional' status (1987: 288). Crisell gives a concrete example of how this hierarchy of voices unfolds in the course of a single news programme, *The World at One* on BBC Radio 4. A newsreader in the studio introduces a series of short reports from correspondents and reporters – the newsgatherers – who in turn often include short 'clips' of actuality in their 'voicepieces'. In other words, 'accessed voices' are being 'wrapped' by the voices of newsgathers, whose voices are in turn 'wrapped' by the presenter. Crisell suggests that this is a conscious attempt at creating amplitude and depth in the end product, out of the potentially one-dimensional raw material of voices alone – a compensation for radio's inability to distinguish between explanation and illustration in the same way that visual media can through the contrasting use of, say, voices on the one hand and pictures or graphics on the other. The arrangement of voices is a central concern of radio production, Crisell concludes, because only through the creation of this hierarchy of voices, with a narrator at its apex, can we get 'a sequence of "framing" which gives the listener a sense of being led deeper and deeper into the story' (1994: 103–13).

Yet other forms of radio – even other *news* programmes – can work just as effectively through a *minimal* use of audible narration. Crisell picks the example of BBC Radio 1, which aims for a younger audience interested more in the pop music which forms the bulk of its output than in the occasional news bulletins which pepper its schedule. Here, reporters in Radio 1's *Newsbeat* programme are often treated as witnesses to events rather than commentators on them; sometimes their voices are not identified at all. The newsgatherers, in other words, are much less 'foregrounded' than in the Radio 4 example, and the actuality of real people is hierarchically *equal*, perhaps even dominant:

> [The programme] suppresses its newsgatherers and instead conveys its air of authority through authenticity – by a mode of presentation which is closely linked to actuality. And these differences of format seem to illuminate the basic differences between quality and popular news in any medium: for whereas the former broadly depends for its authority upon its 'literary' resources, upon the number and accuracy of its reports and the way in which they are set in context by editorial judgement, the latter draws its authority from its nearness to reality, from its pictures or sounds of the people in the news. (1994: 117).

This broad distinction between the form of 'popular' radio news and the form of 'serious' radio news means that news producers work within anticipated boundaries of 'house style'. Each newsroom or station will have its 'style book' – though producers and reporters will only occasionally consult it because they quickly claim to know intuitively how a news story is to be conveyed to ensure a consistency of tone throughout a given station's news output: shorter and more frequent soundbites of actuality, perhaps, for a commercial station (especially if it is music-led), a greater emphasis on slightly longer voice-reports and 'wraps' by reporters, perhaps, on a speech-dominated public-service station.

The degree of institutional *narration* is, then, a vital ingredient in determining the overall 'house style' of radio news. But the broader issue of how to balance illustration with explanation – how to give coherence to raw actuality – is a central concern of *all* radio production. To some producers, authenticity is utterly destroyed by any amount of narration: the voice of a presenter 'linking' slices of actuality is simply too dominating, too didactic, too often 'getting in the way' of reality – a reality which should be trusted to speak for itself. This perspective usually leads the producer towards *montage*, in which a story is told through actuality alone. The effect can frequently be to create a more elliptical programme, with no conclusions being spelled out, and it is commonly used to explore more abstract ideas – such as loneliness, pride, human frailty, or human endurance, for example – in which narrated links would be somewhat reductive in the central task of creating a composite *impression*. The approach brings to mind the philosophy of the 'Direct Cinema Movement', in which Robert Drew made a distinction between the 'lecture logic' of narration, and the (more admired) 'dramatic logic' where 'the thread' of a film is contained *within* the images and dialogue themselves: 'narration', he argued, 'is what you do when you

fail' (Drew 1996: 272–3). What is noticeable here is that even advocates of montage admit that an *unspoken* narrative order has been
produced, that sounds, and words, and music and silence can often
tell a story without the need to 'point the finger':

> Even a soundscape I did of Barcelona had a sort of story – though
> admittedly not an easy one to find. You'd have to describe it in musical
> terms. You could say the programme begins with the *prelude*, then it
> goes into the *allegro*, you have an *andante* – you have a siesta – then
> you have a carnival, a *finale*. So, there is a story even there. Sometimes,
> of course, a presenter really is the shortest way between two points,
> and the best way. But it [narration] usually only really works when the
> presenter is part of the fabric of the story, when they have a real part
> to play, they are 'in it'. (Plowright 1999)

Radio producers do not, in any case, make a straight choice
between *either* using an 'institutional' narrator to link actuality dis-
passionately *or* dispensing with narrated links altogether. Many areas
of production, ranging from the broadly factual to music shows,
phone-ins and light entertainment, need narrators – narrators who
explicitly do not distance themselves from the raw material of sound,
but on the contrary inject a hefty proportion of their own personality into a programme: in other words, *presenters* – or what the industry calls 'the talent'. The central importance of these personalities in
giving coherence and character to a programme is shown simply by
the vast number of radio shows named after their presenters. The
task of the radio DJ, for example, is defined by McLeish:

> to be unique, to find and establish a distinctive formula different from
> all other DJs. The music content may vary little between two com-
> peting programmes and in order to create a preference the attraction
> must lie in the way it is presented. (1994: 166)

The 'unique' quality ascribed to radio presenters as a breed gives
them considerable leverage within the production process: the most
sought-after can command huge salaries and threaten to go elsewhere
if dissatisfied. McLeish observes that 'the journalist and the DJ, the
presenter and the performer, frequently regard themselves as the pre-
eminent component in a mixed sequence' (1994: 257). While he was
at BBC Radio 1 in the mid 1990s, Chris Evans became for a time
the UK's highest-paid radio presenter, with a fee of over £1 million.
The then managing director of BBC Radio, Liz Forgan, admitted
that the original plan for the *Chris Evans' Breakfast Show* looked as
if it had 'nothing in it' and would not work, but that what 'carried'
the programme was Evans himself (Garfield 1998: 105–6). It was

also thought that hiring Evans brought not just his talents as a broadcaster, but also (since he had his own television shows and a tendency to appear in the columns of tabloid newspapers) what was called 'media equity' – a publicity value which could help associate the station as a whole with his high profile elsewhere (1998: 102). Similarly, in the USA, Howard Stern – who has so far surpassed Evans in having a major Hollywood film made about him – tripled the morning drive-time audience for his first Washington station (WWDC-FM) and was rewarded with a $10 million five-year contract when he signed up for Infinity Radio's K-Rock station in New York in 1990. Unsurprisingly, Douglas notes, he has had a tendency to be 'relentlessly self-absorbed' (1999: 302–6).

The producer's role in this is somewhat contradictory. Although the producer is in a creative partnership with the presenter – a partnership in which programme ideas are 'bounced to-and-fro' – he or she is also concerned with maintaining the sought-for balance between the different elements of the narrative hierarchy: to ensure, in other words, that one element of the programme (in this case, the presenter) does not use sheer force of personality to dominate other elements in the programme (which could be interviewees, music, or any other form of actuality). The importance of this sought-for balance is illustrated by various battles between the *Breakfast Show* and Radio 1's managers over the playlist during Chris Evans' tenure at the station:

We had a lot of playlist problems with Evans. Matthew [Bannister, Radio 1's Controller] would say to me, 'Well, I really like the playlist all day long, but when Chris is on he doesn't seem to keep to it. Will you go and speak to him?' In the initial negotiations over the playlist, John Revell [the *Breakfast Show* producer], who thought he knew a thing or two about playlists, having run Virgin [Radio], said to me, 'I'm not playing all these bloody new records, this is hopeless, Chris doesn't know anything about new music, he wants to play records he likes and feels comfortable with, banging out great oldies by the Police and Bryan Adams.' Within a matter of weeks that had been completely turned on its head, because Chris had come back into the music business, and he wanted to appear very hip, and suddenly it was, 'I don't want to play all these old records, I only want to play Black Grape.' Chris and Revell and his team were all basically twenty-five to thirty-five-year-old white people, and they all liked indie and guitarpop, which is why you never heard any black music on the Chris Evans show, never any dance unless it was sort of Prodigy or Chemical Brothers white student dance, but they just didn't like Shola Ama or R&B, and I found that a real problem. Radio 1's proposition is that it is about generality, it's not about niche, because everyone else does niche. (Trevor Dann, then Radio 1's Head of Music. Quoted in Garfield 1998: 116)

This is, in fact, a quite typical example of the sort of tensions created by the need to employ a high-profile DJ to give shape and identity to a programme: the programme producer is here clearly forced to act as a go-between between the presenter and the radio station which has commissioned the show. What is less typical, but an interesting development in radio production, is that the programme producer is in this particular example employed by an independent production company owned by Evans himself: the producer is institutionally aligned more closely with the presenter, who is also his employer, than with the station to which he also answers. The station is in fact his client – and, in this case, a client rather desperate to hold on to the product he is helping to provide. Sometimes, then, we have to regard the producer's role of achieving the sought-for balance in a programme as residing at a higher, managerial level rather than with individual programme makers – in this case, with the station's Head of Music. Of course, where the producer is employed by the station, as is still normally the case, he or she is institutionally aligned more closely with the goals of the station than the presenter in any negotiation over content, style or decency.

Having established the proper relationship between the different voices, or elements, of a programme at any given time, the radio producer has to turn to establishing its shape *over time* – its linear narrative, or story line. The very nature of radio is defined by time, a subject to which I will return more directly in chapter 4. Here, my concern is how considerations of time dominate the ways in which radio is produced. Other media involve the manipulation of space. In newspaper production, stories are arranged over the physical area of a page; television involves in part a consideration of the use of the physical area of the screen; the full content of a radio programme, on the other hand, unfolds *only* through time (Crisell 1994: 5–6). Hence the incessant need for *linear* narrative structure in all radio programme production, whether it is for small individual elements of output – such as trailers, adverts, news reports or interviews – or for the longer arcs of 3-hour programmes and whole parts of the day. Take, for example, one common radio building block, the *script* of a short voice-report for a news bulletin, factual magazine show or documentary, in which McLeish suggests the producer-writer pays due attention to linear structure:

Radio is an immensely 'switch-offable' medium, you're talking to a very non-captive audience, so the very first sentence must be interesting. Don't spend a long time 'getting into' the subject, start with an idea that's intriguing, relevant, or at least unusual. . . . 'The first sentence must interest, the second must inform'. . . . Now you go through your lists of points linking them together in a logical way, threading them in a sequence like beads on a string. . . . We started with an interesting sentence, and it's often a good idea . . . to end with a reference back to that same thought. It reinforces the point and can act as a 'trigger' for the later recall of what you said. Of course, if you want to leave your listener with a specific thought, or motivate him to a particular action, then these points must come right at the end. What I'm trying to say here is that there *must be* an end, – not a sudden stop, or a drifting away, – but a clear 'rounding off'. A resumé perhaps, or a provocative question to stimulate the listener to further thought. Openings and closings – without doubt the most difficult part of any broadcast – but the final word is often how you'll be remembered. (1994: 65–72)

For whole programmes, which may consist of countless small 'narratives' like this, a larger narrative structure is created most explicitly through the production of a *running order*. Put at its simplest, the running order merely determines the order in which individual elements of a programme are transmitted, but it is very often constructed according to the conventions of traditional story telling. Take, for example, the following five elements in the running order for a typical DJ show or magazine-programme:

■ First, it will often open with a 'menu' which signposts to the listener the range and quality of the material to come – in terms of records, competitions, regular and special features, and so on: it attempts to 'hook' the listener into staying tuned by the promise of events – *action* – and introduces the presenter (or presenters) and guests – the *characters* in this drama. This menu will never be a full recital of the programme contents because it is designed as a 'tease', in which certain items are signposted in deliberately partial and mystifying ways.

■ Secondly, if there is to be a competition, say involving listeners phoning-in to answer questions for a large prize, the competition will be scheduled in a series of carefully positioned 'episodes' in which the prize is only finally won in the closing stages of the programme, after a series of increasingly nail-biting near misses by other contestants: callers would need to be screened, of course, to ensure that any dramatic tension is not dissipated within the opening stages of the programme by a contestant with the right answers being put on air first. This careful staging thus creates a narrative arc of 'rising action', complete with complication, suspense, tension, climax, resolution and even the occasional dramatic twist when no-one wins and the prize is 'held over' for another day, perhaps increasing further in value.

■ Thirdly, the various tracks of music would be positioned to ensure a predetermined flow in which the 'exclusive' playing of the latest release by a major artist would invariably be very close to the end of a show, and records would move in a carefully staged progress towards dramatic peaks and troughs of tempo and energy – with the 'strongest' tracks interspersed at regular intervals through the programme and positioned at either side of less popular elements such as the news.

■ Fourthly, the news bulletins contained within these programmes will be changed slightly each hour, so that even if very little has actually happened, the subtle variations in a bulletin's running order or its use of different ways of telling each story in different bulletins will create the impression of an unfolding narrative of its own.

■ Fifthly, adverts may be scheduled so that each self-contained commercial also acts as an episode in a larger 'drama' built over several hours. Characters introduced in one slot will re-appear at twenty-minute intervals, but within a changing story line designed to sustain listeners' interest rather than irritate them through tiresome repetition of slogans: the technique of 'instant-response' advertising is exchanged for a more subtle 'drip' campaign with greater longer term effectiveness (RAB 1998b).

Needless to say, this concern for linear narrative structure operates over the course of the *day* as a whole too. It is heard, for example, in the daily news 'cycle' in which stories are prepared each day in order to be 'broken' in the morning, subsequently explored through the day from different angles, and then 'summed up' in the extended drive-time news programmes. And linear narratives are produced across the *week* as a whole – in a competition, say, which takes several days to 'find' a winner, or where different tracks from a newly released album are played on consecutive days. Throughout all this, considerable production effort goes into positioning 'trails' and 'promotions' throughout all programmes. A presenter will, for example, always precede a news bulletin or set of adverts with a 'trail ahead' of what is still to come, both immediately after the news and in the course of the programme as a whole, and even later in the day or the week. This is not just to establish a programme's (or station's) identity, but to make 'visible' the 'invisible' future of it's own large-scale linear narratives.

It is important to note that this production of narratives – complete with the tricks of dramatic tension, suspense, characterization, conflict and surprise designed to keep the listener listening – is characteristic of the *medium as a whole*, and to a large extent of *broadcasting as a whole*. It shapes the production of factual programmes just as much as entertainment programmes. Radio journalists, like their television colleagues, invariably speak of news 'stories', and depend on some degree of conflict for a story's news-value. Music programmers want to know the 'story' of a record – that is, what the artist might be doing in the way of tours, interviews or publicity stunts in order to make playing it not just an act of music policy but part of a bigger story to be chewed over by presenters, guests and listeners phoning-in (Marr 1999). And talk-show producers, magazine programme producers and documentarists constantly plan their running orders with the need to 'have a beginning, middle and end', in which the minimum requirement is to 'start strongly' and 'finish strongly', and in which strong characters in sharp conflict might put in an appearance along the way. It is this essential need for narrative in broadcasting which explains why, even when the documentary producer observed by Silverstone had gathered vast amounts of information, 'something' was felt to be 'still missing entirely':

> It is any sense of a story, of an adventure or of a quest; there are as yet no clear heroes or villains, no way of expressing or managing emotion, no people with whom to get involved. No life. No death. No pain. No sorrow. No joy. No passion. (1985: 31)

The producer, then, in attempting to 'make sense' of the unordered world, does so largely by the means most readily at hand, and most readily understood by audiences, namely through constructing narratives. I have suggested that this approach to production extends across both factual *and* entertainment programming areas. This is not to say that there is a single pattern of production for all of radio: some programmes are clearly more tightly structured by rules than others. But the key point, as Crisell reminds us, is that much of radio's output – and particularly the ubiquitous DJ-led talk-and-record-show – is composed, not according to the 'rules' of one genre or another, but on the basis of being a 'virtual matrix' of many traditionally separate genres:

> Such output has an infinite ability to incorporate extra programming elements such as adverts, jingles proclaiming the station or the presenter, news summaries, weather and travel reports, competitions, studio interviews or discussions, trailers, phone-ins, live music sessions

and so on. . . . In miniature all radio is here: the snatch of dialogue in an advert is a tiny play or sitcom; the location report in a news bulletin is a brief commentary or outside broadcast; the on-air telephone caller answering a competition question is one of a series of challengers in an intermittent quiz show. (1994: 65–6)

For such radio programmes, the producer has to piece together a programme which constructs and keeps alive several narrative threads at one time – the unfolding drama of a competition, the build up to a particular record, the changing news coverage, the presenter's own take on the events of the day – in order to create a larger narrative, and one that might just be more than the sum of its various parts. The individual programme producer may call on other 'producers' to provide each individual element – drawing, for example, on the separate efforts of a newsroom, commercial production department, and trails producers – but it is the producer or presenter in charge of a particular programme who *blends* these elements: he or she decides the precise order in which these are pieced together to create the final programme. The narrative tasks involved in much radio production, then, cast the producer, not just as director, editor and technician rolled into one, but also as story teller, advertiser, entertainer and informer rolled into one.

Producing 'liveness'

Crisell observes of radio:

> The fact that its codes are auditory and therefore exist in time explains the greater sense of 'liveness' that we get from radio (and the visual media) than we do from literature; for when we start to read a book we know that the last page has already been written. But radio, even when its programmes are pre-recorded, seems to be a 'present-tense' medium, offering experiences whose outcome lies in an unknown future. Like theatre, film and television, then, it seems to be an account of what *is* happening rather than a record of what *has* happened. (1994: 9)

Liveness, then, defines the main competitive edge broadcasting has over print media, which can only capture events already a day old, and even the Internet, which still usually takes a matter of minutes and sometimes hours to circulate its material around the globe. Radio and television can offer us access to events 'as they happen'. Live coverage of an event is, in some sense, the original, authentic media version of that event: it is not a 'reproduction', and as more and more reproductions *are* made in the form of recorded highlights and repeats and rebroadcasts on different channels, the 'non-reproductive character of the original work' – the original live cover-age – becomes more and more 'valuable' a cultural commodity (Thompson 1995: 21). This 'value' placed on liveness encourages a great deal of production effort in *all* forms of broadcasting towards creating programmes that are live – or *appear to be* live, or are at the very least topical. Radio, though, has a further competitive edge over television in producing topicality: the relative technical simplicity of producing radio means that it is significantly easier and cheaper to produce live radio than to produce live television. For television to cover a live event, a considerable amount of planning in advance is involved just to get crews and cameras to the right location and be able to get live pictures back for transmission; for radio, it could just be a matter of getting someone to talk on the other end of a micro-phone or phoneline. Live radio is not just cheaper than live televi-sion, but it is generally *cheaper than any other form of radio*: the only time in which relatively expensive resources such as editing, studio and transmission equipment are required is for the period of the broadcast itself. 'Pre-production' – the preparation of material, fixing of guests, planning of running orders, writing of scripts – often takes up a large amount of the total production schedule, and if 'going live' only demands the time and effort of one or two staff, who may in any case represent fixed overheads, considerable sums of money can be saved. Liveness, and its corollary, newness, therefore appeals both to radio's need to distinguish itself from other media *and* to its goal of reducing costs.

Radio producers, then, aim to make programmes that are somehow current, and if not enirely *live*, then certainly *topical*. To pre-record a programme requires extremely accurate and time-consuming editing to ensure it fits a station's schedule precisely. More importantly, pre-recording commits a producer to a 'final version' which can be overtaken by events. Most often, therefore, a programme is presented live: it may have pre-recorded elements within it – such as records, interviews, short features – but a running order will always make room for as many live elements as possible. And as a programme nears its transmission time, some live and pre-recorded items will be dropped in favour of even newer items – items so new, so topical, that perhaps they can *only* be covered live. Radio programmes structure themselves to accommodate this:

> programming tends to become a continuing process into which can be fitted units of almost any length without drastic upset of pre-disposed listener expectation. In fact, listeners are coming to expect

the unexpected, the real, the 'now'. (Don Quayle. Quoted in Ledbetter 1997: 115)

Producers therefore tend to 'fill' each programme 'from the bottom up', by which they mean they start planning a programme by positioning the least topical items in the least important parts of the running order, and only fill the all-important opening slot as near as possible to transmission time, in order to guarantee the most topical-sounding start to the finished product.

Indeed, radio's emphasis on topicality means that most production effort is always highly perishable. The time that elapses between the occurrence of an event and its coverage in a programme must be as short as possible. Donovan notes, for example, how the morning editorial meeting of the *Today* programme on BBC Radio 4 sees producers dismissing some story ideas as too 'day two-ish' (1997: 176). And the Controller of BBC Radio's first 24-hour news service, Radio 5 Live, Jenny Abramsky, stated her measure of the station's worth quite unequivocally when she said that 'our real test will be covering sudden events as they happen – will we be able to get to them quickly?' (Hendy 1994: 15). In broadcast journalism, Schlesinger concludes, 'news is "hot" when it is most immediate; it is "cold" and old, when it can no longer be used during the newsday in question' (1978: 87).

Though Schlesinger's focus was broadcast news, Wilby and Conroy make the point that the three most widespread genres of popular radio – DJ music-shows, phone-ins and news-and-talk – all 'depend on the "here and now" factor which itself provides a distinctive edge and excitement to the radio experience' (1994: 207). Most radio producers, whether dealing with music or speech, entertainment or information, therefore use a combination of whatever quick-wittedness they possess combined with the technology at their disposal, to 'go live'. Recorded programmes, suggests the former BBC manager John Tusa, may have the virtue of allowing repetitions, clumsy formulations, hesitations and the 'mental throat-clearing' of interviewees to be edited-out so that the listener gets 'full informational value for its money', but live broadcasting may often produce a 'better result': 'It is stimulating; it is dangerous; it is direct; it imposes discipline on all those taking part; it is more lively to do' (Tusa 1993: 7–9).

Such an emphasis on liveness is indeed now an integral part of producer culture. So much so, in fact, that Shingler and Wieringa suggest there has been a loss of a sense of proportion:

It could be said that so-called live radio is more important to the producer than it is to the consumer, who wants information and entertainment, and considers the question of how s/he receives it to be irrelevant. . . . Evidence that producers will disguise pre-recorded interviews where possible indicates the importance live broadcasting has within the industry; perhaps 'radio hacks' want to preserve a sense of mystery and wonder about the nature of radio or even their own skills. (1998: 103–5)

I would go one step further, and suggest that the technological ability for radio – not just news but *all* radio – to be live, creates a number of inherent tensions in the production process itself. One is the way that an emphasis on radio's topicality can lead to a certain 'flattening-out' of the medium's aesthetic potential. 'Hard' news cannot afford to spend time being 'playful' with actuality: it sees the medium in purely informational, rather than aesthetic terms. When, for example, NPR sought to become more a part of the Washington mainstream political and media establishment in the 1980s by increasing its 'hard' news coverage, it turned away from the campus and Pacifica 'alternative' stations that had once been its major recruiting grounds and hired staff from newspapers instead. These new recruits dismissed much of the actuality-led feature-making of older hands as 'ear candy' (Ledbetter 1997: 119–23). The hard-news advocates have been in the ascendant since, and Douglas describes their victory as part of a trend towards 'sensory conformity' (1999: 324).

Another tension lies in the recurrent need to balance the competitive demands for 'immediacy' and 'reliability'. Hasty production – whether aimed towards true liveness or just a fast 'turn-around' of raw material into broadcastable coverage – can lead to identifiable mistakes and inaccuracies, untested interviewees being exposed, garbled presentation (Schlesinger 1978: 89–90). More than that, though, its appeal can lead to a form of trivialization:

A 'breaking story' is manna from heaven to a 24-hour news-network, but when the first day of [BBC] Radio Five Live coincided with the stabbing of a schoolgirl in Middlesborough and violence on the streets of Johannesburg, the response was uncertain. Fergal Keane, the BBC's admirable Southern Africa Correspondent, came on the line with news important enough to interrupt a studio discussion, but somehow not deemed important enough to be included in the next regular bulletin. And when a police-officer from Middlesborough was interviewed live on the telephone, he had very little information to offer and the listener was forced to return to another studio discussion (this time on children in Bosnia) which had been interrupted. The effect of these uncomfortable changes of theme on the listener was unsettling. Teething problems perhaps, but the question remains: is it always wise to place a news story in the public domain before at least a modicum of facts and background have been gathered? Certainly, any impulse to talk to people who have nothing to say and to discuss facts which do not yet exist does not seem to fit well with the Birtian 'mission to explain'. (Hendy 1994: 16)

Liveness, then, is not just capable of becoming a fetishistic concern of radio producers, but also a goal which can clash with that other production task, namely creating a fully worked out 'narrative'.

A further tension for the radio producer to resolve is that between satisfying the listener's demand for topicality and satisfying the same listener's deep-rooted need for *familiarity*. Topicality demands unceasingly new material and has the potential for constant variety, but *too much* variety may destroy a programme's identity, which is itself largely a product of a consistent style:

> The most potent reason for tuning in to a particular programme is that the listener liked what he heard last time. This time, therefore, the programme must be of a similar mould, not too much must be changed. It is equally obvious however that the programme must be new in the sense that it must have fresh and updated content and contain the element of surprise. The programme becomes boring when its content is too predictable, yet it fails if its structure is obscure. (McLeish 1994: 169)

In other words, liveness, and topicality, and all the unpredictability that goes with it, must have its limits – it must all be anchored, *packaged*, in familiar ways. And this constraint is only one of several in the production process as a whole. A radio producer's original ideas are shaped – squeezed-down some might say – at each stage. To be expressed at all they must be given voice by real people and sounds; if they are to be coherent they will need structuring according to readily understood narrative conventions; if they are to be relevant to the radio audience they must be topical at the same time as being coherent. These, though, are largely aesthetic dilemmas – constraints determined by the contradictory aspirations involved in producing 'good radio'. Beyond such artistic concerns, there are other more prosaic constraints which, though perhaps more 'external' to those questions addressed so far, are nonetheless central to the whole production process. Specifically, these constraints are of time and of money.

Time and money

The common thread which runs through the radio producer's various tasks is best summed up in McLeish's description: 'to reconcile the desirable with the possible' (1994: 250). Producers may generate pro-

gramme ideas and even resolve their aesthetic dilemmas over narrative structures, topicality and so on, but their chosen strategies must
always be practicable in terms of resources – resources of money, facilities, people and time. Of these four resources, it is the limitations of
money and time which are the fundamental constraints which shape
all others, and which I now wish to address more directly.

First, then, money. Each producer operates within a programme
budget which will, for example, limit the amount of travelling time
available to collect interviews and other actuality, the amount of live
music that can be recorded, the time spent in studios on mixing and
editing. Although, in theory, a producer may be free to choose exactly
how to spend this money as long as the programme stays within
budget, in practice he or she faces other more diffuse financial pressures. The BBC's 'Producer Choice', for instance, establishes an
'internal market' in which producers have nominal freedom to 'buy'
the services of other departments within the BBC, or even look
outside the Corporation. Previously, a producer only needed to be
concerned with 'above the line' expenses which are generated for
each individual programme – such as travel, contributor's fees, copyright, technical facilities and so on; 'below the line' expenses – such
as fixed office and studio overheads, engineering support, secretarial
support, transmission costs and capital depreciation – were met by
the Corporation as a whole (or at least 'directorates' within it), and
rarely impinged upon the producer's consciousness (see McLeish
1994: 263–5). While this was seen to encourage a cavalier attitude to
below-the-line production costs because it concealed the true *total*
costs of a programme, it at least made budgeting a relatively narrow
area of concern for producers and, arguably, allowed them to focus
on the more 'creative' aspects of their job. Producer Choice, however,
aims to encourage more prudent budgeting by transferring a share
of the various overheads to each programme-unit and thus 'shift' the
responsibility for spending it onto the programme producer. This
shift allows the BBC, in common with other broadcasters, to claim
to be spending 'more' money than ever on programme-making, but
what this conceals is that much of the 'extra' money is simply there
to meet the newly-added overheads of production, and will quickly
be spent on costs over which the producer, in reality, has little
control. It can be argued, therefore, that this common approach to
budgeting gives producers a sense of control over resources which is
somewhat spurious – and which is at the cost of diverting ever more
of their time and energy into financial bureaucracy and away from
the creative dimension of production.

Of course, many decisions over resources are still made not by
individual producers, or even programme units, but by managing

editors and network controllers making strategic decisions on behalf of larger areas of production. This may lift some of the burden of budget-keeping from the producer's shoulders, but an institutional atmosphere in which costs are under constant discussion inevitably comes to shape the producer's horizons: he or she is always *aware*, at least, of the broader budgetary restraints within which a programme has to be made. And if an institutional effort to make costs transparent is the prelude for a concerted attempt to *reduce* them – to make 'efficiency savings' in the jargon of the industry – then the producer will often come to anticipate and replicate the managerial obsessions with cost. Of course, as I suggested earlier in this chapter, a broadcasting organization may not always wish to make only the cheapest programmes: more expensive productions may bring cultural kudos and public-service credibility. Nevertheless, the overarching pressure to reduce costs leads to a culture of production in which the creative advantages of more expensive techniques – like producing heavily edited and 'textured' features – always have to be weighed carefully against the budgetary advantages of cheaper practices – such as producing a live interview or simply playing another record. Undoubtedly, the latter approach often wins out.

The producer is, here, in a pivotal – and not entirely comfortable – position. He or she is expected to have ideas, perhaps an individual vision, and certainly to 'reflect and anticipate' the concerns and interests of the listening community (McLeish 1994: 249); he or she is therefore part of the pool of *creative* talent in radio. At precisely the same time, this same producer is also *managing* – reigning-in – the creative aspirations of programme making, in order to ensure production conforms to institutional expectations of cost and efficiency as well as acceptable standards of taste and house style. The radio producer, in other words, is required to act, not solely as *co-producer* of the output alongside a presenter, but also as *director* – guiding a presenter who most probably sees his or her role as in some sense an individual and spontaneous performance subject to the notions of artistic freedom – and further, as *manager*, acting on behalf of the station in ensuring a creatively impulsive individual somehow operates within limits deemed acceptable.

This tension between creativity and management is thrown into even sharper relief by our second concern – questions of *time*. Radio, like television, has to be produced against a mostly unshiftable *deadline*, with transmission times determined and publicised in advance, and an audience expectation that a show will start and finish at consistent times of day and during consistent days of the week. And since, as we have seen, there is great stress on *immediacy* as a measure of success in the competition with other stations, the demands of topicality narrow the time frame of production further. The more topical the programme claims to be, the less time there can be to produce it. Schlesinger referred to the 'stop-watch culture' this fostered in broadcast newsrooms (1978: 83–105). But although the degree of journalists' obsession with time may be peculiar to the processing of news, a professional concern with the stopwatch defines radio production as a whole. There is an inherent expectation among all programme makers that their primary responsibility is to be ready with their programme *on time*, and to ensure it runs *to time*. This does not just time-limit the producer's schedule of work at any given moment, but shapes radio's whole production system.

Yet, while deadlines *squeeze* the time available in which to produce, and lead to ever shorter 'cycles' of production, the total number of hours that need, ultimately, to be filled with some form of programming or another *stretches* ceaselessly ahead. Very few programmes are one-offs: most are in some sense 'serials' – programmes which build their identity through repetition and regularity, which have to be somehow familiar to the listener and yet also offer something a little bit different every time. This means that the inherent challenge of production is how to achieve the continuous *re*production of these *short* 'cycles' over *long* periods of time – day in day out, week-by-week, and year-by-year (Scannell 1991). Both the unpredictability of worldly events and the capriciousness of individual producers and presenters working in broadcasting offer a potential threat to the achievement of this task. Production, then, has to ensure that it is only ever chaotic, rushed, or spontaneous on a *superficial* level: at base, its rationale will always tend to aim at 'control and prediction' (Schlesinger 1978: 87). The most efficient means of controlling and predicting is the *routinization* of production – by the adoption of familiar (and therefore more effortlessly executed) production habits, by the creation of programme templates which can accommodate changing content within a recurring structure, and by the 'locking in' of programmes to regular transmission time slots. In other words, *formatting*.

Formats

We saw in chapter 1 that formats can be understood as devices to 'enable radio stations to deliver to advertisers a measured and defined group of consumers' (Fornatale and Mills 1980: 61). From the perspective of those producing radio, however, they can be described as a means of institutionalizing 'standardization and predictability' (McCourt and Rothenbuhler 1987: 106). Both definitions are to all intents and purposes two sides of the same coin: a standardized product is likely to be the best means of predictably securing a given audience – an audience which is drawn to a certain station or programme by the promise of a given product. Or, to put it rather mechanically, the 'production' *of* a certain audience involves producing *to* a format. Producing to a format, though, operates in several ways. There is the task of creating templates for each individual programme – the running order and tone it might present to the listener, for example. There is also the need to set the stylistic boundaries of an entire station – deciding, say, that it is to be a Contemporary Hit Radio station (CHR), or a Talk station. And cutting across both these strata of formatting is the need for programmes to fit into regularized patterns of scheduling across each day and across each week. These three aspects – programme formats, station formats and scheduling – are of course seamlessly connected and shaped by each other, but I will attempt here to focus briefly on each one in turn.

Programme formats

Whatever the overall format of the station, or the genre being produced, each radio programme will be produced according to its own particular format. This 'template' establishes the structure and style of the programme: its precise *content* will vary from one edition to the next, but the *structure* and *style* will always be essentially the same, at least until there is felt to be a need for refreshing it further through *re*-formatting. It provides the listener with a perceptible programme identity because it makes each separate edition sufficiently familiar, and it offers producers the security of a framework to which they can habitually work. In one sense, this is no different to the typography and layout which characterizes each newspaper, or the set design of a television programme. But while their format is instantly recognizable, we know that the structure of a radio programme is invisible, and is only *partly* revealed at first hearing – perhaps by the voice of its presenter and the style (language, pace, degree of formality) with which it is deployed: a fuller sense of its structure is revealed only gradually in 'real time' during actual transmission. Therefore, a programme format, though clearly concerned with the *sound* of the programme at any given instant – the tone adopted by the presenter, the tempo and texture of the jingles, and so on – attends most of all to its overall shape as it reveals itself over time.

The most pervasive means of establishing this temporal structure is by building a running order based on a 'clock format' (see figure 2.1). In a given hour of, say, a DJ-presented music-show, all the

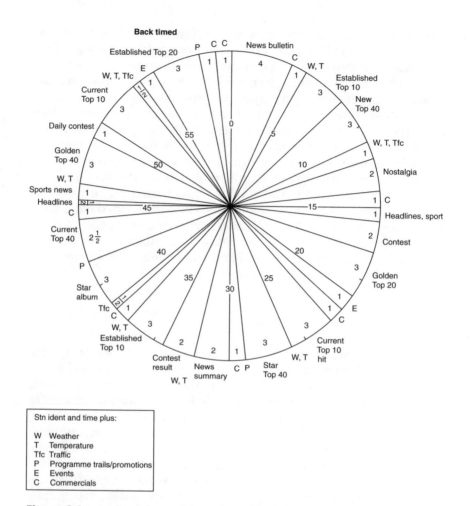

Figure 2.1 A clock format for a breakfast show on a typical UK commercial-radio station with an MOR or Gold format comprising:

- News on the hour, summary on the half-hour, headlines at quarters;
- Eight minutes of advertising in the hour, employing news-adjacency;
- Music/speech ratio of about 60:40;
- Speech includes current information, sports news, 'short' programme contest and station daily competition.

Source: McLeish 1994: 159 © Robert McLeish, *Radio Production*, 3rd Edition, published by Focal Press

ingredients – records, competitions, trails, news bulletins, weather reports, and so on – are distributed at fixed points throughout the hour: this is represented graphically as points on a clock face, so that their planned transmission can be checked against the actual position of the minute hand as it passes around the studio's own real clock. In this way a skeletal structure of absolutely fixed points – such as the news on the hour or at exactly 20-minute intervals (a '20-20' clock format), can be fleshed out with target times for each of say three or four ad-breaks, and a pre-planned distribution of certain types of record. Thus, for example, an up-tempo and familiar chart hit will be required immediately after the news bulletin: each hourly bulletin will be followed by a different record, but all records in this slot will conform to the clock-format's requirement that they be 'up-tempo and familiar'.

In this way, the three interrelated demands of production have been met. First, given that each programme will have a slightly different way of distributing its individual items around the clock, listeners come to know both the particular placing of individual programme elements and the unfolding *direction* of a programme. Secondly, producers have solved the 'problem' of reproduction: considerable thought, research and experimentation may go into creating the clock-format's first ever 'cycle' of production, but once it has been effort*fully* worked out in detail for one hour, it can be effort*lessly* repeated in the very next hour, and the many more hours to come after that. Thirdly, it allows for the demands of broadcasting to achieve constant 'newness' in the context of an overarching familiarity. McLeish suggests that 'the clock' is very much at the service of the producer, here: it provides 'a solid framework from which a presenter may depart if need be, and pick up again just as easily. It imposes a discipline but allows freedom' (1994: 158).

Crisell suggests that the fact that each individual item within this 'solid framework' – record, ad-break, bulletin, and so on – is of roughly the same duration creates, in theory at least, limitless possibilities:

> The segments which make up talk and music sequences on the radio are much more apparent, more discrete and detachable than those which co-operate in a 'built' programme such as a play or documentary. To a far greater extent they can be added, subtracted or reordered without discernible damage to the whole. (1994: 72)

Yet the overall effect of such infinite variety is often to create a great deal of programming that somehow ends up very similar in its overall *feel*, whatever the precise 'individual' clock format it employs. In part this is explained by the recurrence of common assumptions in formatting strategies: the attractiveness of news every 20-minutes for example, or the need to 'hammock' unfamiliar music by placing known hits on either side, or the need to distribute ad-breaks evenly. But more important is that, while producers have to bend their ideas to fit programme formats, these programme formats in turn have to bend to broader constraints: in particular, they must conform with the overarching format of the station or network which carries them.

Station formats

We saw in the last chapter how the vast majority of radio stations adopt a particular format – an overall style and range of programming, defined most commonly in terms of the music genres played, or whether the speech is devoted to 'news', sport or more general 'talk'. I suggested that this formatting is not designed to provide diversity for its own sake. Indeed, I tried to show the negative impact on diversity at an industry-wide level of such formatting. Here, I wish to outline how this 'standardization and predictability' is actually *produced* at the level of each radio station.

For some in the industry, formatting has long been regarded as more concerned with producing *style* than producing content. One British commercial radio manager asserted in the 1970s that:

> We are a radio station, not a collection of programmes . . . our programming is clinical and disciplined, and the way you do things in radio is actually more important than what you do, it's a 'how' medium. . . . Style must come before content. . . . The typography of a station comes before everything else. (Bob Snyder. Quoted in Barnard 1989: 78)

A consistent typography will demand that each individual programme within a station's schedules, while offering something somehow different from all other programmes, will somehow also be audibly – and above all else – *of* that station. It will be required to share the same broad stylistic framework – the same package of jingles, the same package of scripted 'liners' spoken by the DJ to identify the station and its particular catchphrase, the same fixed points on the 'clock' in terms of news, travel information and ad-breaks. But if such typography defines a station's 'brand' image, it is not quite the same as defining a station's format: indeed, a 'brand' is really what stations use to help differentiate stations of similar or identical formats. The format, *in part* defined by style, is in truth very much more concerned with *content*. It is, if we recall McCourt and

Rothenbuhler's words, a definition of the *boundaries* of what a station will present to the listener (1987: 106). Berland offers a clear description of what this means in practical terms in the particular case of a *music* station:

> Every format follows a complex set of rules for programming, including the style and range of music selections, size and origin of playlist, quotas for musical repetition, relative numbers of current and past hits and their usual sequence, conventional relationships between music and speech, and so forth. A major change in any one of these is inconceivable without a subsequent change in all of them and in the relationships amongst them. For instance, a switch from Middle of the Road (MOR) to contemporary hit radio (CHR) would demand (besides a new music director) a new on-air style, different news, a smaller playlist with higher weekly rotation and faster turnover of hits, and above all, a successful transition to new sources of advertising revenue for the less affluent but presumably larger market. (1993a: 107–8)

Production, in this case, becomes above all else a matter of 'gatekeeping' the content. In music radio, for instance:

> The radio gatekeeper may appear to mediate between [record] manufacturer and consumer, in the same way that record reviewers in newspapers do, but his responsibilities ultimately lie elsewhere. Radio gatekeepers have a responsibility to the public only in the vaguest sense: their primary concern is to serve the *particular* publics that the stations' managers or owners have delineated. (Barnard 1989: 114)

Thus, just as newspaper editors choose which few – out of the huge universe of available stories – are the best to follow up for his or her particular readers, radio producers are constantly determining which music will most fit the editorial profile of their station. The programmer of a 'Soft Adult Contemporary' formatted station, for example will automatically exclude from its playlist any record with a 'rougher' guitar-led sound, and will look for tracks with a softer, more smoothly produced, melodic feel.

Significantly, these 'gatekeepers' will rarely be the producers of individual programmes. Indeed, individual producers or production teams, whose loyalty can lie primarily with their own programmes, represent an inherent threat to such gatekeeping. Garfield relates the description by one DJ at BBC Radio 1 of 'entrenched production teams' at the station as being like 'a series of Italian city states . . . baronies [which] never talked to each other' (1998: 3–8), and a second DJ talked of programme teams as 'laws unto themselves, to the extent

Table 2.1 Some current station formats in the USA

Format name	Other names, sub-formats and brand examples	Brief definitions
Country	Traditional Country, MOR Country, Contemporary Country.	Country music. Broad age-range appeal, though strongest in South and Midwest of USA and among 'blue-collar' audiences.
Adult Contemporary (AC)	Urban Adult Contemporary, The Mix, Hot AC, Triple A, Lite, Soft Rock	Current mainstream pop, excluding hard rock. Music often presented in uninterrupted sweeps or blocks of ten minutes or so. Very strong in 25–49 age group.
News/Talk	News, News/Talk, News Sports, News Plus, Talk, All-Sports, Tourism, Talk 'n' Rock	Diverse. Mostly all-speech, though with increasing numbers of stations mixing in music to catch younger listeners. All-News formats catch slightly younger and more affluent audience than All-Talk stations.
Gold/Classic Rock	Urban Gold, Classic Hits	Classic Rock and Classic Hits focus on rock hits of the 1970s and 1980s.
CHR	Top 40, 'Churban' (which includes 'urban and rock hits')	Concentrates on only the current fastest-selling records. Usually a very tight and breezy presenting style. Core audience is teenagers.
Album-Orientated Rock	AOR, Modern Rock	Non-chart rock, drawing from wider playlist than either AC or CHR stations. Core audience: 18–34 year-old males.

Format	Variants	Description
Urban Contemporary	Urban Adult Contemporary, Urban Gold	Targetted mostly at Black and Hispanic listeners in large metropolitan areas. Emerged from Disco formats, now includes broad range of dance, R 'n' B, Latin and Rap.
Nostalgia	Oldies, Big Band	Oldies focus on music from 1950s and 1960s, Nostalgia/Big Band on music of 1940s and 1950s. Both captured listeners from Easy Listening stations in the 1980s.
Ethnic	Hispanic, 'The Groove'	Covers similar range of musical styles, such as more contemporary and more traditional services, targetted at different age-groups. 'The Groove' mixes Motown with Latin pop to target Hispanic women.
Beautiful/Easy Listening	Soft Adult, Lite and Easy	Instrumentals and soft vocals of established songs, with emphasis on lush orchestration. Core audience is over-50s.
Religious	Contemporary Christian	Some stations are all-speech, including conservative talk-shows with a moralistic agenda; others include music with 'a Christian or life-affirming perspective'.
Full Service	Middle-of-the-Road (MOR), Variety	The 'not-too-anything' format. More news and information during drivetime, and DJs given more opportunities for patter. Losing listeners to revitalized Easy Listening and Soft Rock/Oldies formats.
All-Children	Radio Aahs, Disney Radio	Teeny-pop music, competitions, stories.

Source: Keith 1997: 70–83; Stavitsky 1993

that, because the music was hand-picked, producers would deliberately schedule listener-unfriendly records at the end of their shows to dent the inherited audiences of the show that followed' (1998: 35). Station managers, aware of the dangers of such 'hand-picking', more often than not *centralize* gatekeeping in the hands of one person or department. Hennion and Meadel show how music is selected 'externally' to the programmes at RTL-Radio Luxembourg. At the station, which is entirely typical of most pop stations, music is:

> Very autonomous vis-a-vis producers and presenters, who see very clearly that they do not control this element. . . . Most of the programming is done according to criteria which seem to ignore the producers, by a department with which they have little contact and which appears to them to function quite apart. (1986: 289)

This 'centralization' of one key element of production – the selection of music content – aims to leave little to chance in an environment where consistency is seen as the safest way to 'deliver' an audience. On a day-to-day basis, such consistency is enforced through the use of centrally managed computerized systems, such as *Selector*. This involves a centralized 'inputting' of data onto Selector about each song, combined with the inputting of clear 'rules' about which types of record can be played (and when) across the station as a whole, with only subtle variations allowed for different times of day and different days of the week. Selector then matches the 'rules' with the available data on each song in order to calculate a running order which is then issued to each programme producer (McLeish 1994: 160; McCourt and Rothenbuhler 1987: 105). This running order can be printed out, so that the presenter or producer can make some changes and incorporate some of their own choices of material. This element of 'free choice' – long the exception rather than the rule – is now rare: much more often, the running order of music is incorporated *directly* into a larger system of 'automation', in which instructions over presenters' spoken links, the choice of jingles, adverts, trails and competition-features are sent *directly* to the 'on air' studio computer – which subsequently 'retrieves' each item from its hard disk and arranges it in order. Programmes can then be presented in what is called either 'live-assist' or 'fully automated' ways. In 'live-assist' production, the presenter in the studio will let the computer run through playing a sequence of records, jingles, and so on, but will stop it every now and then to intervene – perhaps to make some comments, or to take a phone-call from a listener. In 'fully automated' production, even the presenter's links are pre-recorded as separate items in the studio computer, and then 'time-shifted' so that the computer automatically plays-out the links – along with all other elements of the programme – in an entirely pre-programmed order without the need for either presenter or producer to be present (Head and Sterling 1990: 338–9; Powell 1997).

Head and Sterling point out that this automation *makes more possible* the syndication of programme material across networks of stations, while retaining the pretence that they are entirely local in character:

> Radio automation tends to break down distinctions between local and nonlocal programming. . . . In live-assist programming, automatic equipment relays a syndicated music format with breaks for local DJs to add live patter between songs. . . . In automated programming, all music, commercial, and promotional content is automated without the help of . . . local staff. In a twist that combines the advantages of both syndicated formatting and the presence of a live radio personality, a single on-the-air disc-jockey may speak for dozens of stations while playing a single music tape interspersed with commercials, weather and announcements appropriate to each participating station's community. Using microprocessors and two-way interconnection, one orchestrator can command pre-recorded tape cassettes of local advertisements and regional weather to play at each of dozens of stations. . . . So far, rapid blending of programme sources cannot be achieved with the same ease in video as in audio; . . . radio continues to lead television in evolving new distribution processes. (1990: 338–9)

Most managers within the radio industry regard the technology of automation and computerized music selection as 'neutral' – that is, that it does not *in itself* shape a station's output (Powell 1997). And indeed it is undoubtedly true that, as with all computer technology, the precise rules over what is or is not permissible on a station are originally determined by a living being, who may indeed have real and passionately held feelings for particular music or types of entertainment or news. Even so, once these rules have been set, the precise role of automation is to *police* the 'boundaries' a station establishes more effectively than is humanly possible – indeed to make the transgression of the format, once agreed, a near *impossibility*. To this extent, automation is a significant trend in ensuring that station formats, once regarded as nothing more than vague statements of intention, are now rigidly enforced aspects of the whole production process.

Schedules

Radio, as I emphasize repeatedly throughout this book, is as much about a succession, or *flow*, of programmes as it is about individual shows. And that flow needs to be coherent in order to create not just radio programmes but what those in the industry call a radio *service*. The distribution of a station's whole array of programmes across the hours of the day and the days of the week – a station's schedule – is therefore a central concern of programm*ers* (as distinct from programme makers). One reason for such concern with scheduling, which I will address more fully in the next chapter on audiences, is the obvious need to provide listeners with a familiar pattern: only by 'locking' programmes into regular time slots, so that they recur from week to week on the same day and at the same time can a regular pattern of output become a routine and accepted part of the listener's daily expectations (see Scannell 1988b, 1991). But scheduling does more than establish the routine times of transmission for the listener's benefit: it also allows broadcasters to position and sequence programmes in ways which might help attract certain audiences at certain times of the day, and keep them listening for longer periods: it may *reflect* audience habits, but it also seeks to *manage* them in order to establish a competitive advantage over rival broadcasters. More than that, even, the broadcaster's understanding of which audiences are available (and what sort of programmes they say they like) at certain times of the day can *predetermine* which are the most appropriate programmes for each time of day. In other words, programmes are rarely made in advance of being scheduled: they are commissioned to *fit* the pre-ordained requirements of a given slot on a station's schedule.

What, in practice, does this involve? The starting point in any scheduling process is some understanding of what audiences appear to want at a given time of day. As Head and Sterling put it, effective scheduling is about 'complementing typical audience activities with appropriate programmes' (1990: 287). Audience research, which is discussed in more detail in the next chapter, gives us the broad patterns. BBC Radio 4 analysed its audience in 1997, in advance of major rescheduling, and concluded, for instance, that:

■ The audience for the *Today* programme at breakfast time – the largest for the whole day – is 'broad' and contains 'a large number of light listeners' who 'have lots of activities and tasks they need to complete during the morning'. Many stop listening when they go to work, but even those who stay at home 'are choosing other stations' by 9 am. The new schedule would aim 'to encourage the non-working *Today* audience to stay with the network through the morning', and notes that 'there is a large number of educated, older women who are available to listen'.
■ Between 9 am and 10 am, people still 'worry about being dis-

tracted': they 'want intelligent radio but with a clear structure
they can dip in and out of'.

■ In the late morning, 'listeners are gradually becoming more
outward-looking – less obsessed with "getting my work done"',
and may be looking for radio which is a little more 'energising
and fun'.

■ There is a second peak of listening at lunchtime, when people
wish to catch up on the news and actively seek it out. For the
rest of the afternoon and early evening, the audience is smaller,
except when there is a news programme or an edition of *The
Archers* soap opera. Listeners say there is still work to be done in
the afternoon around the home, and they cannot guarantee
catching every episode of a running drama or even take 45
minutes out of their domestic schedule to listen to something
demanding, but they could ' "mentally", if not actually, sit down
to listen' to something like a half-hour single drama.

■ After 4 pm in particular, younger listeners are returning to the
network, but it is a busy time 'particularly for those with families'. There is a demand for news, 'to reconnect with the world'
in ways that are energising and not in too much depth.

■ Listeners in the evening are much smaller in number. In the early
evening, listeners 'seek programmes that are easy to listen to and
which relate to their leisure activities'. By the mid evening,
however, those choosing to stay with radio and avoid TV are
more committed: they 'regard the evening as a time when they
can concentrate on specialist or intricate programmes'. In the
late evening, listeners are 'looking for narrative forms and entertainment'.

This research has been translated directly into clear guidelines for
programme makers. In the evening, for example, producers are told
explicitly that programmes between 6.30 pm and 8 pm should
be 'entertaining', while those between 8 pm and 11 pm should be
'informing'. In the afternoon, more bulletins would have to be produced to 'provide useful entry points for the listeners', and particularly strong programmes were needed after *Today* and *The Archers*
in order to avoid throwing away the network's biggest audiences.
The precise brief for one particular programme slot is shown in
Figure 2.2.

The example of BBC Radio 4 reveals some of the consistent
scheduling strategies, employed in broadcasting more generally. The
most important of these is *zoning*, in which each day is divided into
a number of 'dayparts', such as 'breakfast', 'mid morning', 'drive-
time' (late afternoon), and so on. Each daypart will tend to define a

BBC RADIO 4 COMMISSIONING BRIEF   Category: OPEN

SLOT

Day: Monday–Friday

Time: 13.30–14.00

[Repeats on: 13.30 Sunday]

Programme type or title: Quiz

Estimated no. of programmes available: 104

Guide price (£):   **3,500–4,250** (5,000)

AUDIENCE PROFILE

There are currently around 800,000 listeners at 13.30, falling to under 700,000 by 13.45; there is a need to hold the post-news audience, including some who are lighter listeners.

The audience is mainly retired, with some middle-aged women at home and middle-aged working men in cars – it is a slightly younger profile, but not quite as AB as during the news.

Around 500,000 Radio 4 listeners are choosing other stations – they are a mix of men and women and different ages.

This time is still part of the lunch-time/washing-up period for many. Listeners feel they have to justify to themselves staying with the radio, particularly if it means postponing chores. If they do stay listening they feel they can give it more attention. They want a change of tone after the news.

EDITORIAL GUIDE

This will be a series of challenging quizzes to stimulate and entertain the middle aged and retired lunchtime listeners.

There must be a genuine competitive element and the score must matter. The level of learning and questioning will be high; the chair a figure of friendly authority who may well have proven expertise in the particular field of questioning.

Word games, as well as those testing knowledge, should be proposed.

Proposals for interactive quizzes, involving the listener at home over the phone or by letter are also welcome, as are programmes recorded on location.

The structure must be clear and easy for the listener to follow. Winning might be over the series, or in individual programmes.

Figure 2.2   A typical commissioning brief issued by BBC Radio 4 to independent production companies – in this case for an early afternoon quiz-show slot
Source: BBC Radio 4 Commissioning Guidelines, 1998/9, 2nd Edn

Quiz continued

INFORMATION FOR JANUARY 1998 ROUND

1. What we have commissioned or shortlisted

General listeners participation quizzes:

Brain of Britain	General knowledge
New quiz	General and specialist knowledge
Wildbrain	Nature and wildlife

Quizzes with experts/pundits:

Quote Unquote	Quotes and sayings
Inspiration	Science and technology
The Write Stuff	Literature and writing
Who Goes There	Biography
Trade Secrets	Jobs and professions
Hidden Treasures	Antiques and heritage

Games with experts/pundits:

Foul Play	Who dunnit?

Specials with celebrities:

Wireless Wise	Radio

Music quizzes:

Counterpoint	Listener participation – general knowledge about music
Full Orchestra	Expert participation – music and playing music
Word and Music	Listener participation – lyrics, songs

Pilots:

One Across Two Down	Crossword puzzles
Puzzle Panel	Puzzles, lateral thinking games

2. Implications

▪ Less was commissioned than expected particularly in the music category.
▪ Some of the new titles may get a second run during the 98/9 year.

3. Editorial reflections

▪ It has not proved possible to commission as many music based quizzes as hoped.
▪ New proposals for music quizzes which offer a different approach, but one still suitable for this very mainstream older audience, are welcome.
▪ Proposals for general knowledge quizzes or more 'questions to a panel' quizzes are likely to be less well received than offers for inventive games, puzzles, trea-

---

sure hunts and the like, involving either listeners, experts or celebrities.
PROPOSAL TO INCLUDE

Sample questions which indicate the range, tone and intellectual level of the quiz or game must be included. Proposals must include the name of the chair and details of how the quiz will be structured – individual programmes and over the run – e.g.: will each programme be an individual game with winners and losers, or a round in a larger game? Where appropriate please include details of possible panellists and quizsetters.

Figure 2.2 *Continued*

particular style and pace of programme output. In a music station's schedules there will, for example, be a prescribed clock format for each daypart, with breakfast programmes being locked into a faster-paced format than mid morning or afternoon programmes (see Keith 1997: 88–90). In the case of both music and speech stations, such zoning is usually accompanied by two other strategies: *blocking* and *stripping*. Blocking 'seeks to maintain audience flowthrough by scheduling programmes with a similar appeal next to each other', while stripping 'tries to create the habit' of daily listening by 'scheduling episodes of a series at the same time every day of the week, usually for months on end' (Head and Sterling 1990: 289). BBC Radio 4's consistent division of evening programmes into a 6.30 pm–8 pm zone of 'entertainment' and an 8 pm–11 pm zone of 'information' five days a week is thus an example of blocking. Although the network does not schedule exactly the same programmes each night of the week, it does use a modified form of stripping by scheduling the same *genres* of programme at the same time each night, such as documentaries and discussions between 8 pm and 9 pm and science programmes between 9 pm and 9.30 pm (BBC Radio 4 1998). Radio stations in general might also engage in *counter-programming*, in which they offer very different programmes from their main competitors in order to steal their audiences: a music station might, for instance, seize on the time slot of a rival's news bulletins as the very best time to schedule an extended 'all music' sequence.

In all these scheduling strategies, the guiding principle is to control *audience flow*: the 'flowthrough' of listeners between different programmes on the same station, and the 'outflow' or 'inflow' of listeners to and from competing stations or networks (Head and Sterling 1990: 287). Blocking, and other devices designed to blur the distinction between programmes, helps 'flowthrough' and minimizes 'outflow' by trying to keep the audience for a popular programme listening to the one which follows. Counter-programming is a strategy for achieving 'inflow' of listeners retuning from other stations.

All this is common territory for programmers in television as much as radio. But where radio scheduling differs from television scheduling is in the sheer rapidity of its scheduling strategies. With the exception of channels like MTV, most television consists of relatively long 'built' programmes, and audiences tend to flow – zap – from one channel to another very promiscuously at key points, such as commercial breaks. Radio is in one sense much less prone to outflows, because retuning, up till now at least, represents quite some effort from the listener. The task in radio is therefore much more about *retaining existing listeners* than about dramatic attempts to attract new audiences at certain times of the day – though this latter goal may of

course be a *long*-term objective. However, music radio in particular
consists, not so much of discrete programmes, but of a very large
number of very short programme elements, such as records, bulletins, competitions and so on. The number of points on the clock in
which programme content actually changes is therefore much more
numerous on radio than on television. Scheduling on radio consequently attends as much to the minute-by-minute distribution of
records, competitions and so on, as it does to the key junctions
between each show or daypart. As Hennion and Meadel observe in
their study of RTL-Radio Luxembourg, this involves a more subtle
layer of scheduling that cuts right through and across individual programmes. Commercials, for example, only relate to the programmes
within which they are broadcast in terms of their listening figures
(which determine their price) and are 'conceived and scheduled
externally to the programme's inner schedule' by the station's so-
called 'traffic' managers (1986: 289). The programme within which
a given song is scheduled to appear is even more irrelevant: what is
important is organizing the distribution of records in a way which
creates an overall sense of homogeneity and continuity across *all*
programmes:

> by cutting across the hour unit, music and advertising give a material
> content to the unit of the week, which is in danger of not being noticed
> – and with it the station's identity, which is reduced to a series of pro-
> grammes separated from one another – if it is only presented to
> listeners as the abstract recognition of a regular repetition of pro-
> grammes. The vertical salami-slicing of the schedule, which makes
> each content person work on a single time slot, in ignorance of what
> takes place in the others, and which thus ensures a strong unity of tone
> and a differentiated personality for each time slot, is set off by
> a common quasi-material framework made up of the regular repeti-
> tion of the 'milestones': music and advertising; lines laid out by
> the central mapping departments according to an overall plan
> independent of the landscapes thus surveyed. (Hennion and Meadel
> 1986: 292–3)

We can say, then, that scheduling exerts further powerful constraints upon the programme-making process in radio in two significant ways. First, the practices of zoning, blocking, stripping and so
on, will suggest to station managers that only a certain prescribed
range of programme ideas and styles can be produced in each pre-
existing slot: programme makers can rarely make a programme and
then hope for a slot – the slot comes first, and establishes its own
boundaries of action. Secondly, in very many formatted music radio
stations, whole areas of programme content, such as songs and

adverts are removed entirely from the province of individual programme makers and controlled by 'central mapping departments' explicitly in order to limit the individual identity of programmes and ensure a unity of tone for the station or network as a whole.

Creativity versus predictability

I began this chapter by suggesting that radio was, perhaps even more than television, a 'producer's medium', and that the job of the producer was, first and foremost to have ideas. And ideas, as McLeish asserted, 'are not the product of routine' (1994: 249). Yet I have also described a powerful array of constraints upon the producer's room for creativity which have the precise effect of making radio production a largely *routine* activity. These constraints range from an underlying notion of the need to interpret audience desires in preference to the producer's own, through an innate requirement to conform to the rules of narrative and topicality, all the way to the systematic necessity of working to budget and to time, and to make programmes that are both internally consistent *and* compatible with a predetermined station format.

Given that the producer's role is one of constant mediation between the creative urges of the programme maker and the business sense of the institutional broadcaster operating in the market, a process of 'internalization' is often demanded of the job. It is seen to be an essential part of the *professionalism* of the producer, that his or her own personal values, beliefs and tastes are never made explicit in the process of deciding, for instance, *which* stories – or records – are selected for broadcast, and *how* exactly they are treated on air: the judgement is deemed to be reached by an informed, but professionally detached, assessment of what fits the requirement of the station and the broader ethos of the industry. As Scannell notes:

> Programme-making appears for those involved, at every level, essentially unproblematic. What is done is done according to accumulated institutional experience, well-tested rules-of-thumb, established precedents, etc. Everyone, more or less, knows what they're doing. (1996: 9)

The producer's skill is acknowledged implicitly to be what Barnard described as 'a kind of notional independence based on self-censorship, the skill of *knowing* without having to be told which stories are acceptable and which are not' (1989: 114). Hennion and Meadel observe how this 'knowing without having to be told' comes to be inculcated at all levels in the production process in the course of playlist-meetings at RTL-Luxembourg:

> It is a question of establishing within the team a sort of 'directed con-sensus'. . . . Everybody throws in titles in turn, including the Head of Department. She doesn't cut short discussion by making a decision. There has to be a sort of unanimity before a record goes forward. But at the same time the Head remains the point of reference: tacitly it is she who has to be persuaded. And nothing works better than this silent search for approbation of the group and one's superior, to make the programmers internalize the constraints of broadcasting, to anticipate audience reactions, to give up 'pleasing oneself' by suggesting this record or that according to their fancy. (1986: 295–6)

As Gallagher (1982) points out though, to 'know' without being told, and to act as one's own censor, is not just to be aware of orga-nizational constraints, but to be absorbed into a *value system* – a system which, at the very least, is capable of encapsulating a certain ideological position. The ideological implications of such 'value systems' are explored more directly in the course of chapters 4 and 5. But what is worth noting at this point is that, regardless of whether they reflect a particular ideology, notions of internalization, or professionalism, as mechanisms for managing the organizational constraints of production, are not unique to the medium of radio. Television producers, newspaper editors, commissioning editors in book publishing, film producers, also have to provide what Aber-crombie calls the 'management of creativity' (1996: 111). Radio producers, though, since they embody *several* roles in the whole production process, have an additional burden: they have to manage not just the creativity of others – such as presenters – but of *themselves*.

What most differentiates radio from other media, though, is the *degree* to which formatting – and the process of automation which helps police it – often now squeezes the individual producer out of the production process altogether. Formatting is both more wide-spread and more intensive in radio than in television. Though multichannel television has undoubtedly 'segmented' the viewing audience, much of it still consists of stations with general or 'mixed' programming that demands at least some flexible and ad hoc activ-ity and broader boundaries of content. The radio market – if only because it consists of many more services in total – has divided its listeners into smaller and even more tightly defined niches. The common assumption is that these niche audiences – whose tastes and preferences are minutely researched – are secured most reliably by the production of programming which is entirely consistent with those tastes. Radio, a medium in which the technical simplicity of production makes individual creativity *potentially* so much easier than in television, has therefore surpassed the latter medium in its routinization of production, in its taming of unpredictability, its institutionalized loathing for aberration. Douglas, who is generally optimistic about radio's potential – who, indeed, argues that it has 'expanded' the public's imagination in a way that television has not – sees the turn of the millennium as what she terms 'the age of the mechanical DJ':

> The disc jockey walks into the studio. Before him is a computer print-out and often a computer monitor as well that tell him which songs will be played in which order throughout his shift. Pre-positioned on the printout, between the songs or sets of songs, are bullet points, some more scripted than others, that tell the DJ what he should say when about station promotions, upcoming concerts, or the music. The log also tells him exactly how long he has to talk. The program or music director, away in another office, has developed this list with the help of audience research, consultants, and computer software programs like Selector. Selector makes sure that musical sequences don't vary too much in tempo or mood, keeping 'the music from becoming too depressing, too uplifting, or roller-coastering back and forth between the two.' Also, if your audience is primarily male, Selector will regulate to a minimum how many female performers appear in any given hour. The computer draws from a tight playlist and helps determine the rotation of songs to assure the right sequence of new and repeated songs. (1999: 347)

In this automated reality, some of the familiar debates about the need for producers to 'internalize' their own creative visions become somewhat redundant. As do many of the producers themselves. Stations once staffed by twenty or thirty presenters, producers, journalists and technical operators, can – and do – quite easily transmit around the clock with a staff of just two or three. This small handful of people simply manage the 'intake' and repackaging of satellite-delivered syndicated material, and ensure that the various pre-recorded items that make up a programme are continually re-arranged and updated in a predetermined pattern of 'spontaneity' transmitted automatically, with or without a presenter in the studio. McLeish argues that in radio production, 'ideas are not the product of routine . . . they need fresh inputs to the mind' (1994: 249). But the constraints set by an industry 'so powerfully centralized and consolidated, so in the grip of research, consultants, and investment groups' seem overwhelming (Douglas 1999: 356).

Of course, Douglas reminds us, radio is a medium of what can be called high 'technical insurgency' – the ability to constantly reinvent itself, and be exposed to new talent and practices through its relatively low entry costs and technological egalitarianism. The thriving micro-radio scene in the USA is one vivid illustration of this. What is more, the automated production of format radio – dominant in the highly commercialized mainstream radio market of the USA which Douglas describes – does not yet represent the entirety of the radio spectrum elsewhere in the world: the industry, as we saw in the last chapter, is decidedly more pluralistic. All radio stations, as we have seen, are acutely aware of the need to attract audiences, but where programming is at least marginally less formatted (and typically, this can occur on public-service stations serving a more general audience, or on pirates or micro-stations which do not need to raise advertising revenues) production can still take a less predictable course. It can be geared towards capturing the public imagination, to produce programmes, rather than merely audiences. As Wilby and Conroy imply, the radio station has historically made *so much* investment in its relationship with its listening community, that a failure to react to wider social changes – even to anticipate them – would in some sense be a failure of production:

> The 'edge' to radio's product is its point of contact with the listener at each unique 'here and now' point in that listener's ever metamorphosing cultural experience. This edge would not be achievable if the business of making radio programmes were simply one of putting the resources and production techniques together in slightly different ways while conforming unflinchingly to formats and style policies. The essence of live – 'living' – radio lies in the responsiveness of its programming to the very conditions (weather conditions, traffic conditions, political conditions, cultural conditions) that prevail and that are experienced by listeners at the moment at which they interact with radio's text. (1994: 230)

But if Douglas' vision of the 'mechanical' age of radio production appears too bleak in the more pluralistic radio landscape outside the USA, Wilby and Conroy's vision of a living, *organic*, mode of production also now seems hopelessly optimistic, and too influenced by the public-service traditions long dominant in UK radio. Given the broader industrial trends we observed in chapter 1 – and particularly the ever more rigid, ever more segmented nature of the global radio market as a whole – the resources and production techniques of radio – not all radio, but much of the mainstream of radio – are, it seems, steadily geared more and more towards conforming unflinchingly to formats. If this is the case, the critical question then becomes whether or not the medium still has anything to say to – or about – the society within which it operates. We need, in fact, to move our attention outwards, from the internal concerns of the radio industry and individual radio stations to the wider society with which they are most directly concerned, their body of listeners.

3

Audiences

Radio is always and everywhere produced *for audiences* – for *us* – whether we are counted in hundreds or in millions. Each station or network will always have a particular audience in mind when constructing its format – indeed, as we saw in chapter 1, the audience is often *the* product of radio: commercial radio needs audiences to generate advertising revenue, public-service radio needs them to justify its public funding. Getting listeners – the right sort and in the right number – is what it is all about. Producers may design programmes to deliberately attract certain audience sectors – and they will always have some notion of who they expect to listen. These concepts of 'the radio audience' shape programming, and mould our listening experience. But while they deal with statistical averages and generalities – while, just like the television industry, they deal with us as a *mass* of some size or another – radio listening is also a peculiarly *individual* phenomenon. The study of radio is littered with certain recurring phrases – it 'paints pictures' in the 'mind's eye', it is the most 'personal' and 'intimate' of the mass media (McLeish 1994, Wilby and Conroy 1994). Such phrases place this individual dimension centre stage in any discussion of the radio audience. There is, then, a gulf to be explored, between a concept of the audience as a community – and even a market – and the highly personal nature of the listening process.

Parallel to this, and intimately connected with it, is another apparently unbridgeable gulf: between a concept of the radio audience as one which is very much in control of the medium, using it for our own ends and interpreting it in our own ways, and a rather different concept of the radio audience as more vulnerable to manipulation, as unwitting consumers of radio's 'messages'. There are, then, two underlying themes running through this chapter: the relationship between the *mass* and the *individual* aspects of our listening, and a debate over whether we are more '*active*' or more '*passive*' in our relationship with the medium we consume. In the process of exploring these themes, we need to touch upon several wider theories of media consumption, and question some of the methodologies of audience research. But I would like to begin with an exploration of the act of listening itself.

The act of listening

Listening to the radio is not quite the same as listening to all the other sounds which surround us. Even so, a brief discussion of how we listen to the sounds of the world in general has proved a useful starting point for many studies in seeking to understand the listener's relationship with the medium. One recurring theme is the way in which we assume that the *images* seen on television screens, billboards, films, magazines, are inherently more powerful, more affecting, than the *sounds* to which we are also exposed. Thorn (1997) draws attention to what he calls an assumed 'hierarchy of the senses', in which most hearing is ranked 'a poor second', after seeing. We all tend, after all, to listen to the sounds around us while doing other things – it is a *secondary* activity. Indeed, we often don't really *listen* to these sounds at all: we simply *hear* them, barely registering them, and certainly only rarely turning our full attention to them as we would habitually when looking directly at the various images around us. But Thorn draws our attention to the importance of sound in pre-literate communities studied by anthropologists. Drawing on the work of, among others, Classen (1993), Feld (1994), Stoller (1989) and Gell (1995), Thorn explores the importance, specifically, of the *soundscape* in people's understanding of their environment. He notes, for example, that the Suya Indians of the Brazilian Matto Grosso, use the term 'it is in my ear' to indicate that they have learned something, even something visual such as a weaving pattern: sight is considered an 'anti-social sense' cultivated only by witches (Classen 1993: 9). Among the Umeda of Papua New Guinea too, hearing something, rather than seeing it, is what makes that 'something' real. Thorn quotes Gell's conversation with an Umeda man who described being chased down a path by an ogre:

> 'Yes, yes', I said, cutting him off, 'but did you actually see the ogre?'
> My informant looked at me in perplexity. 'It was dark, I was running

away, it was there on the path, going hu-hu-hu'. . . . When, I won-
dered, was an Umeda going to admit to actually seeing one of these
monsters? But that, of course, was a misapprehension bred of a
visually based notion of the real. For Umeda, hearing is believing, and
the Umeda really do hear ogres. (Gell 1995: 239)

The issue here, as Thorn suggests, is not whether or not on this particular occasion a man had been pursued by an ogre, but that what
constitutes evidence for the existence of ogres in principle is *aural*,
rather than visual. Other anthropological studies, of say, the Songhay
and Kaluli peoples, have drawn similar examples of the way in which
a sense of a specific place is defined in largely aural terms – the sound
of a place, rather than its appearance is what marks it off from other
places. Sound, in many non-western societies cannot, then, be
omitted from any attempt to understand the nature of knowledge:

The soundscape characteristic of any particular set of cultural and
geographic circumstances, produces 'the foundation of experience'
for those whose whole way of life is built on that foundation. (Thorn
1997: 4)

These anthropological insights provide a firm basis for examining
radio's impact in many parts of the developing world, where literacy
levels are low and oral culture is more widespread – a subject pursued
a little further in chapter 5. Here, though, the critical question is
whether the privileging of sound over image found in Papua New
Guinea and the Brazilian rainforest is rather culturally specific –
thrown up in large part by the conditions of the rainforest, in which
little is clearly visible but a great deal is concretely audible. If it is
culturally specific, it may not really tell us very much about the
importance of sound in more literate, western society. Certainly,
Synott suggests, the use of the alphabet and of writing in highly literate cultures immediately demands a 'shift' in the sensorium away
from the oral-aural and towards the task of *looking* at the printed
page or image (1993: 210). Thorn, though, draws attention to a
research project in which he asked young people in Britain to write
about the way in which their personal soundscapes had meaning.
They wrote about 'dad's razor being scraped night and morning,
giving me a sense of security', 'the sound of the key in the front-door
meaning dad was home and everything was alright', and 'the sound
of family moving about the house after I'd gone to bed giving me a
sense of security and belonging'. Sounds may have lost their primacy
over images in western society, Thorn concludes, but they do still
help constitute a person's sense of both time and place: all human

experience is contextualized in a soundscape, and the aural bound-aries of a soundscape can be marked temporally (by associating different sounds with different times of the day), personally (by associating different sounds with different people), and spatially (by associating different sounds with different spaces) (1997: 5–6).

What is also clear from Thorn's findings, is the *emotional* quality of his respondents' descriptions of sound. Storr suggests that 'there is something "deeper" about hearing than seeing' (1992). And the cognitive basis for this broad assertion is described by Douglas:

> When information comes solely through our auditory system, our mental imaging systems have freewheeling authority to generate what-ever visuals they want. . . . When sound is our only source of infor-mation, our imaginations milk it for all it's worth, creating detailed tableaux that images, of course, preempt. (1999: 28)

This ability – indeed this *need* – for our brains to 'fill in' any missing visual data, is the psychological basis for the platitude that radio, as an aural medium, 'stimulates the imagination'. We may often use our imaginations when watching television or a film, but being presented with an image is a pre-emptive strike which inevitably *narrows* the options for creating our own mental images of how things look; in denying us an image, blindness – and radio is, of course, a blind medium – forces us into more powerful, and ultimately more plea-surable, cognitive activity. This imaginative potential for sound is illustrated vividly through the findings of one psychological study in the USA:

> When two groups of children were given the beginning of a story – one group via radio, the other via TV – the children who had heard the story created much more imaginative conclusions than those who had seen the television version. It is interesting that children who see a story on TV remember the action better; those who hear it on the radio remember the dialogue better. Children also draw more imagi-native pictures when they hear a story on the radio. Imaginativeness is a skill that you develop and get better at, a skill that radio enhances. (Douglas 1999: 26–7)

The radio listener, then, is actively *participating* in the creation of images to an extent that, say, the television viewer cannot. Radio the-orists have frequently pointed out that, in being a blind medium, radio does not, therefore, have to always disguise or compensate for its lack of visuals, but can instead celebrate, indeed *exploit* the imagi-native potential of the aural domain (Douglas 1999: 28–9; Crisell 1994: 6–10; Shingler and Wieringa 1998: 73–93). In watching a television drama, or a stage play, for instance, Crisell points out that the images on offer cannot be 'abolished' from the viewers minds:

> In radio, however, we are free – forced – to imagine everything. . . . However often we hear them, and in however much detail they are described, we will be required to picture them in our own way . . . [Radio dramas] make *us* 'construct' the appearance and movements of a character as much as or more than the actor who plays it, force *us* to build the scenery instead of a stage carpenter. . . . But as we are already well aware, there are as many potential realizations of the play as there are listeners, and this, together with the fact that radio can accompany the listener wherever she goes, renders the play not so much an external event as the private and unique creation of each person who hears it. (1994: 153–4)

Douglas, though, widens the debate over the power of aurality beyond the relatively narrow confines of radio's much-proclaimed ability to 'paint pictures' in the mind's eye. She does this in three ways. First, she suggests that, 'the more we work on making our own images, the more powerfully attached we become to them, arising as they do from deep within us' (1999: 26). In other words, it is not just that radio 'stimulates the imagination', but that the innate pleasurability of such cognitive activity helps forge a strong *emotional* attachment to the radio medium itself, even in a predominantly televisual age. Where there is a modern-day nostalgia for radio, then, it is a nostalgia not only for *what* we may once have listened to, but also for *how* we may once have listened.

Secondly, she points out that radio's role as a purveyor of music brings further associational qualities to the medium. Drawing again from the work of neuroscientists, she notes that the auditory system of the brain feeds into the limbic system, the part of the brain from which we derive emotions and memory. The limbic system generates a host of associations and mental states, and once activated in a pleasurable way, it may want to sustain that level of arousal. Music is in many ways the perfect vehicle for this, and music that is in one way or another *familiar* is particularly resonant:

> The brain apparently becomes accustomed to patterns of music based on exposure to different musical traditions and stores knowledge of certain kinds of musical sequences in groups of cells. Based on these stored connections, the brain will predict which notes will come next in a sequence. When this prediction is right, the connections between the brain cells where these sequences have been stored become even stronger. The more we listen to certain kinds of music, then, the more we learn to like it. While the brain seems to like the surprise that comes

> when musical expectations are violated – such as through syncopation, dissonance, or unusual melodies – evidence suggests that predictability produces more pleasure. Successful music in a range of styles handles this paradox by setting up our musical expectations and then toying with them before providing a familiar resolution. (1999: 32)

This, it would suggest, helps explain the emotional attachment we feel, not just to music in general, but specifically to music *on the radio*. We can associate music with our own memories and emotions, but also more specifically use radio's predilection for programming the 'new-yet-reassuringly-familiar' to feed deeper neurological cravings for predictability.

Thirdly, Douglas draws our attention to a defining characteristic of radio beyond its aural dimension, namely the *sociable* dimension of the listening experience. When Storr says that there is something 'deeper about hearing', he also goes on to argue that there is something about hearing other people which fosters human relationships even more than seeing them. Douglas supports this by quoting the suggestion made by one researcher on perception that, 'Listening is centripetal; it pulls you into the world. Looking is centrifugal; it separates you from the world' (1999: 30). Sight, Douglas argues, may allow us some power to gaze and dissect at a distance, to be apart from our surroundings; sound, in contrast, 'envelopes us, pouring into us, whether we want it to or not, including us, involving us' (1999: 30). Listening to others is, in other words, a more inherently *sociable* act than reading about others, or even watching others. And listening together *at the same time* is the key to this sociability:

> Orality generates a powerful participatory mystique. Because the act of listening simultaneously to spoken words forms hearers into a group (while reading turns people in on themselves), orality fosters a strong collective sensibility. People listening to a common voice, or to the same music, act and react at the same time. They become an aggregate entity – an audience – and whether or not they all agree with or like what they hear, they are unified around that common experience. (1999: 29)

Most of us, of course, tend to listen to the radio alone, rather than in a small group of friends or relatives. But while we listen alone, we are also somehow aware of *others* elsewhere, listening to the same words or music at precisely the same time as us. Since this auditory experience is live – and therefore fleeting, perishable, immediate, it encourages a concentration on the present. 'It is', Douglas suggests, 'this evanescent nature of what we hear, this absolute simultaneity of experience, that drives us to bond together'. Radio thus ties together utterly diverse and unknown people 'by the most gossamer connections', to create not just a mass of individual listeners, but an *audience* with some sense of community (1999: 22–30). This sense of community is not simply engendered by radio producers exposing the sounds of the world to us through their programmes, but also by the sense of shared experience we gain for ourselves from listening to a broadcast medium.

Shared experience can, of course, be more illusory than real: other listeners, like the radio presenters themselves, are never visible to us, and we are unlikely ever to meet them – they have to be *imagined* into being. The various ways in which this process might contribute to people's sense of *identity* are explored in chapter 5. For now, though, it is relevant to note that these imagined communities are rarely fixed in time or space. The geographical reach of 'shared experience' is, of course, determined by the physical reach of the radio station itself: the footprint of a station's transmitter helps define the boundaries of the community it serves, whether national or local. But the experience does not have to be based on geography or political boundaries: to listen to a sports station, or a religious station, or a jazz station, for instance, is to become – if only temporarily – a member of a community of interest which ignores location. Sometimes, we will be listening to something which makes us feel part of a national entity, at other times we may seek niche stations which offer a conspiratorial sense of *difference*. Listening might allow us, for example, to experience our identity in terms of our generation: most of us develop our musical preferences as teenagers, and for many of us, the establishment of mental 'groovings' makes us reach a point where we are reluctant to take on board new, unfamiliar music – so that music has a generational quality, and choosing a certain music station is also an expression of membership of a particular generation. Radio, in other words, gives us the potential to experience at the same time *multiple* identities: not just one 'kinship web', as McLuhan envisaged it, but many.

The act of listening to the radio is, then, quite paradoxical. It prompts us to explore our innermost thoughts and memories, but it also takes us out of ourselves. It stimulates idiosyncratic mental images, but also panders to our desire for the familiar song and the shared experience. In the end, then, the act of listening to the radio is defined by this paradox. It is more personal, more intimate, more innately prone, at a cognitive level, to individual interpretation than the process of watching television or reading the newspaper. It is also, and simultaneously, an act which is *replicated* countless times among members of the wider audience. And the sense of this wider phenomenon *is part of the individual experience*. This, at least, is what listening to radio offers *in theory*. It marks radio's potential. The critical question arises, though, as to whether or not we take advantage of radio's potential. Or, to put the question another way: how do we, the radio audience, most often *use* the medium *in practice*?

The radio audience

What, then, do we actually know about how radio is being used in the domestic and private sphere? Certainly, not as much as we would like, though there have been several wide-ranging academic studies, both quantitative and qualitative since the pioneering work of Lazarsfeld and Field in the USA (1946) and Silvey in the UK (1974). The radio industry is, of course, very active in day-to-day audience research of its own, if only because the ability of each station to sell advertising slots is crucially dependent on providing evidence of the precise size and composition of its audience. Public-service broadcasters, keen to compete, follow suit. There is, then, a sizable industry in audience research, and a consequent torrent of data delivered to stations not just daily, but sometimes hourly. In America, Arbitron is the market leader in measuring 'ratings' with several thousand stations contracting its services; in the UK, radio audiences are measured by RAJAR, which is jointly owned by the BBC and the commercial companies; elsewhere in Europe, companies such as Gallup and Ipsos, with broader interests in public-opinion polling and advertising, are the main players. Much of the information these companies generate is supplied to subscribing stations on a confidential basis as a tactical tool in competing with rivals, but a great deal is also publicly available, and can be drawn on here.

First, though, we need to understand a little of the methodology of audience measurement – not just *how* the data is collected, but also what *questions* are asked of it. All these organizations base their data on a *sample* of the total audience, based on a cross-section of the total population by age and sex, in order to then extrapolate figures for the audience as a whole. But what differentiates these measurements is the way in which these samples are collected. The most common techniques are through street interviews, telephone interviews and listening diaries. Tyler and Laing (1998) identified the main advantages and disadvantages of each approach. They suggested that while street interviews allow a station to gauge the success of current or ongoing programme changes, they are less reliable for measuring past listening. Telephone interviews are useful for gathering a wide range of qualitative information, but can underrepresent those sections of the population which cannot afford telephone lines. The listening diary is perhaps the most widely embedded of the three techniques, though it is also the one which faces the most frequent criticism. In this technique, diaries are placed in homes and respondents are asked to log their daily listening over a week, noting every time they turn on or change station. Arbitron, for instance, uses data from about 1 million diaries distributed across the USA; in the UK, RAJAR bases its figures on between 650 and 2,500 diaries for each of 30 separate survey areas. Tyler and Laing note that such diaries can produce quite detailed information covering every quarter or half-hour of a station's schedule, but also that they tend to be fully completed only by the most middle-class and authority-conscious of listeners. Others have criticised the listening diary system for failing to ensure that the listening habits of younger more marginalized members of a household – such as teenagers listening in their bedroom – or more transient groups as a whole – such as students – are reflected. Recall the example in chapter 1 of the Oregon progressive-rock station KAVE-FM. When it was forced to change to a syndicated format following low Arbitron ratings, station staff suggested that 'their listeners weren't the kind to fill out ratings books' (Stavitsky 1993: 84). A similar situation confronted the early days of London's 'alternative' music station, XFM, which consistently fought off criticism of low audience figures with the defence that one of its target audiences – the city's large student population – was not able to make an impact in a diary system orientated towards settled families.

Audience research organizations have, to be fair, been sensitive to such criticism and refined their methodology in recent years. Most use a mixture of methods to gather their data. And in the UK, RAJAR revised its whole approach in 1999, making one person in each household responsible for diary keeping, and monitoring the entries more closely and more frequently. The first published results of the new regime immediately revealed more radio listening overall than previously thought and a particularly marked increase in the amount of listening to many of those stations which appealed to children and teenagers (RAJAR 1999a, 1999b). Further changes are likely within the next few years, with electronic tracking of each respondent's listening being developed by several companies. Arbitron, for example, is developing a pocket-sized 'people meter' based on 'the latest military technology' which is designed to eliminate the diary altogether.

For the time being, then, the raw data on radio listening remains imperfect. The way it is then processed can also follow a number of different paths. In each case, the research companies' prime objective is to estimate the total size of a station's audience, given *either* as a percentage of the number of adults living within a station's transmission area (which is here defined as its 'TSA', or 'Total Survey Area'), *or* as a percentage of all radio listening within the station's given 'market', whether that is local, regional or national. The latter option, which tends to produce a higher percentage, is – unsurprisingly – favoured by radio stations. The audience size can then be presented in any or all of four ways:

■ 'Average Audience'. This estimates how many people are listening to a radio station for a given 15-minute slice of time.
■ 'Reach' or 'Cume'. This estimates the cumulative number of different people who have listened to a radio station at some time or another – even if only for five minutes – over a longer period of time, such as a day or a whole week.
■ 'Core'. This estimates the number of listeners for whom the station is their primary choice – that is, that they listen to it more than any other station. In the USA, for example, Arbitron distinguishes between P1, P2 and P3 listeners, according to their loyalty: a P1 or First Preference listener tunes in to one radio station almost exclusively, while P2s and P3s are more 'promiscuous' with the dial (Douglas 1999: 354).
■ 'Share'. This is a percentage of the total listening audience in a given market which listens to a station within that market.

Radio stations and networks inevitably use whichever figure most suits their needs. If, for example, increased competition in a given market means a station's 'share' goes down, it might be able to boast that more people are sampling its output *at some point or another* – that its 'reach' is up; where 'reach' may be down, a station might console itself with the knowledge that its 'core' audience is up, indicating hardening loyalty for those who have chosen to listen. Advertisers, though, are particularly keen on the measurement of 'share' because it gives the most direct indication of the best outlet in any geographical area for reaching as many people as possible.

Given all the imperfections of this data, we can nevertheless sketch out some broad patterns of listening. In the UK, 89 per cent of us listen to the radio at some stage or another each week. On average, in the UK and the USA we listen for about 22 hours each week – just a little less time than we devote to television (RAJAR 1999b; Douglas 1999). The figures are similar elsewhere. In Europe, Tyler and Laing's calculations (1998) suggest that most people listen for something between 17.5 and 28 hours each week. Listening is highest in Belgium, Denmark and Poland, and lowest in Bulgaria and Spain. These figures probably reflect a combination of factors, possibly related to measurement methodology, possibly cultural, but certainly including the range of rival leisure pursuits on offer and the respective range and quality of each country's television and radio services.

One striking contrast between European listening and that in the USA, is the share between public-service and commercial stations: the European average is about 49 per cent of the audience listening to public-service radio, and 51 per cent listening to commercial radio – which, coincidentally, is the exact figure for the UK itself (Tyler and Laing 1998: 6); in the USA, by contrast, public-radio stations capture some 22 million listeners – less than a tenth of the country's total population (*New York Times* 1999). On both sides of the Atlantic, however, it remains the case that for national audiences as a whole, broadly based pop music stations tend to attract the largest audiences – though, as Seymour-Ure notes of the UK, the relatively small numbers of middle-class listeners tend to prefer 'full-service' speech stations like BBC Radio 4 and listen to more radio overall than working-class listeners who, in general, are more inclined to pop music stations, especially commercial ones (1991: 126).

Ever since television overtook radio in the mid 1950s as the main household activity in the evening, radio's daily ebb and flow of audiences has remained quite distinctive. The peak time is in the early morning, when we get up, have breakfast and go to work, but those working in the home or listening at work ensure that quite significant numbers still listen through the mid-morning and lunchtime. The numbers steadily decline in the afternoon, building briefly during the late afternoon rush hour, before falling off sharply in the evening, when television sets are being switched on (see box 3.1).

Box 3.1   Listening patterns during the weekdays: the example of BBC Radio 4

The following is an extract from BBC Radio 4's 'Commissioning Guidelines', in a section which provides independent production companies with details of the network's most recent audience research. The section asks the question, 'when do people listen to Radio 4?'

Although the total weekly audience is over 8 million, the actual audience at any one point is much smaller – it fluctuates between a peak of 2.3 million at 7.45 am on a weekday and a low of around 140,000 at 9.30 pm on a Sunday.

Weekdays

The chart below shows how the Radio 4 audience varies throughout a typical weekday. The general pattern is similar each day.

Continued

There are three quite sharp news peaks around meal-times, connected by dips or 'hammocks' in between.

The grey line shows how the number of listeners varies through the day; the black bars show how Radio 4's share of the total radio audience varies through the day. Audience share provides a useful measure of how a slot is performing. It provides a fair comparison by adjusting for changes in the total radio audience at different times of day. The evening broadcast of *The Archers* is a good example of this. Although the audience size in terms of **number of listeners** is very similar to that for *The World at One*, the **share** of the total radio audience is twice as high. In other words, the evening *Archers* is getting a bigger slice of the smaller available listening cake.

Although Radio 4's demographic profile is never radically different from that outlined above, there are some variations during the day. These differences are highlighted in the annotated boxes.

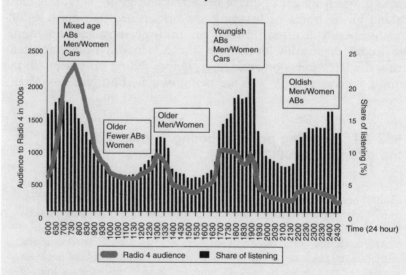

Radio 4's weekday audience

Source: Rajar, Q2 1997

Source: *BBC Radio 4 Commissioning Guidelines* 1998/9, 2nd Edn

Significantly, however, the pattern is different for teenagers, who tend to listen noticeably less in the mornings and much more in the evenings. Carroll et al. (1993) conducted a survey of American teenagers which revealed the consistency of this over the last four decades, and suggested an underlying cause for the phenomenon. Drawing on the earlier audience surveys of Troldahl and Skolnick (1968) and Weintraub (1971), as well as more recent data of their own, they noted that adolescents in their mid-teens spend more time with radio and less time with television than both slightly younger and slightly older teenagers:

> In the earliest stage of adolescence, radio listening is tentative, much like the probes into peer groups as they begin the process of separation from the family. As peer group affiliation becomes stronger, so does involvement in radio listening. And just as older teens change in their social affiliations, their listening tastes also change and many appear to reject the radio medium they embraced when younger. (Carrol et al. 1993: 173)

Radio, in other words, is being used by teenagers as an escape route from family life and into what is described as the 'privatism' being sought for at a particular moment in their psychological and social development. This chimes with the observation by Barnett and Morrison that for all of us:

> Television has become the 'social' medium, allowing the family to share a leisure activity in its own living room; radio, on the other hand, has become 'asocial' – a solo medium which is isolationist rather than communal. (1989: 1)

There are two important caveats to this casting of radio listening as somehow more 'private' or 'asocial' than watching television: first, it underplays the changing relationship between the way we use various media in the home, and secondly, it underplays the sociable dimensions of radio listening itself.

First, then, the question of competing media in the home. In the years since Barnett and Morrison made their observation the number of television sets per household has risen considerably throughout the western world. Specifically, many teenagers are now just as likely to have a TV set in their bedrooms as a radio. The domestic consumption of television is therefore becoming much *more* like listening to radio – namely an affair now more capable of being conducted in the private, rather than communal, spaces of a household (Abercrombie 1996: 171–2). At the same time teenagers are no longer quite so dependent as they once were on the transistor radio as their means of withdrawal from the family: the better off among them are now likely to have their own CD players, computer games, even Internet access. These offer entry to a whole range of 'asocial' activities other than radio, and their presence in households appears to be making teenagers more discriminating – sceptical even – about the radio output on offer (Carroll et al. 1993). Radio usage is therefore being somewhat squeezed by rival media, and many younger listeners certainly *predict* that they will be listening to less radio in the first years of this century (BBC NRRA 1996).

This is not, however, a story of unequivocal decline: not only is the fall in radio use among the young very small, but greater use of the Internet may itself help cushion any future drop. Research on the use of the Internet in British homes in 1999, for instance, suggested that while more than a third of people spend less time watching television and a quarter spend less time reading magazines since they have gone 'online', a quarter claim to spend *more* time listening to the radio (*The Times* 26 February 1999). In a similar survey in the USA, radio listening was actually down slightly in households which were online, though television watching was hit more severely (Arbitron 1999). Radio, in other words, is the medium which is most complementary to one of the fastest-growing leisure activities, namely surfing the net. This should not, of course, be surprising given radio's use as a secondary medium, listened to *in the background*, and precisely because it is eminently 'consumable' *while doing other things*. We do not so much 'listen' to radio as 'hear' it while bathing, dressing, cooking, driving, working in shops or factories, or, of course, surfing the net. So, if rival media are crowding radio out of its once-special status as *the* 'private' leisure pursuit in domestic life, a fundamental human requirement for some form of accompanying soundtrack in our lives seems to be ensuring its ultimate survival.

This brings us to our second caveat to radio's 'asocial' character, namely the danger of underestimating its own forms of sociability. As Barnett and Morrison themselves note, describing radio as 'asocial' does not somehow do it justice, for 'the corollary of isolationism is comfort and company, an antidote to boredom and a solace for loneliness' (1989: 1–2). Often, then, people listen to radio not so much to *escape* from social contact altogether as to *opt in to a different one* from that offered by the family circle. Radio's use as a vehicle for sociability operates here on at least three overlapping levels. First, as I mentioned earlier, we are always aware, even if only subconsciously, that others too are listening to the same programme as we are at precisely the same time: to use Douglas' vivid phrase, we are connected to invisible others by 'gossamer' threads, making

us part of a 'community' of fellow listeners, united by the simultaneity of experience. Secondly, and rather more prosaically, we use
the sound emanating from the radio sets to fill a vacuum in our
domestic spaces, to somehow make us *feel* less alone. In interviewing their respondents, Barnett and Morrison found, for example,
that:

> the sudden and unaccustomed absence of children was a common
> theme: 'I dreamt when they were all sort of young that one day I could
> just have a quiet house – but I miss the noise'; 'I can't get used to dead
> quiet now. If everything's dead quiet I feel uneasy.' These lessons are
> being passed down the generations. One mother was gradually helping
> her daughter to feel comfortable in the house on her own, despite the
> unnerving scraping noises of her pet hamster: 'I have told her that if
> she's by herself and she feels it's quiet, if she keeps hearing noises, put
> the radio on.' A teenage girl had recently moved away from home: 'I'd
> moved into my new little room and I was lonely. I wanted someone to
> talk to, so I said to the radio "talk to me"'. For one teenage boy, radio
> could relieve simultaneously the problems of loneliness and boredom:
> 'You've got music, keeps you a bit of company listening to people
> singing; otherwise it's just boring sat at home on your own doing
> nothing.' A travelling salesman was a self-confessed addict to his
> car-radio: 'I was without one for a fortnight and nearly went off my
> head.' (1989: 3)

Thirdly, as well as connecting us to other listeners and filling our
domestic spaces, radio is used by listeners to forge a direct relationship with the broadcasters themselves. As another of Barnett and
Morrison's listeners says: 'You feel at one with the radio . . . [the DJ]
is talking about certain things and you're listening, you feel that he's
with you and . . . he's talking to you personally' (1989: 3). The radio
presenter's concern to write scripts, or speak spontaneously in a style
that makes it seem as if he or she is speaking, not to a mass, but to
us individually, is therefore a contrived reaction to the knowledge
that, for the most part, radio is listened to *alone*.

This 'relationship' between broadcaster and listener is resonant
with meanings, and will therefore be explored a little further in the
next chapter. Here, I will just make one point about this relationship
– namely, that it creates a rather peculiar paradox. On the one hand,
the concept of radio as friend, company and background noise, as
something to 'alleviate the monotony of a boring job or journey',
tends to imply that the precise nature of programme *content* is unim-
portant in radio – the medium is somehow fulfilling its function
simply by being *on*. Listeners, Scannell points out, would generally
be taken aback by being asked whether they had a particular reason,

a *motive* for turning on the radio – or, for that matter, the TV. 'It is', he points out, 'hard to give good reasons for watching and listening':

> We do so because we can't find anything else, anything better to do. In this way, the activities of listeners and viewers appear unmotivated. They are nothing more (or less) than pastimes, ways of spending 'free time'. (1996: 24)

This, Scannell suggests, is what underpins broadcasting's desire to provide talk *for talk's sake*, a mission to entertain that makes *how* people talk on the radio or television just as important as *what* they talk about.

But radio is perhaps even more extreme than television in this respect, because whereas viewers tend to seek out programmes rather than channels, for radio listeners it is the station which counts more than anything else. Radio, in other words, is often not really about listeners choosing programmes at all, but about them choosing to opt into a fairly undifferentiated stream of music or talk. It is 'tap-listening', in which we turn on, dip in, turn off, several times a day, very often with no special attempt to 'catch' the beginning of a particular show. And the broadcasters themselves accept this: programmes, as we saw in chapter 2, are constructed on the very assumption that people do not listen to a full 3-hour show, but to perhaps twenty minutes or half-an-hour or so of it – that programmes should, in fact, not really be very self-contained at all, but open-ended. Segmentation of programming into bite-sized chunks is not just a strategy which suits the producer, then, but one which is ideal for the listener:

> it allows her amid the many other demands of her life to drop in and out of radio content without feeling that she has missed anything of major importance. Even in all-news formats segmentation works well since it usually consists of a repeated sequence of bulletins, interviews and short features which allows the listener to 'step aboard' at any time. (Crisell 1994: 215)

Mendelsohn's early characterization of listening as an experience in which listeners do not greatly distinguish between different kinds of content (1964: 239–49), is thus still pertinent.

On the other hand, the sort of 'relationship' often forged between a listener and a particular show suggests that, despite our distracted and taken-for-granted approach to listening, the *content* of radio may well be extremely important to us. As Barnett and Morrison found out from their respondents:

Passionate feelings were expressed about disc jockeys, phone-in hosts, quiz presenters and programme formats; at times daily patterns were constructed in order to coincide with favourite programmes. It is fair to say that not even the most casual listeners were indifferent to what they heard. (1989: 3–4)

A similar tale of discernment was uncovered by Carroll et al. in their study of American teenagers. They note that, whereas in the early 1970s teenagers suggested that 'time filling' was one use for radio and they were not especially concerned with the medium's 'meaningful content', by the 1990s – when time filling could be satisfied just as easily by recorded music or computer games – teenagers were failing to mention it at all in relation to radio. Instead, they were expressing irritation at too much news, or with DJs who talked too much and didn't play enough music; they also expressed a strong desire to interact with programmes, through requesting songs, making dedications, and calling into on air competitions (1993: 166–9). They were, in other words, quite prepared to turn off, join in, or attempt to change output, if it didn't quite live up to their expectations.

This paradox, between what appears to be a rather undiscriminating tap-listening, and a rather more engaged attention to actual content, is explained by Douglas in terms of our different 'modes' or 'repertoires' of listening:

We can passively hear, but we must actively listen. While much radio listening involves conscious attention to the program at hand, listeners can also shift cognitive gears and zone out into a more automatic, effortless mode. . . . In fact one of the pleasures of radio may come from the ability to move between such dramatically different states of awareness. (1999: 27)

Tap-listening and 'concentrated' listening are not, then, two mutually exclusive habits, but extremes we all move between many times of day, and from moment to moment. While we usually enjoy the benefit radio offers of not having to talk back, or even pay complete attention, we can suddenly be moved to shout back at our set, or sing along to a record which somehow grabs us. Douglas, in fact, suggests we should think of *three* major repertoires, which people rapidly and easily switch between in the course of a single day:

■ Informational: in which we listen for information. This is 'a relatively flat kind of listening: we are taking in dates, names, times, concepts, and the like but are not asked to imagine much' (Douglas 1999: 33).

■ Dimensional: in which we are working a little harder, paying a little more attention, and where listening is potentially all the more gratifying, because it is largely an experience of our own invention. This mode is activated by a range of programming, such as drama, sports commentary, even music, where we might be memorizing lyrics or focussing on the performance of the musicians themselves.

■ Associational: in which music in particular is associated in our minds with a particular event, or place, or period in our lives.

Whichever of these repertoires is dominant, Douglas suggests, is partly a matter of people's level of education, their race, their gender, their age, and so forth (1999: 35). But most of all, it is about exactly *how* and *when* and *where* each and every one of us are listening at any given point in our daily lives. For it is precisely the fact that we listen to the radio while carrying on with the rest of our lives that gives it a role in our domestic culture. Television is often an escape *from* everyday life – it demands, and we frequently give it, a great deal of our attention – but radio is almost always an accompaniment *to* everyday life (Crisell 1994: 69–70, 204). It is interwoven with ritualized routines, such as reading the paper, preparing for work, eating meals, having a bath, going to bed. It marks time so intimately, in fact, that cause and effect are difficult to establish. Do we, for instance, listen to a programme because it happens to be on when we prepare supper? Or do we prepare supper at precisely that time because it means we can listen to the programme? Scheduling, as Scannell says, is a matter of broadcasters adjusting their output 'to be grossly appropriate to what people are doing and when', but it is also true that our sense of time in our domestic lives 'is always already in part determined by the ways in which media contribute to the shaping of our sense of days': radio 're-temporizes', by steering us into regarding certain times of day as *the* time to get up, shower, eat or whatever (1996: 148–56). That radio often achieves this *even more powerfully than television* is demonstrated by the way in which scheduling changes on radio are invariably attacked by listeners. Take for example this despairing comment by one BBC Network Controller: 'You can move a TV programme from Monday to Thursday and no-one gives a hoot, but if you move a radio programme by five minutes there are questions in the House [of Commons]' (David Hatch. Quoted in Barnett 1994: 228).

It seems, then, that we are fiercely utilitarian about our use of radio. We may find company in the voice of a presenter, or memories in hearing a particular song, we may use it to feel connected to other people, or to events in the wider world, and, above all perhaps, we may use it to help structure our daily lives. As such, listening to radio is a vivid example of the so-called 'uses and gratification' approach to audience studies, in which the central task is to identify what people do with the media – the '*uses* to which they put them and the satisfactions or *gratifications* they obtain from them' (Crisell 1994: 209).

Most studies of this kind come down to identifying four main kinds of gratification, which echo the habits of radio listening we have so far described: the need for a diversion from life's routines, for companionship and social integration, for some sense of self-awareness, and some knowledge about events in the world (see Katz et al. 1973; McQuail 1983; Lowery and De Fleur 1983; Fiske 1990). People, it is suggested, constantly choose *between* the different media and choose *when* to consume the various media, according to the perceived effectiveness they offer in satisfying these needs. Put thus, radio rarely emerges spontaneously in people's minds as the *most* 'useful' medium: audiences may nowadays prefer to get their news from television or, if wanting a little more context, turn to their newspaper or, if wanting an escape from the news, go to the cinema or listen to their favourite CD. But, as many authors remind us, radio's everyday 'usefulness' is quite often concealed by its very taken-for-grantedness. All the empirical evidence suggests we *do* use it to satisfy all four of an audience's perceived 'needs' at various times and in varying degrees – using what Douglas calls 'multiple and overlapping listening competencies' (1999: 33) – but we frequently fail to acknowledge it:

> Radio is unique in being a secondary medium and . . . this is what enables it to be used in a casual, desultory way that television cannot: we can slip into and out of its content as our circumstances dictate. (Crisell 1994: 219)

All this certainly casts us as listeners in control of the medium, rather than controlled *by* it, even if only in the sense of choosing to become engaged at times that suit us. When we are *dis*engaged, hearing but not listening – and this, it appears, is most of the time – it is rather difficult to imagine that the medium could be seen to be anything other than the passive partner in this relationship. And yet, suggests Crisell, we must be alert to another, more subtle process affecting the listener:

> she may hardly be listening, but unlike television, which she experiences while disengaged from most other activities and which she is

therefore much more likely to recognize as extraneous to her personal situation, her radio is simultaneously with her primary activity. This means that whatever their proportions relative to each other it is often hard to separate first-hand experience from vicarious 'radio' experience: 'Where did I hear that story? Did someone tell me at work or was it Simon Mayo on Radio 1?' It may be that precisely because it is ignored radio is capable of strong effects, that its content can infiltrate the listener just because her conscious faculties are primarily engaged elsewhere and her mental defences therefore down. This is a plausible challenge to the conventional view that the most influential media are the visual ones: there seem good reasons for arguing the opposite, that they are the more resistible for being perceived consciously and being perceived 'out there', as separate from the events of our own lives. (1994: 221–2)

What Crisell alludes to is what the radio advertising industry calls the medium's ability to sneak 'under the radar' – for messages to be absorbed by the listener with little clear sense of where, and when and how they were absorbed.

So where does this take us? As Crisell himself admits, by their very nature the existence of unconscious media effects is, of course, almost impossible to prove. Even so, it should give us pause for thought. Audience studies have long been concerned with a much wider debate over whether we are 'active' or 'passive' audiences for the mass media. The weight of both academic writing and the evidence so far discussed in this chapter certainly supports a picture of an active audience for radio. It would appear to reject what has come to be called the 'media effects' approach, which argues that the mass media are capable of having a profound effect on what we do or think. But Crisell's observation about radio's powers of 'infiltration' certainly chimes very well with Douglas' vision of a medium which 'stimulates' the cognitive recesses of our brains. This would suggest that the 'active' – 'passive' audience debate is somewhat more finely balanced in the case of radio than might at first sight be assumed. It is, then, a debate worth revisiting.

The active audience?

We have seen the many ways in which listening to radio can be seen to be an active and enabling process: stimulating our mind's eye, connecting us to wider communities, informing and entertaining us, or simply keeping us company, while we carry on with the rest of our lives. But we also now know that it has many features which can be described as genuinely passive: our habit of leaving the set tuned to one station, regardless of exactly what programme might be on, or to favour the relatively undemanding – because *familiar* – music of our youth over any output which stops us in our tracks and grabs our attention too often. Listeners such as this (and that includes all of us at some time or another) are, in short, radio's equivalent of television's couch potatoes. For Adorno, all this passivity makes the act of listening full of danger:

> the most familiar [music] is the most successful and is therefore played again and again and made still more familiar. . . . Not merely do the few things played again and again wear out . . . [they] are transformed into a conglomeration of irruptions which are impressed on the listeners by climax and repetition, while the organization of the whole makes no impression whatsoever. (1991: 32–6)

In this interpretation, to listen to the radio, with all its familiar and rather bland music and repetitive speech, is to succumb to a narcotic which induces a false sense of tranquillity. There is, in common with the other media, a process of mass deception going on, in which consumers are controlled by being 'regressed' into demanding what they think is novel and exciting but which in fact is rubbish – a trivial and standardized product which further lulls their critical faculties and therefore induces a harmonious view of the world, allowing the forces of capitalism to flourish.

Though Adorno clearly had a tendency to get a little carried away, his perspective shares some of the ideas contained in the more restrained – and longer-surviving – 'media-effects' or 'stimulus-response' theory of the media. This approach, again first adopted in the 1930s, argued that audiences react to deliberate messages in direct, largely predictable, and sometimes dramatic, ways. The classic example invoked in the case of radio – though not always convincingly – is the effect of Orson Welles's 1938 adaptation of H. G. Wells's *The War of the Worlds*, in which several million listeners apparently believed the drama – complete with mock news bulletins and 'live' commentary – was real, and prepared to flee a Martian invasion (Cantril 1940). With the benefit of hindsight, this particular incident can perhaps more accurately be seen as a less dramatic reaction to a number of historical factors – not the least of which was the threat of war. The debate over media effects has been enacted and re-enacted in more recent times though, particularly over the issue of violence on television. And what links these more general 'stimulus-response' approaches with Adorno's more specific point about music, is a set of three interconnected assumptions, identified by Abercrombie (1996):

- The content of programmes is *trivial*;
- The mode of viewing/listening is *passive*;
- The set of effects on the audience is *narcotizing*.

Of course, Adorno, and with him the work of others in the Frankfurt School, has been roundly condemned as simplistic and outdated: too elitist, too dismissive of the audience's powers of discrimination, too influenced by the totalitarianism of Nazi Germany, perhaps even racist in its condescension toward popular music forms like jazz. Yet, Adorno's ideas find a clear echo in the much more recent work of the Canadian theorist of radio, Berland. She believes that, while Canadian radio can be 'the best in the world', most stations work within tightly defined music formats in which the continuous, lulling rhythms of sound teach the listener 'addiction and forgetfulness' (1993b: 211):

> Format radio depends on distraction for its existence. Its primary goal is to accompany us through breakfast, travel and work without stimulating either too much attention or any thought of turning it off. In this respect it is mutually interdependent on the daily life for which it provides the soundtrack; more specifically, it is designed to harmonize all the contradictions of domestic and working life that radio could illuminate and transform. (1993a: 104–5)

The three elements, both of Adorno's and the broader 'stimulus-response' perspectives, are all here. The output of radio is designed not to grab too much of our attention (it is *trivial*), we don't actively engage with it enough to turn it off or stop doing other things (our listening is *passive*), and in encouraging us to accept – 'harmonize' – life's contradictions, it has a clear effect (it is *narcotizing*).

The concept of the passive audience is, then, still lively and pertinent. Yet it has consistently faced three main criticisms in terms of its relationship with radio. First, that it can only be accurately associated with a particular historical moment of industrialization and urbanization. Secondly, that it cannot be applied in a *pluralistic* media landscape. And thirdly, that it underestimates the freedom of listeners to make of the 'messages' what they like – even to ignore them altogether. I will try in this section to examine the strengths of these three critiques in turn.

First, then, the historical argument. Blumler and Gurevitch point out that the domestic propaganda machines of Fascist regimes of the 1930s appeared, at least, to be remarkably successful in ensuring mass conformity. If audiences were susceptible, it was because of broader changes in society taking place at the time:

The dissolution of traditional forms of social organization under the impact of industrialization and urbanization had resulted in a social order in which individuals were atomized, cut off from traditional networks of social relationships, isolated from sources of social support, and consequently vulnerable to direct manipulation by remote and powerful elites in control of the mass media. (1982: 243)

The suggestion is that this process of industrialization and urbanization is now largely complete, and the social disruption which went with it – and which cut people off from reliable, local, sources of information – is largely absent. Yet 'industrialization and urbanization', and the social dislocations that are associated with them, are precisely the ongoing conditions of many parts of the world today. Mass migration, for instance, is of huge proportions at the start of the new century: war, ethnic conflict and famine have turned some seven million Africans into refugees; in Latin America, there are recurrent seasonal migrations of labourers throughout Columbia, Venezuela, Bolivia, and elsewhere (Held et al. 1999: 283–386). The pattern is replicated in Asia and eastern Europe. In each case, large numbers of people are uprooted from their 'traditional networks of social relationships', and are often reliant on new and unfamiliar sources of support and information. In the developed world too, several writers describe the continuing effects of *globalization* in terms very similar to Blumler and Gurevitch's earlier sketch of a dislocated 1930s Europe. Giddens has pointed out how *powerlessness* in the face of a diverse and large-scale social universe is 'one theme which unites nearly all authors who have written on the self in modern society':

As the forces of production develop, particularly under the aegis of capitalistic production, the individual cedes control of his life circumstances to the dominating influences of machines and markets. What is originally human becomes alien; human powers are experienced as forces emanating from an objectified social environment. Not only the followers of Marx have expressed such a view; it is also found, in somewhat different guise, in the works of the theorists of 'mass society'. The more extensive modern social systems become, according to this position, the more each individual feels shorn of all autonomy. Each, as it were, is merely an atom in a vast agglomeration of other individuals. (1991: 191–2)

The 'alienation' wrought by global forces – a process long begun but by no means complete – is thus cast in similar terms to the earlier processes of industrialization upon which Blumler and Gurevitch focused.

Giddens, though, describes the theory of 'alienation' in order to distance himself from it. He accepts that the 'globalized connections' of modern life can expropriate control from our lives in many ways, but sees many opportunities for people to forge new, and often more intense relationships at the more personal level – to *reappropriate* control (1991: 192–3). Albrow provides an analysis of how this reappropriation might be taking place on a large scale:

> The social activities which transpire in any one area are disconnected from each other, but equally are parts of social worlds which may extend beyond localities and national boundaries to the globe as a whole. This applies not simply to the more obvious economic linkages, work for a multinational, or a retail outlet of a national firm, but equally to kin, friendship and special interest relationships. These can all be sustained actively at a distance. (1996: 156)

In other words, while people are certainly disconnected from local relationships, they are not so much alienated as actively engaged in 'intense social construction' of new relationships, across large distances around the globe which can be of equal value to those relationships forged in pre-modern communities of geographical proximity. Systems of communication are central to this process of 'social construction': what sustains relationships is the power to communicate at a distance, through letters, the telephone, air travel, and so on.

Does listening to the radio, as just one of several 'space-binding' media, have a special place in this network of communication? Possibly, if we attend to Giddens' emphasis on the importance of *intimacy*. Drawing on the work of Bensman and Lilienfeld (1979), he points out that the expanded horizons of organizations and of human experience have a perceptible consequence at a much more personal level:

> Much of life becomes run along impersonal lines, within contexts remote from the ordinary individual, and over which she or he has little or no control. A flight into intimacy is an attempt to secure a meaningful life in familiar environments that have not been incorporated into these larger systems. (1991: 94)

Giddens pursues intimacy in the context of family relationships, but intimacy is, of course, precisely what *radio* claims to offer. It may be an intimacy beamed at us from afar, but – as we know – it 'speaks to us' as individuals and it makes us feel part of a community: 'We listen to radio . . . to keep from being depressed or isolated, to feel connected to something, to enfold ourselves in its envelope of pleasure, information, power' (Berland 1993b: 211). The more isolated we feel, Berland implies, the more likely we are to be drawn to a medium like radio. Our relationship with the medium, however, is not entirely constructive, in the way that Albrow might envisage. The community is not real but imagined, the intimacy is synthetic. Remember the actual programming we are talking about – banal, repetitive, familiar, reassuring: we are, Berland implies, not seeking anything innovative or attention-grabbing, but something akin to an aural narcotic. As such, listening leads to a form of passivity in which we lack discernment. And it is precisely this which, in turn, makes us vulnerable to any messages embedded in radio's 'continuous rhythm of sound'.

Again, this notion – if accepted – is resonant with cultural and ideological implications, and will therefore be explored further in the next two chapters. Here, though, it is worth noting that the broader sociological discussions about the effects of globalization prompted by Giddens (1991), Bauman (1992, 1998), and others, give a fresh impetus to the stimulus-response debate in relation to radio. The original concept of a kind of 'magic bullet', in which crude propaganda is aimed at the audience with the clear hope of directly shaping its behaviour has shifted to a more subtle perspective, in which radio's impact on the audience is less dramatic, more insidious: it no longer shouts at us, but it does gently massage away the pains and confusions of modern living, drawing us into a passive acceptance of the world.

The second criticism levied against the notion of a *passive* radio audience inherent in the 'stimulus-response' theory, is also historical in tone. Crisell suggests the notion was only plausible 'when the media were newer and fewer than they are today': 'Scepticism about their messages was not natural in an age less inured than ours is to the clamorous and conflicting voices not only of newspapers and radio but of multi-channel television' (1994: 206). Certainly, where the media are genuinely pluralistic, the clamour of 'conflicting voices' provides an environment in which listeners are not only exposed to a range of opinions, but can learn to be discerning about them – to weigh difference, and reach reasoned opinions of their own. This idea – that a plurality of voices in the media is a necessary condition of democratic life – is used both by those in favour of market liberalization and those wishing to protect the public-service sector of broadcasting to argue their case, as we shall see in chapter 5. Yet, for many millions of people, the debate is rather academic. Between 70 and 90 per cent of the population in many parts of the developing world still live in rural areas. They are frequently beyond the reach of the electricity systems needed to sustain television, or the distribution networks needed for daily newspapers. Illiteracy may be widespread, and the reliance on *oral* communication consequently even stronger. Radio remains for them the *only* consistent source of information – and where the range of programming on offer is restricted to state-controlled services or market monopolies, listeners are less able to marshall arguments against any dominant message. Even in the liberalized, 'multi-channel' western democracies, it can be argued that the pluralism of the media does not always constitute the range of voices and sounds often claimed. Recall our discussion in chapter 1, over the effects of steady commercialization, the impetus of expanding radio companies to achieve economies of scale through takeovers and syndication, the trend towards internationalized 'brands', and my suggestion that even the multi-channelled future promised by digital radio may bring large amounts of recycling. And recall too, our discussion in chapter 2 of the way in which producing formats involves a rigid process of excluding many cultural products through 'gatekeeping'. All these discussions lead us towards the conclusion that plurality does not guarantee diversity – particularly given the steady 'fragmentation' of the listening public into many smaller 'niches' to be served with a safe and familiar diet to match (rather than disturb) their own minutely researched tastes.

Again, the *cultural implications* of these trends are worth further exploration – and will be addressed both later in this chapter and in the following two chapters. The point I wish to make here, though, is that these trends can be seen to limit the radio listener's perceived *exposure* to the range of ideas, voices and sounds that Crisell sensibly offers as a potential protection against undue media influence. Indeed, some writers go further, and suggest that gatekeeping contains an *agenda-setting* function which actively precludes any changes in attitude in audiences. In this view opinions which conflict with the 'dominant ideology' of those in control of the media are filtered out, so that audiences cannot hear issues in any other terms – or, indeed to hear any other *issues* – than those 'on the agenda' prescribed. Murdock applies this reading to the audiences for radio soap operas. 'Serials', he suggests:

> concentrated on the doings and attitudes of the upper class and the better-off sectors of the middle-class. They therefore provided a powerful conduit for the downward transmission of dominant views and assumptions. (1981: 156)

This analysis, Crisell claims, casts listeners as something more than just passive dupes, crudely vulnerable to media messages in the sense that they will think whatever they are told to think, but as people whose mental responses are *nevertheless* still 'confined by the limits set by the imaginative and ideological world' presented by the serials (Crisell 1994: 208; Murdock 1981: 156).

Most radio, of course, is *music*-radio, which – superficially at least – seems devoid of agenda-setting. Attali, however, has seen the sort of 'trickle-down' effect which Murdock identified in relation to radio soaps as applying to the music which happens to most typify contemporary format radio. He draws our attention to the dominance of mainstream Anglo-American genres distributed by large multinational corporations. Radio is the prime agent for broadcasting and popularizing Anglo-American music globally (Held et al. 1999). By implication, therefore, the medium is complicit in what Attali sees as a 'strategic use of music by power to silence [through] massproducing a deafening, syncretic kind of music, and censoring all other human noises' (1985: 32). Homogenization of radio output, in other words, is stifling our ability to experience *difference* – an impact which does not just reinforce dominant cultures, but also *dehumanizes* the listener in the process: he or she is *disempowered* from an active engagement in what ought, in the case of music at least, to be a spontaneous and *participatory* experience.

How does the balance sheet lie now, between thinking of radio audiences as predominantly passive recipients or as predominantly active consumers of programming? Certainly, our accumulated experience of the mass media undoubtedly means that for many of us, persuasion will only work when it is hidden rather than overt: any broadcast perceived as manipulative will be less likely to succeed as it once could have done, simply because we are now too sceptical to be vulnerable to crude propaganda. And although we may still be in the midst of a long-term displacement from our traditional social networks, radio can help us forge new and more widely spread communities of interest, binding disparate individuals through Douglas' 'gossamer connections', and offering an intimacy otherwise missing from our lives. There are, though, several objections from a broadly *political-economic* point-of-view to the assumption that the modern-day listener to radio is entirely beyond manipulation. In these analyses, the notion of radio's actual *content* is more important than its fundamental ability to communicate: a *plurality* of channels, theoretically offering us almost infinite freedom to discriminate between different sounds and ideas, may carry an *homogeneity* of music and talk, with, in Attali's phrase, a 'power to silence'. This is not simply a case of listeners being disenfranchised by a lack of real choice, but of them being *pacified* by radio's preference for the predictable and reassuring, the banal and the trivial, whether in music or speech.

Thus described, the argument seems quite evenly poised. But there is, of course, a third area of criticism of the 'effects' theory, as applied to radio – namely, that broadcasters can never be entirely sure how their programmes are actually being regarded in the actual places of reception, the homes and cars of the listeners themselves. We listen to radio in so many different ways, in so many different circumstances, that we may each have a very different sense of what exactly it is we are listening *to*. A sense of the way in which listeners use radio, which contrasts particularly with Attali's assessment, is conjured up in a study by Hamm (1995a). He traces the way in which one particular piece of music, the single 'All Night Long (All Night)' by Lionel Richie, was received in the specific setting of black townships in South Africa. The record itself, released in 1984, conformed to an internationally appealing 'Motown' sound. It was not a purely American urban black working-class music, as would have been the case with the label's much earlier material, but a more generalized sound: the lyrics and music were 'shot through' with references to Afro-Caribbean and Afro-Latin cultures, hints of Latin street fests, of reggae, of calypso. But 'the song as a whole was none of these things' (1995a: 252). In other words, it was, according to Hamm, 'open-ended' (1995a: 254). The record was played on a request show of the Radio Zulu service run by the South African Broadcasting Corporation for a specifically Zulu audience. To an apartheid regime which sought to intensify ethnic and 'national' identity among the various black 'tribes' of the region at the expense of black unity, while simultaneously maximizing 'the sales among the black population of commodities produced by white-controlled capital', the record seemed usefully devoid of political content: the lyrics were rather obscure, Lionel Richie had no visible history of political activity, and the popularity of music by black Americans would help attract listeners to the station. But when women heard the song on the radio, they saw in the references to dancing, not a metaphor for sex, but a simple description of communal activity; the specific African words sprinkled throughout the song were from Swahili, which was not the language of the South African townships, so words were not understood literally but perceived as generically African; when Lionel Richie sang of 'Tom bo', whatever its literal meaning, it was immediately perceived by black South Africans as a reference to Oliver Tambo, the then-head of the outlawed African National Congress. In other words, the ambiguities of the record were crystallized in specific ways by its South African listeners, transforming it into a much more politically resonant artifact than many western listeners, in say the USA or Britain, would have recognized (1995a: 249–69).

Hamm's intention is to make a specific point about music in general: that it is not given 'immutable and unshifting' meaning at the point of composition, but that meanings are fully realized 'only at the moment of reception'. The broader implications for the construction of meanings in *radio* programming are picked up and explored in the next chapter. What is important to the current discussion is Hamm's underlying conception of the importance of listening, and specifically the listener's ability to *resist*, even if rather subconsciously, any attempt to reinforce political or economic power through the diffusion of a *dominant text*. In its purest expression, such a perspective draws deeply on structuralist notions of the 'text', in which true authorship resides, not with the original writer, but with the reader: in the case of radio, one would say that a programme's full meaning is generated not by the producer or the station, but by individual listeners, each of whom, in the very act of listening, enacts a totally idiosyncratic 'decoding' of what the programme is about.

This approach to audience studies is often applied to television, where programmes can be described as polysemic – that is, containing (either consciously or unconsciously) a number of possible meanings, and therefore allowing a whole range of interpretations by an active, discerning audience (see Fiske 1989). In one sense, radio is inherently *more* susceptible to such 'open' readings than television, because of what we have already discussed about its lack of visual images demanding a great deal of effort by each listener to create mental images at a cognitive level for themselves. Take, for example, Crisell's earlier point about how we listen to drama on the radio: he suggested that the play is 'not so much an external event as the private and unique creation of each person who hears it'. Radio's ability to 'stimulate the imagination' has, then, as its logical conclusion the concept of the fully active listener, able to dominate the text and make of it whatever he or she pleases.

This, though, is not quite what Crisell, Douglas – or indeed Hamm – are saying. Hamm, in fact, makes clear in his study that the 'moment of reception', the hearing of a record on the radio, is never an *entirely* open, polyvalent event. It is 'shaped by the cultural capital of the listener' (Hamm 1995a: 249–51). There are always clear limits, as Pickering and Shuker argue elsewhere, to the way in which the 'same' music can be experienced in radically different ways by different audiences:

> This exaggerates the extendibility of textual meaning and valuation, because the extent to which the meanings of a piece of music can be adapted depends on the particular range and combination of discourses upon which those audience members are able to draw. So all music cannot be all things to all people. (1993: 50)

In the case of Hamm's study, the fact that the listeners concerned are members of the disenfranchised black township communities of

South Africa is central to *their* interpretation of the Lionel Richie song on Radio Bantu. More generally, it is implied, *all* radio listeners can only bring to bear on a programme a set of interpretations which is *predetermined* by their class, gender, age, environment and cultural milieu.

Indeed, any ability which listeners may have to 'resist' the dominant meanings of a 'text' and construct ones of their own may be based less upon the 'openness' of the text itself and more upon the broadcasters' sheer inability to control the circumstances in which we listen. This is illustrated by Scannell with the rather farcical instance of the infant-BBC's negotiations over the live broadcasting of the wedding of Lady Elizabeth Bowes-Lyon to the Duke of York in 1923:

> In the end permission was refused because the Dean of Westminster feared that 'men in public houses might listen with their hats on' (Wolfe 1984: 79). If this seems a more than faintly ludicrous objection today, it was entirely correct in anticipating the implications for sacred events of their live coverage by radio and television. What the Dean rightly foresaw as a fundamental difficulty for the authorities (for those in charge of the management of such events) was the impossibility of controlling the behaviours of an absent audience of listeners. (1996: 77)

As Scannell notes, the records of Mass Observation show that audiences for the Duke's coronation some 14 years later did indeed listen in ways that might have alarmed the organizers – some, to be sure, reverential, but others asleep, laughing, or just getting on with their shopping or cooking. The listener's status as 'absent' from the event itself is the key to his or her power here. When the event is broadcast it enters the worlds of the listeners, where people are free to listen 'in a wide range of possible settings and with a correspondingly wide range of possible dispositions and demeanours' (1996: 77–9). Broadcasters, Scannell suggests, have long come to recognize that their output must therefore somehow adapt itself to, and seek to enter into, the contexts in which it is being heard. Given that these domestic contexts are, as we have seen, places where we are just as likely to turn off our radio sets and do something else as we are to listen attentively, there is a deeper implication too:

> The relationship between broadcasters, listeners and viewers is an unforced relationship because it is unenforceable. Broadcasters must, before all else, always consider how they shall talk to people who have no particular reason, purpose or intention for turning on the radio or television set. (1996: 23)

Here, it is suggested, lies the ultimate power of the audience – what makes radio listeners truly 'active': the ability to take or leave the product itself on largely their own terms. The broadcasters themselves, as Scannell makes clear, know and understand this, and always seek to 'bend' to their audiences accordingly: they will not, because they *cannot*, always get their way. Hennion and Meadel seek to draw out the wider point, when they assert the difference between *industrial* products like cars or soap, which are simply processed and then consumed, and *cultural* products – such as radio programmes – which are 'constructed in and through interpretations':

> Culture is not the content of a message which follows a linear path through production and consumption; it does not force any entry into people's lives, but is a material constructed by a constant process of iteration between all the actors. (1986: 284)

As listeners, then, we are the *co*-producers of radio. We all create our own images in listening to radio, and we each inhabit domestic worlds which mould our listening in different ways. At the same time, we take radio so much for granted, take so little notice of it infiltrating our minds, generating associations and feelings of intimacy and companiability, that we almost certainly underestimate the reliance we place upon it. We are, in short, neither a fully 'active', nor a fully 'passive' audience for the medium.

This is not a paradox free of tensions, however. For while broadcasters may recognize that we each listen in different ways and that they must therefore try to talk to us all as individuals, they also have to treat us, institutionally at least, as a *mass* to be 'segmented' into manageable audience markets. No radio station has a method of audience research so precise that it can 'get to know' every single member of the audience. Yet to make the sort of day-to-day production decisions about which records to play, what sort of news to transmit and when, a station has to make 'gross' assumptions about who we are and what we might want – and to act accordingly. Thus, for example, when the BBC tells aspirant programme makers that at 9 o'clock on a weekday morning the listeners to its speech-based network Radio 4 are 'not as "middle-class" as during the *Today* programme' and that their average age is 57, it is clearly trying to characterize a much more diverse *actual* audience in a necessarily simple way (BBC Radio 4 1998). Just as BBC Radio 1 does in telling its programme makers that '86% of 15–24 year-olds go clubbing', and – with obvious purpose – reiterating the station's interest in dance music (BBC Radio 1 1997). From the producer's point of view, these gross generalizations may be necessary in order to plan their programmes, but their effect on listeners is for them to be divided up from each other before being offered a host of carefully crafted and tightly defined formats from which to choose. In the end, it is the *station* not the listener which has *formed* the market, and defined the programming parameters accordingly. And, according to Douglas, this 'segmentation' exacts a toll on the listening process itself:

> Is radio, as one analyst put it, not something we listen to anymore but something we just "sit in"? . . . Audience research indicates that many Americans want this kind of safe, gated-in listening. It goes with our increasingly insular, gated-in communities and lives. Indeed, in the 1980s listeners used new technologies, most notably the Walkman and the boom box, either to isolate themselves from others or to enact hostile takeovers of communal auditory space. Industry representatives also note that many people listen for only ten minutes at a time and move among six different stations; programmers are at the mercy of such habits, they emphasize. Their point is that people have become more selfish and less tolerant listeners, and that stations must cater to this. But in the last twenty years the radio industry itself has cultivated this kind of caution in listeners, so that many have lost – or never acquired – the patience and playfulness needed to learn about other music, especially the music of the young. . . . The radio industry and its advertisers, which successfully forged a national market in the 1930s, have now helped us see ourselves as members of mutually exclusive auditory niches, willing and able to listen in only a few ways. (1999: 348–9)

The increasingly formatted and segmented radio industry, in other words, is predetermining, squeezing-down even, our listening experience – an experience which ought, from Douglas' point of view, to be open, communitarian, and exploratory. And, so the argument goes, we cannot help but collude with this narrowing of experience because the industry has cultivated our desire for such narrowness.

This conclusion may seem a little bleak, and perhaps a little out of place in, say, a European radio environment where there are many examples of flourishing national networks of mixed programming. But Douglas' concern is merely a reflection of a more general point raised much earlier by Elliott (1974): that the audience's 'needs' detected in uses-and-gratifications theories, are themselves *learned* through social experience – including, naturally enough, our experience of the media. In which case, we should remember that radio might well be gratifying needs which it has in some sense helped to create. Crisell, let us remember, believes that any influences on the radio audience are likely to be both more powerful and more difficult to prove in the case of radio than for television because it is simultaneously more closely integrated with everyday life and more invisible. He concludes, therefore, that:

> The fact that even the most inattentive listener is in some sense using the medium does not preclude the possibility that it might be 'using' her, too – that she might be subject to its influence in almost subliminal ways. (1994: 224)

If listeners are in any sense more 'gated-in', to use Douglas' phrase, and yet it is *they* as consumers who help 'construct' the meaning – and the cultural resonances – of radio output produced 'for' them by the industry, the inevitable question arises: what *sort* of meanings, what *sort* of cultures, are actually being generated by radio in this dialectic between its producers and its audiences? That is the subject of the remaining two chapters.

4

Meanings

So far we have looked at the two 'ends' of what has traditionally been seen as a quite linear media activity. At one end, the *production* – at both an industry-wide scale and by individuals and small teams – of radio output; at the other end the *consumption* by audiences of that output. Yet I have suggested, in common with many media analyses, that the two processes are not really so detached, that the listeners to radio are in some way the co-producers of radio. But what exactly do I mean by this? *What* exactly are the co-producers involved in co-producing? The answer, in short, is radio *as text* – something more than a one-dimensional product to be taken just at face value, a product possibly rich with *meanings*, and specifically designed to be taken in and interpreted, 'read' if you like, by listeners. A radio programme, or the larger stream of radio programming, might have a particular set of meanings to the radio producer – other than simply providing a source of income, of course – and a slightly different meaning to his or her employer, and almost certainly many more meanings to the people who end up listening to it at home, at work, or in the car. There may, then, be many different meanings attached to a single radio 'text'. But that is not the end of the matter. For it is also worth asking whether or not these meanings *add up* to something more – a general *meaningfulness* for radio as a whole in contemporary society. An exploration of these meanings, and their collective meaningfulness form the subject of this chapter. We need to take a broad sweep, and look at the way radio helps 'construct' our sense of who we are, our sense of time and place, and above all, our sense of what radio is *for*. To begin with, though, we need to focus on radio's most obvious and all-encompassing function – that of somehow *communicating*.

Radio as communicator

Radio, like television, often presents itself as a window on the world. Where a pane of glass is pure, the image of life outside is barely refracted: we simply see what is there to be seen. By analogy, radio merely allows us to hear what is there to be heard. This self-proclaimed status ascribes to the medium very little intrinsic meaning, beyond contributing to human knowledge and experience by acting as a conduit of other ideas and events. This may be a significant role in itself, by helping to forge what has come to be known as the 'public sphere' – a contribution to political life which is examined critically in the next chapter, along with radio's other claims to shape our individual and communal cultures. In this chapter, we need to ask a prior, and more fundamental, question: in what ways might this 'window' actually *distort* our impressions of the outside world, so that radio can be seen, not so much as a distributor of other material and other meanings, but as something which inscribes fresh meanings on what it transmits, and which gives the medium itself a meaningfulness in modern life? Certainly, most recent studies of radio have suggested ways in which meanings – often specifically ideologies – are lost, generated or changed by the medium. Talk on radio, for example, is similar – but not identical – to our everyday conversations; listening to music on the radio is a *bit* like listening to our record collections, but is certainly not the same as putting on a series of CDs; hearing a live pop concert or the commentary of a football match is a chance to 'join' an event, but certainly not the same as 'being there'. What is the significance of these differences? Or more pertinently: in what ways do these differences allow us to see, *through the form and content of radio programmes themselves*, ideological and cultural meanings inscribed by the settings in which they are produced and heard, namely the radio studios of broadcasting institutions and the homes or cars of listeners?

One central conflict in much analysis of radio's meaningfulness, is the question of whether or not radio's intrinsic communicative properties are entirely benign. Higgins and Moss (1982, 1984), for example, in their various examinations of Australian talk-radio, have suggested that the medium tends to construct and impose a 'pseudo-reality' in a never-ending spectacle for its audiences. Callers to radio phone-ins have their views filtered through the dominant ideology of the programmes – one in which all the apparently unrelated elements of output coalesce into a planned flow of messages which – taken as a whole – foster a consumerist culture, ultimately disempowering the listener: callers may illustrate through their declared experiences that life is tough, but the radio station's own adverts will offer them the possibility of buying a better future. The theme of radio as an *anti-dote* to reality is pursued in most analyses of music radio. Barnard describes how programming as a whole – the songs played, the patter of the presenters, the phone-ins and dedications – generally avoids the negative and disturbing aspects of life to celebrate the romantic and idealistic through a tone of 'good-time camaraderie marshalled by the disc-jockey' (1989: 154). Similarly, Hennion and Meadel (1986) and Negus (1993) have shown how any records that may disturb the expectations of listeners for the familiar and the melodic are squeezed from the schedules.

Radio, then, provides familiarity. But it also offers some form of escape from isolation and tedium. Hobson (1980) has described how daytime radio's male DJs – they are mostly male – are required to act as romantic figures in the isolated lives of housewife listeners. Taking his cue from the songs he plays, the radio presenter talks to his listeners in intensely personal ways, linking any nostalgia for the personal freedoms of youth to an acceptance that others too have now learned to live with the burdens of family life: they are special, but not alone and should therefore be reassured that they have made the right choices in life (Coward 1984). The danger this entails is raised explicitly by Berland in her study of the 'political phenome-nology' of Canadian radio (1993b). She draws a picture of the radio experience in which listeners are promised a sense of belonging to a listening 'community' in which 'pleasure, information, power' envel-op us – but in which the community is in fact entirely illusory:

> The absence of any spontaneous or innovative event, or any specific (vs. abstract) intimacy, contributes ultimately precisely to depression, which after all is merely a sideways description of powerlessness, of being prevented in various ways from achieving anything spontaneous or innovative, of having or living a new idea. (1993b: 211)

The implication of all these approaches is that radio, despite its own claims to intimacy and friendliness, instead contributes to a growing sense of *alienation* in contemporary life, created by global patterns of transience, mobility and rootlessness. They also cast radio, in varying degrees, as inducing a rather passive, and therefore rather uncritical, form of listening, as we saw in the previous chapter.

These perspectives might help explain why certain radio pro-grammes do or do not get made, but they are less concerned with another important concern: explaining why radio programmes *succeed* – or, to put it another way, why, despite any possible alienat-ing tendencies or any lack of expressive motivation on the part of broadcasters, listeners persist in listening in a way that suggests that *they* at least find meaningfulness in the medium. Scannell (1991, 1996) shifts the focus to this second question by placing radio more positively within the fabric of our routine lives, and implying that listeners have a more active role in generating meaning. In providing an arena of sociable interaction for its own sake, in bringing us face-to-face to the everyday and its concerns, through showing us a world in which people are particular persons with their own voices, radio – Scannell argues – retrieves and proclaims the social character of human life. Through letting us hear (and in the case of television, see) real people – not as some mass but as individuals living in what Giddens calls a 'peopled world' – broadcasting 'rekindles the life and fire of the world in all its live and living being' (Scannell 1996: 164–5). Despite this power, radio is positioned by Scannell as a taken-for-granted part of everyday life. Indeed, it must be so – though not necessarily for any covert ideological motives: what intention there is, whether to inform or to entertain, is not concealed and malevolent, but is there to be heard by any competent listener using common-sense inference. What distinguishes this theory of broadcasting's *communicative intentionality* from, say, the work of Higgins and Moss or Berland, is that the significance of radio is being located not so much in the hidden motives of those who make its programmes as in the way radio somehow fully discloses its own intentions to all who care to listen:

> All programmes have an audience-orientated communicative intentionality which is embodied in the organization of their setting (context) down to the smallest detail: there is nothing in the discourses of radio and television that is not motivated, that is not intended to generate inferences about what is being said by virtue of how it is being said. . . . All broadcast output is, knowingly, wittingly *public*. (Scannell 1991: 10–11)

In other words, whatever the intentions of the programme-makers might be, they will be realized and expressed in every aspect of their creations – creations, moreover designed so that 'anyone can enter into any programme at any time' (Scannell 1996: 177).

There is then a tension in studying the meaningfulness of radio, between perspectives which emphasize its manipulative and alienating properties, and ones which emphasize its ability to nourish the social life into which it is woven. But there is a third approach to radio's powers of communication which, to some extent, bridges this gap by assessing the varying effectiveness of radio at conveying specific 'messages' to its listeners. Crisell explores the usefulness of this semiotic approach to radio. He takes as his starting point the broad distinction between an *icon* – a sign which resembles the object it represents, such as a photograph – an *index* – a sign directly linked to its object, in the way that smoke is an index of fire – and a *symbol* – a sign which bears no resemblance to its object, such as a national flag (1994: 42). Crisell argues that since radio is a 'blind' medium, all its 'signs' are auditory, and exist evanescently – and thus rather precariously – in time rather than space. Without the context of visual images and written text, radio broadcasters *and* listeners have to fight against the ever-present risk of misinterpretation.

Let us take a specific example. Although many of the different kinds of sounds broadcast by radio occur naturally, the real world's soundscape would be so bewildering when thrown at the human ear without visual clues that broadcasters are compelled to prioritize these sounds, foregrounding the most important ones and eliminating the irrelevant ones:

> Radio does not seek to reproduce the chaotic, complex and continuous sounds of actual life: it may tolerate them to a degree, but seeks to convey only those sounds which are relevant to its messages and to arrange them in a hierarchy of relevance. (Crisell 1994: 45)

This process of selection and arrangement, in which a given sound might be combined deliberately with other sounds, speech, music or even silence itself, inevitably alters the original meanings of a sound, and conjures up new ones. The hoot of an owl, for example, can be transformed from an indexical sign in a natural history programme to a more symbolic one, perhaps suggesting the occult in a radio drama: it has become an example of an 'acoustic shorthand', a convention which can replace or absorb much of the adjacent language. Such signification is not fixed, but can shift according to context and the preconceptions we bring to it. Thus, Crisell suggests that the voice of a radio station's continuity announcer may be interpreted simply as the index of a human presence, but may also be interpreted as the index of a certain personality, even as an index of the radio station or an entire nation. He also illustrates the way in which music, less bald and more indefinitely suggestive than speech, can give a radio programme various connotations (see box 4.1). All this, as Crisell makes clear, does not reduce the listener to an entirely passive recipient of radio's messages. Indeed, his recurring theme is that the medium's sole reliance on sound for its codes, rather than a fuller communicative package complete with pictures and written text, demands more of its listeners: in requiring them to 'fill in' the 'missing' information through the power of their own imagination,

Box 4.1   Music as a 'framing' or 'boundary' mechanism

The following is an extract taken from Crisell's wider discussion of music's role as a 'code' in radio's text:

Musical jingles (sometimes known as 'IDs') identify or 'frame' radio stations just as signature or theme-music frames an individual programme by announcing its beginning and/or end. Station IDs are similar in function to the voice of the continuity announcer; they set the style or tone of the station and could be seen as both index and symbol.

. . . As a way of framing individual items theme-music is also common in film and television, but it is of particular significance in radio because of the blindness of the medium. . . . Silence, a pause, can also be used as a framing mechanism, but unlike that of film and television it is total, devoid of images. To give the programmes connotations, an overall style or mood, music is therefore an especially useful resource on radio – less bald, more indefinitely suggestive, than mere announcements.

Let us take a formal but lively piece of eighteenth-century music played on a harpsichord – a gavotte or bourree composed by Bach, perhaps – and consider its possibilities for the radio producer. It is highly structured and symmetrical in form and therefore commonly regarded as more cerebral or 'intellectual' than the Romantic compositions of the following century. She might therefore regard it as ideal theme-music for a brains-trust or quiz programme.

But its characteristics have other possibilities. The 'period' quality of both the harpsichord and the music is unmistakable and might lend itself to a programme about history or antiques. Alternatively the 'tinny' tone of the instrument combined with the rhythmic nature of the piece might introduce a children's programme about toys or music boxes or with a faery or fantasy theme. You can doubtless imagine other possibilities for yourself, and I would simply make two further points.

The first is that depending on the specific contents of the programmes I have suggested, it would be possible to discern all three modes of signification in such theme-music – the symbolic, the indexical and the iconic.

Second, I would stress that these are extrinsic meanings of the music: we could not say that it is 'about' cerebration or history or toys. Another way we might describe them is as 'associative' meanings: in a serial, for instance, the theme-music will bring to the listener's mind what he already knows about the story-line: even more than this, it is a 'paradigm' of that genre of programme (Fiske and Hartley 1978: 169).

This function of music as a framing mechanism . . . [is] noticed by Goffman (1980: 164–5).

Source: Crisell 1994: 50–1

radio offers its listeners a more rewarding, imaginative experience than TV can ever offer to its viewers. Listeners are in this sense fully involved in meaning-making, simply because the communicative deficiencies of the medium mean they *have to* be.

In recognizing the role listeners play in meaning-making, Crisell's semiotic perspective does provide something of a bridge between what could loosely be termed the 'alienation' approach favoured by Higgins and Moss and the 'repersonalization' approach suggested by Giddens and Scannell. Nevertheless, Scannell (1991) has argued that 'encoding-decoding' approaches to radio tend to reduce its communication to a technical problem to be overcome – namely getting a 'message' across clearly. Thus, for example, much radio dialogue is categorized as 'anchorage' for adjacent sounds, employing Barthes' term for the way words are used in captions for photographs to 'fix' meaning in the face of the 'terror' of uncertain signs which might otherwise be misread (Barthes 1977: 39; Crisell 1994: 47–8). In Scannell's critique, judging radio by its effectiveness at conveying specific 'messages' to its listeners is certainly valid, but perhaps rather one-dimensional: implicitly, the model views communication as a one-way process rather than as interactive, and it risks overlooking what Scannell calls the '*expressive* dimensions of communication – *how* things are said, why and for what possible effects' (Scannell 1991: 10–11). Radio, he suggests, is knowingly constructed with its audiences fully in mind. Given this, all the perceived limitations of broadcasting to distant, distracted audiences, are seen not so much as *threats* to the communicative process but *inherent* to its very form and function.

This approach widens our focus from the so-called 'codes' of radio – speech, music, sound, silence – to encompass a broader canvas in which we have to address the circumstances in which radio is listened to – and, even more importantly, the circumstances in which both producers and consumers *come to understand* and take for granted what is being asked of them in listening. The meaningfulness of radio can therefore be found in the way it relates as a whole to our sense of time and our sense of place, as well as through the particular sounds it emits at any given moment. For this reason, the later part of this chapter will go on to explore radio's place in everyday life. Before that, however, we must ask: if radio exhibits 'communicative intentionality', *how* exactly is this realized in the form and content of its programmes, through its talk and through its music?

Radio texts: talk and music

Talk

In most studies of radio's forms of communication, talk is *the* central focus. As Shingler and Wieringa point out, talk is 'everywhere on radio' (1998: 30). Even where music and the other sounds of the real world are in play, some explanation of those sounds is needed – and it is invariably provided by speech. Talk is therefore almost always described as the 'primary code' of radio, which contextualizes all other sounds. It is not, though, simply a matter of the words themselves which are being spoken: words are provided by particular *voices*. *How* those voices behave, and how the different voices on the radio are organized – how, in a sense, they are allocated roles – is therefore just as important to radio's communicative powers as *what* those voices say. Our task, then, is to examine words, voices *and* the interplay of different speakers.

We can start by exploring the ways in which talk on the radio is essentially different, both to the sort of scripted, formal language of public lectures or speeches or written texts on the one hand, and to the talking we do in everyday, face-to-face conversations on the other. In everyday conversation, which we often regard as 'normal' or 'mundane' talk, we are usually close to one another, and within sight of each other. Crucially, we use facial expressions, gestures and whole postures to clarify and add meaning to the words we use. The talk is also two-way, and, although it is spontaneous, unspoken ground rules are rapidly established to allow for such simple taken-for-granted processes as taking turns and beginning and ending conversations politely and efficiently (Goffman 1981; Garfinkel 1984). *Mass* communication however, whether in the form of speaking directly to an audience gathered in a hall, or through broadcasting or the press, allows many more people to be 'talked' to, but seems to lack the personal contact of face-to-face chat which usually ensures an unforced mutual comprehension for those involved. When people speak on the radio, their audience is distant, unseeing, large and diverse. As Crisell has observed, the massed readers of books and newspapers are provided with the compensations of a permanent text, and the many millions of television viewers can of course actually see a speaker's gestures and expressions, but listeners to radio have neither visual clues nor the opportunity to 'decode' its speech at leisure. Much of the talk on radio is, then, shaped with this in mind: it has to employ formal strategies to overcome the limitations of the medium and so minimize the risk of ambiguity or even complete communication failure (1994: 5).

But these formal strategies – in which radio talk has to work self-consciously at compensating for its lack of visual clues – always have to be achieved while also considering the absent listeners' preference for a relaxed and apparently spontaneous style of chat. When two people on the radio are apparently talking to each other – for example in a studio discussion or a telephone phone-in – the talk cannot be quite the same as in everyday face-to-face conversations: they are not, as Scannell observes, locked in a private discourse, but engaged in talk which is *intended to be overheard* – indeed, which has been produced specifically for the absent listeners rather than the studio participants (1991: 1–4). In other words, since programme makers want people to listen, they have to make programmes listenable-to. This rules out an entirely relaxed and spontaneous conversation on the one hand, and the sort of formal didactic style employed by many early radio programmes – when many listeners to the BBC, for example, constantly complained of being talked down to by speakers – on the other. Even if radio was a public forum, it was rapidly discovered that listeners, receiving it as they did in the private spaces of their own homes, expected to be spoken to in a familiar, friendly and informal manner (Scannell and Cardiff 1991: 153–78).

On balance, therefore, the overall style of radio talk is tilted towards the manner of communication which appears most natural to most listeners. It is why certain phrases and syntaxes we might regard as normal in literature become entirely inappropriate for voicing aloud on air. Crisell provides several examples drawn from radio news scripts: contractions ('we'll' for 'we will') are used, sentences are usually short and often verbless (1994: 97–8). Stylebooks commonly in use in radio newsrooms also suggest that sentences should be written to be active rather than passive, and present tense rather than past tense ('The Prime Minister says . . .', not '. . . said the Prime Minister'). The incantation to radio scriptwriters is to write in a way that sounds natural *when spoken*, because the words always have to be voiced by someone in order to reach their audience – and the more natural and spontaneous the speaker sounds, the more intimate will be the broadcaster's relationship with the audience.

These spoken phrases are, of course, embodied in a written text – self-consciously planned to sound live, natural and flowing – and this underlines the fact that a relaxed and spontaneous style does not just happen: it has to be worked at. It can be achieved in systematic ways by broadcasting institutions issuing stylebooks and professional guidelines which 'routinize' the language and presentational practices of staff; but it is also achieved through smaller, but no less significant, unscripted turns of phrase, changes of voice and conversational sparrings which go out on air moment by moment. As Brand and Scannell note, any lay speakers suddenly given the radio DJ's tasks of providing spontaneous, unscripted talk, would almost certainly be dumbstruck (1991: 216–17). A presenter's patter is freshly improvised, but drawn from a relatively small reservoir of formulaic phrases: someone thrust into this role would lack, not words as such, but the tag-lines needed to sustain the talk time and time again (Goffman 1981: 324). And time *is* crucial. The continuous flow of sound is everything on radio, and, if only to prevent output grinding to a halt, radio talk must be in some senses constructed and institutionally controlled, even if it is simultaneously infused with informality. These institutional tasks therefore set strict limits on the spontaneity and freedom of all radio talk.

To illustrate this, let us take three specific studies – two looking at the talk of music radio DJs, and, initially, one drawn from phone-in programmes. Hutchby (1991) looked at the way talk is 'organized' during phone-ins on the London commercial station LBC. Members of the public are put on air in the expectation that they very quickly say something worthwhile and interesting, thus actively 'producing' a piece of news. Where they take too long to do this, perhaps choosing to chat informally to the presenter, they are presuming some intimate and equal relationship with the presenter that in reality does not exist, and they are failing to conform to the patterns of talk that are clearly expected of them. The presenter hosting the phone-in might allow some informal 'interpersonal' chat to delay business for a moment or two, perhaps trying to preserve the formal appearance of an interpersonal relationship with the caller ('Frances, good morning'), but he eventually forces the caller into observing the expected routines ('yes, well wha'd'you have to say?'). The message is clear enough: though 'news' is here being achieved through a collaboration between caller and presenter, it is the latter who is ultimately in charge. As long as his programme is going out over the air, he is the organizational 'hub' of the broadcasting institution for whom he works, operating at the interface between lay member and institution; and since the institution's main concern is for its *listeners* at large rather than any particular *caller*, the presenter's task is to 'process' callers in such a way that the listeners get their 'news' in short order. When, for example, the presenter occasionally sums up the gist of calls already broadcast, it may help any future callers to focus their thoughts, but his words are also *designed* to clarify the developing story for the overhearing audience.

Our second example, Montgomery's study (1986) of DJ talk on BBC Radio 1 in the mid 1980s, shifts the focus away from interviews towards monologues. Many radio practitioners are taught that since most listeners are listening in isolation, presenters should talk as if they are addressing an individual listener: *I*, the presenter, am talking to *you*, the listener. But Montgomery suggests that 'you' is here a constantly shifting concept. At times, the DJ seems to be speaking to an individual, perhaps greeted by name ('Ian Schlesser hello happy birthday'), or to particular groups ('. . . anyone who's a typist in a hospital'; '. . . now if you're healthy and you're over ten years old . . .'), and very often speaks to two different audiences at once, switching attention from second to second. This constant shifting illustrates two significant aspects of the talking. First, the presenter is continually addressing different fragments of the audience, but without alienating the majority. Although excluding some sections of the audience from the discourse might relegate them to the status of overhearers rather than participants, the DJ ensures this state of affairs is fleeting and dynamic – a second or two later, and some interpolated asides (very often underlined by a change in the tone of voice itself) will make them participants again. Secondly, the use of direct questions and commands to listeners ('oi! Libra stop that it's dirty') treats them as if they were visible and close. In Montgomery's phrase, this 'simulating co-presence' is 'erasing a sense of distance between speaker and audience' (1986: 429). Taken together, the constant shifts in address and treating the listeners as if they could reciprocate, helps draw the audience as a whole into the radio discourse. The talk does not cast the audience as a homogeneous mass, nor as a unitary subject: just as schedulers break the audience as a whole into different sections across whole dayparts, presenters use their talk constantly to shift between them second by second:

> It is maintained as a thing of many 'voices' addressed to many 'audiences'. . . . On the one hand, it is continuously inclusive with respect to diverse constituencies within the audience in a personalizing, familiar, even intimate, manner. . . . On the other hand, although the discourse may constitute the audience in fragmentary terms, it also manages simultaneously to dramatize the relation of the audience to itself: as listeners we are made constantly aware of other (invisible) elements in the audience of which we form part. (1986: 438)

Our third example of how seemingly spontaneous radio talk is constructed and shaped by its institutional setting is Brand and

Scannell's study of one well-known British DJ, Tony Blackburn (1991). They identify at least five different 'voices' which Blackburn employs during his interactions with callers on the phone:

- Standard: the baseline 'natural voice' that is returned to when speaking 'normally'.
- DJ voice: a hyped-up, upbeat voice routinely used for introducing records and promoting various parts of the programme.
- Authoritative voice: used to assert expertise (e.g. of music or broadcasting), to reassert a formality in telephone interviews, or to give advice and instructions to callers.
- Empathetic voice: imitating the tone of the caller in order to establish an intimacy or a shared point of view with them.
- Various 'camp' or send-up voices: e.g. chat-up, macho, etc.

Blackburn shifts continually between these different voices, in a way which helps establish his overarching identity, and that of the programme. It is a performance, but significantly, it is *intended to be recognized by listeners as a performance*. They are familiar with his style, and more often than not, they play along with Blackburn's verbal games – colluding, for example, with Blackburn's self-evidently manufactured chat-ups. Where callers don't play along, the DJ may be momentarily wrong-footed, or may summarily dispatch them from the airwaves: they have been offered the chance to share in the production of fun, but having failed to do so on the DJ's own terms – having failed, in Goffman's terminology, to have 'co-produced' talk that is 'in frame' – they must be excluded.

Brand and Scannell imply that there is a careful balance of rights and responsibilities revealed by this sort of 'talked' performance. Listeners are provided, over time, with a common knowledge of the programme's discursive world: it is a shareable resource for the production of talk by both presenter and caller. But in entering the discourse of the programme, callers – listeners – have to behave in an appropriate way: the communicative event taking place is public, and controlled institutionally to work for its overhearing audience at large. Tony Blackburn's purpose is to 'maintain fun' for his audience, and he will patrol the boundaries of his conversations rigorously. He is not alone in establishing this tightly constructed pattern. For talk-show hosts such as Rush Limbaugh, Howard Stern and other 'shock jocks', the performance is similar, even if more extreme: 'boring' callers are dismissed, not for the sake of impoliteness itself, but because pulling the plug livens things up a bit – not so much for the caller, of course, as for other listeners for whom this public display is produced.

Talk on the radio, then, is much more like everyday conversation than written text or conventional public speaking, but its spontaneity is worked at for institutional ends. It seeks to 'speak' to listeners in their own language, it tries to simulate some sense of the listener being close to the radio presenter, and it is always hearably produced for the listeners, even when presenters are ostensibly talking to someone in the studio or on the phone. Radio talk is thus 'listenable' talk. Yet it becomes listenable only through a series of self-conscious, institutionalized processes: some talk is scripted to *sound* spontaneous, even extemporized talk is a composition drawn from stock phrases, and lay callers have to adjust to its discourses. Above all, because the broadcasting organization is ultimately the author of all the talk that goes out on air, it manages it rigorously. Broadcast talk, as Brand and Scannell comment, thus bears its 'institutional marks' (1991: 216).

Some analyses of talk have seen in these institutional marks something more significant, namely *ideological* scars. The very act of managing radio talk could be editing out some views and discourses in favour of other, dominant ones, so that the talk 'produces' a particular world view as the unquestioned norm. We know already, from Hutchby and Scannell, that most talk on the radio is shaped and directed by the presenters. Hutchby also shows how a phone-in host sometimes explicitly challenges the morality or common sense of a caller's comments, and how, in summarizing a line of debate the host 'formulates' the conversation: he pares down the 'meaning' of the news 'produced' by a caller. This may be designed to help focus a discussion for the overhearing audience, but may also conspire over time to reinforce certain viewpoints as 'common sense'. This ideological 'structuring' has been located by Higgins and Moss in their analysis of talk on Australian radio (1984). They contrast the treatment of one particular studio guest from a prominent entrepreneurial family with that of several ordinary members of the public on phone-ins (see box 4.2).

In the case of the studio guest, clearly a member of the business 'establishment', the host shapes and directs the discourse but in such a way as to allow the guest to 'voice her text': he is complicit in the text-making process, but since he is evidently sympathetic with her viewpoint, his contribution is to supply leading questions and let his guest 'contribute content' to the text. The exchange, once completed, amounts to a text 'imprinted with cultural meaning', namely that the economic misfortunes of South Australia may reasonably be blamed on the excessive demands of workers. A rather different discourse is prompted by a caller to a phone-in about a proposed piece of legislation. The caller raises issues of free speech and talks of the 'cancer

Box 4.2   Ideological aspects of talk on the radio: two examples used by Higgins and Moss

Higgins and Moss contrast the 'text-making' aspects involved in two interviews. The first is an interview with Dame Nancy Buttfield, the daughter of the first and only indigenous Australian car manufacturer, the second is with a caller from the general public on a Queensland station morning show, who wishes to talk about some proposed legislation.

Interview with Dame Nancy Buttfield

[The interview begins by discussing the origins of her family firm and the book about it which Dame Nancy has just had published]

Host: All the anecdotes, I guess, that are in the book, do you have any favourites?

Dame Nancy: Oh, I think probably the ones about my grandfather; he was a tremendous prankster, a bit erratic, he used to always think up things to impress people. I can remember him, he told a young University student that had come to join the firm, that he was being a bit obnoxious and he better go home and he would ring him when he wanted to see him. So this young man got a bit sick of sitting at home and not being called, so he came back to the office without being told. My grandfather put him in the car, drove him around to the cemetery, and said, 'see all those grave-stones there', he said, 'all those people thought they were indispensable, like you'.

Host: I like that. What about the story that turned up in the review in the paper, I think it was yesterday, about Sir Edward being not allowed to join the Club, what was all that about?

Dame Nancy: Oh yes, that was in the days of the Establishment; they thought that trade was absolutely non-U, it all had to be professions, and anybody who joined the Adelaide Club had to be a professional. But after all, professionals haven't done as much for their country as some of the people in trade.

Host: What do you think we can do for the country at the moment, I'm talking about the sort of enterprise that started the car industry which supports millions of people in employment directly or indirectly?

Dame Nancy:	What can we do today?
Host:	Let's say we make you Prime Minister for a week.
Dame Nancy:	I'd hate to be Prime Minister for a week because I think that whatever the Prime Minister does it will always be wrong whatever party it is, he is just built up in order to throw bricks at. I do think that the Australian workman, good as he is, and I don't think there is a better workman throughout the world, is badly led and if only he could be persuaded to knuckle down and get on with the job instead of always going on strike, I think they would all be more secure in their jobs and there would be better production and the whole country would benefit.
Host:	Yes, you have really got to look without being political, not so much at the Australian worker and whether he wants to go on strike.
Dame Nancy:	. . . at the leadership of the workers.
Host:	Well, it is rather difficult to get to the worker and say is this your strike? Do you really believe democratically that this is the thing to be doing?
Dame Nancy:	Oh, that's right, the poor things are terrified, there are so many recriminations come through if they do happen to stand up against the desire to strike. I don't think the average workman wants to, certainly his wife doesn't.
Host:	Let's talk about the State, let's talk about the things we have initiated in this State and the fact it doesn't really seem to be the most go-ahead State at the moment. After all, it gave birth to the car industry, this State. What would you like to see done to revitalize this State?
Dame Nancy:	I'd like to see us go back to what happened, now you are really touching again on a good part of this book. My father knew in his years of work that this State had to be a manufacturing state, we haven't got the resources to be what the other states are, we haven't got oil, not much anyway, we haven't got all those things, we haven't got the people. He knew it had to be manufacturing. He set out to attract industry here and he did, and I mention many of them that were brought here, but he had a Premier, he would only have to send a cable from London saying, look I've got an industry that is

Continued

interested in coming, such as the Australian Cotton Textile Industry that came, what can you do as an incentive to come here rather than go to any other state, and immediately Sir Thomas would cable back, oh, we would give them this, that and the other in tax concessions or other things; now that's all gone. The incentive for people to come here because it was a better state to produce in is now absolutely gone because we are the worst state to produce in, all these incentives have gone, we are now saddled with long service leave, worker's compensation, you know all these things, which people just say well, if we haven't got the advantages of the mass of people to sell to, why would we go there.

Host: Well Dame Nancy, I thank you for your time and good luck with the book.

Interview about essential services legislation

Caller (female): I want to refer to that lady two calls back. I am utterly amazed that nobody else has rung up and complained at the Essential Services Bill.

Host: Yes.

Caller: The last two days you have hinted strongly to people that if it goes through their freedom of speech would be taken away. But where are they now with their voices all silent?

Host: Well, I guess it's the age-old problem that people don't really know what's in the legislation including the State members of parliament who were supposed to discuss it yesterday. All they were discussing was a summary.

Caller: I think everyone should be ringing their State MPs and saying we don't want this thing. It's a bad thing, and what's wrong with Queenslanders? Are they all a bit trop from having their brains addled by the sun or what?

Host: Well, I hope not. [laughs]. I've never heard it put quite like that before.

Caller: That's what's wrong with them. They're such a lethargic mob! They deserve all they get. This is the time they should be out in the streets, saying, 'No, we don't want this thing!' Next we'll be told what church we can go to, won't we?

Host: Well, let's hope that never happens. But at the same time I talked to Dr Edwards was it

> Tuesday morning? – and as I said to Dr Edwards the end of the legislation – you know – the end of the Essential Services Bill is after they have been out on strike for 48 hours that they're dismissed. Then what? And Dr Edwards had to admit that they didn't have 'a then what'. They didn't know what happens next. Now, if you're setting up legislation to try to create industrial stability and at the end of the legislation is a big stick and the big stick doesn't work, then the whole exercise is a waste of time.
>
> *Caller:*   That's quite right. But the way things are going now it's going from bad to worse. And I've rung you before and said it's time Queenslanders pulled the wool off their eyes and just had a look at what was going on and stopped this creeping cancer of the dictatorship that is coming out of our State Parliament.
>
> *Host:*   *(pause)* Alright, thanks *(pause)*. I presume that was your punchline? *(pause)* Ah, yes – I'll leave it at that. It's 8½ minutes to 10.
>
> *Source*: Higgins and Moss 1984: 359–60, 362–3. Reprinted by permission of Sage Publications Ltd.

of dictatorship in State Parliament' but the phone-in host appears to deflect her, trivialize her comments, and eventually push her off air rather brusquely. Higgins and Moss make the point that the caller has actually succeeded in getting her viewpoint across, but this is clearly *despite*, rather than *because* of the host, who is unwilling to 'use' the caller in an act of complicit meaning-making:

> Although the host is not aggressive in turning the interaction towards dominant meanings, indirectly he indicates the strength of the 'preferred' reading of the situation by closing the conversation immediately after the caller's provocative comments about the State government. By closing in this way and also by classifying her closing statement as a 'punchline', a term associated with comedy routines, the host also makes a deeper kind of structuring for the audience. In effect, he signals the illegitimacy of the caller's messages. (1984: 364)

This ideological structuring may infuse more banal areas of radio talk. For example, Montgomery (1991) has shown how 'Our Tune', a schmalzy on air re-reading of confessional letters about loss, grief and emotional upheaval from listeners to a BBC Radio 1 show in the 1980s and early 1990s, had the effect of conveying certain notions of the family. He notices how the presenter actually spends very little time developing the 'event-line' or plot of the letter-writer's story, and puts most effort into 'managing its reception by the audience' (1991: 141). The presenter frequently focusses the narrative, so that the audience is steered towards getting 'the point' of the story ('. . . it's about basically the way people survive . . .'); he also orientates the audience behind certain experiences faced by the central protagonist ('you can imagine how she felt'); and he establishes certain 'generic maxims' – assumed common-sense wisdoms – that invariably cluster around the idea of the family as the site of emotional upheaval but also ultimately of emotional survival, of endurance and solidarity in adversity ('. . . that's something that you need at those times'). Montgomery suggests that this is an echo of Barthes' 'cultural code', where texts 'mobilize' certain assumptions drawn from common sense, popular science and lay-psychology to make them taken-for-granted truths:

> These codes by a swivel characteristic of bourgeois ideology, which turns culture into nature, appear to establish reality, 'Life'. 'Life' then, in the classic text, becomes a nauseating mixture of common opinions, a smothering layer of received ideas. (Barthes 1975: 206)

In the case of 'Our Tune', the presenter's discourses sometimes portray the family unit as under threat, but also – and more forcefully – the place where the protagonists of these tales 'have their best chance not only of survival but also ultimate emotional fulfilment' (Montgomery 1991: 170).

'Our Tune' was a radio genre with its own very particular discourse, and it no longer survives. But we have already seen other examples, from Hobson (1980), Coward (1984), and Barnard (1989), of how music, adverts and phone-interviews are blended and filtered through the patter of DJs to declare that somehow each listener is – to borrow Coward's phrase – special, but not alone. This is the essence of radio talk: it takes up the lives of ordinary listeners, and tries to speak in something like *their* language to mediate these lives back to the public at large. The words and voices used on the radio to achieve this 'mediation' are clearly not the same as those used by listeners in their everyday conversations, yet the impact of this 'rearticulation' is in dispute in our various analyses. The suspicions aroused by Higgins and Moss would suggest that once private discourses are aired in the public spaces of broadcasting institutions something happens: the messy contingencies of people's lives are rearticulated into consensual forms, perhaps even a dominant ideology. According to the work on voices by Dyson (1994) and Valentine and Saint Damian (1988), this ideological effect is helped by the steady creation – through decades of editing, training, adjusting pitch and a preference for the masculine – of what listeners take to be authority and truthfulness embodied in most professional radio voices. Scannell, too, recognizes that the balance of power in any communicative exchange on the radio is invariably in favour of the broadcasters, but he implies that the rules of the discursive game are made to be self-evident, and therefore that sinister motives need not always be imputed. What is more, talk may often be talk *for talk's sake* – a pleasurable activity created for the overhearing audience, in which the substantive content of the talk may be simply a vehicle for the sociable experience of talking itself: a true case, if you like, of the medium being the message. Listeners are happy to engage with this – it works – because talk on the radio 'speaks' to its audiences *dynamically*. Not everyone is being addressed at once, but the audience at large is always somehow included: words and voices always appear to be 'for *me*', though they are almost always meaningfully available, without any difficulty, 'for *anyone*' (Scannell 1996: 14–15).

Listening closely to talk on the radio – even to the talk on music-led stations – can take us quite far in understanding the nature of radio 'texts', then. But a focus on radio talk in isolation from the music which accompanies it carries a danger. It implies that it is the words uttered by presenters that give full meaning to surrounding sounds, that the records played are not really signifying anything other than themselves. An alternative reading of the relationship between music and speech, is offered by Wall (1999). He argues, instead, that *music* can be seen as the primary code. As part of this argument, he describes some of the ways in which the rhythms and content of much DJ patter can be shaped by the instrumental patterns of the records over which they talk during so-called 'intros' (the opening section of a record before any vocals are heard) and 'outros' (the closing sequence of repeated choruses on which records are faded out). In box 4.3, he analyses a sequence of talk from a drive-time show on a Birmingham commercial station.

It is, Wall suggests, the music – and the DJ's attempts to control it – that explain the pattern of the talk, *not* the other way round. He can, for instance, talk for only as long as the instrumental part of a record allows him to – a factor that clearly sets a limit on the range and sophistication of talk that can be attempted. Wall points out that this sort of DJ talk is far from unusual, and he is surely right. If so, we need to turn our attention more fully to the wider range of meanings that music on the radio may convey.

Box 4.3   What is happening when a DJ talks over music?

R&B track 44 beats per minute
Keith Sweat (..) The new one (.) Twisted (...) Keith Sweat of course appear live and direct at the NEC Arena (.) on July 27th courtesy of Choice 102.2 FM (....)
Bringing you the
   fade starts
better artists in the Midlands (laughs) (....) OK, don't forget of course at 5.30 the
After
   fade ends
Dark Guide (..) with Nurica and Justin (....) Drivetime continues to 6.30. 6.30 to
   low volume sounds on record start
7 the Traffic Jam (.) 7 of course Daddy Crucial with the Crucial Jam. Tonight join
   music now discernable in the mix
Anthony (.) One Step (.) Tyral with the block party through to 3 in the morning (..) From Karen White, an absolute classic (..) Hunger (....) It is now 24 minutes to 5 (...) It's a Friday! (..) oh yea!
   vocal starts   R&B track 52 beats per minute

What is interesting here is the way that the talk relates so exactly to the music being played and other 'hidden' activities of the presenter in the control of the mixing desk which concerns me here. . . . The presenter uses both the beat of the record, and the ability of the music to punctuate and fill spaces in his on air utterances. The first three pieces of talk take up almost identical periods of time in the record, the difference in length of each phrase is compensated for by different lengths of silence from the presenter. The next two statements are much longer, and a space is used to punctuate and emphasize the two key pieces of information (the place and date of the concert).
   . . . [a later gap in the presenter's talk] is longer as the presenter has now shifted his attention to the mixer and he starts the next record. . . . As the music becomes more discernable the presenter's continuous phrasing is altered to fit with the beat and musical pattern of the record. He delivers three statements which fit exactly with the music before he hesitates momentarily. His aim now is to talk up to the moment that the record starts [that is, the point where the vocals begin]. . . . To do so he falls back on easily acquirable information about the time and day (in case the listeners had forgotten!) and finally resorts to a

meaningless cry. Both these last two parts of the utterances are made as exclamations echoing the rising declamatory sound of the music track.

This example indicates how strongly the talk of the programme relates to the multiple tasks that the presenter is attempting to conduct at any one time, and its significance is as much, and possibly more to do with its relationship to the records and their pace and mood, than to do with its content, or its strictly verbal articulation of identity. Such an analysis also highlights that the length and pace of the presenter talk are essential parts of the meaning of the act of talking.

Source: Wall 1999: 21–2

Music

If talk is scattered throughout radio, it is music which forms the bulk of its output. Yet, according to the early radio producer Lance Sieveking, there is no such thing as 'radio music' (1934: 24). Crisell takes up this position, by asserting that music on the radio is generally signifying nothing but itself (1994: 48–50). Certainly, pre-recorded music existed before and without radio, and music radio is in many respects often seen as little more than a shop window for the wares of the music industry. Yet music is the radio programming-tool *par excellence* for delivering the right audience to the right advertisers. As Shingler and Wieringa point out, 'when stations are faced with low audience ratings, the first thing they usually do is rethink their musical style' (1998: 62). The ubiquity of playlists – effecting very tight management control over the music played – is proof enough of its importance to stations in attracting audiences and helping to establish the identity, the 'brand', of a service. I have played to groups of students extracts from radio stations consisting solely of their musical output – all verbal clues to the station's identity have been stripped out – and it is striking how this sample audience recognizes the stations *more* successfully than when similarly confronted with extracts of speech from unidentified talk-radio stations. The result is testimony to the sense in which music has become instantly *categorizable*, in terms of genres, or shades of genres, and as part of this phenomenon music-led radio stations correspond in terms of audience markets tied to particular music categories of taste. Jazz, pop, rock and rap, for example, are assumed to have specific social and cultural connotations attached to them, and consequently to have a specific appeal for particular age groups, classes and ethnic communities. Music has, for many of us, become a way of defining one's identity, and from that, establishing communities of shared interests and even values. Given this, a radio station's decision to choose to play a particular genre of music means it is also choosing a particular audience. This choice of music extends beyond the records being played to the whole gamut of incidental music woven into a station's output – the jingles, music 'beds' and signature tunes that accompany and frame the spoken words: they all seek to say, through their particular texture, tempo and style, that you are listening to *this* type of station not *that* type of radio station, whether 'this' happens to be a CHR, AOR, Soft AC, Classical, or dance-station, and – beyond that – to argue through condensed musical style that 'this' station is *unique*, possessing a personality distinguished from all other stations on the dial, even those in the same format, and that you, the listener, are part of its particular community.

But if music is very often the key factor in attracting audiences, we should ask why this should be so? It might, of course, be simply a case of people liking to listen to music. Shingler and Wieringa rightly point out that music, which requires no visual accompaniment, is of course the ideal background sound for a secondary medium:

> Often at a concert we have to look away from the performers or, better still, close our eyes to really hear the music. One of the advantages of radio is that it closes our eyes for us, focusing our attention on the product rather than the process of musical performance. Radio renders music more important than the performers and, consequently enhances its elemental power. (1998: 61)

We do not always need to revere music in this way to recognize it as having a function on the radio. Indeed, our ability – and our need – to get on with other things while listening to the radio demarcates much radio music, not as something to be *listened*-to, but as something to be *heard* – aural wallpaper in a way that even the blandest of speech cannot be. Provided that the music is relatively melodic, and reassuringly familiar in some way, it can provide texture in our lives and fill the empty spaces of our domestic environments *without demanding too much attention*. As Crisell observed:

> In being largely free of signification it allows us to listen without making strenuous efforts to imagine what is being referred to, but to assimilate it, if we wish, to our own thoughts and moods. (1994: 49)

But the question is, why listen to music *on the radio* rather than music of one's own on CDs? It cannot always be with the educative purpose of finding out about what music is 'out there' to be further and more intensively consumed by buying the record, because radio listeners – even music radio listeners – are by no means all record *buyers*. One possible answer is that we tune into a station not so much for the music as for the way it is 'framed' – for the reassuring and insinuating patter of the DJs themselves. Indeed, Crisell argues that 'music alone is insufficiently meaningful, that the listener needs to have it identified for her in what we have seen is the primary code of words' (1994: 64–5). Moreover, the sort of unrelieved music with no audible human origination provided by CDs and muzak is far less *companiable* than music mediated by charismatic radio presenters: their words provide, not just textual content, but – bearing in mind that we usually listen to radio alone – a much-desired human presence. Indeed, some presenters, as we have seen in our discussion of talk, feel almost entirely unconstrained by the music they play, and will talk about almost anything *but* the records themselves. We can go further in this relationship between speech and music. The very blending together of these two ingredients – oral banter continuously and intimately interwoven with music – contributes to what Crisell has identified as radio's *brokerage* between banality and glamour. Constant references by presenters to the unfolding workaday routines of its listeners are combined with the emotional power of music and all its glamorous connotations, so that even mundane concerns such as weather reports and traffic updates are infused with a sense of excitement and urgency. This, Crisell argues, is one way of differentiating radio from television: television may offer an 'escape' from the passage of time, but radio offers 'a pleasant way of *marking* it' (1994: 69–70).

So speech can often add a significant amount of meaning to the records played on music radio stations. But it remains true that music, *in and of itself*, excites – and music on radio is mythically such a source of pleasure, a defining part of teenage culture, that the music we hear on the radio becomes in some sense the 'soundtrack' to our lives – particular songs not just reminding us of a period in our personal history but evoking real emotional responses. Indeed, as Barnard noted, mainstream radio *habitually* roots musical meaning in 'memory or evocative value', rather than in musical appreciation on its own terms (1989: 146). Barthes wrote of the pleasure, the *jouissance*, that music can invoke on the part of performers and listeners, and although he was never directly concerned with radio, his writings convey some useful approaches to its meaning within a mass medium. In two of his essays, *The Grain of the Voice* and *Musica Practica*, he explored the way in which deeper meanings within music had become concealed by centuries of unhelpful music criticism and a steady decline in the numbers of people actually performing music for themselves. Critics, he argued, had reduced music to being seen as coded expressions of emotions such as solemnity, dolefulness or voluptuousness – a reductive approach which ignored a certain 'voice within the voice'. This voice, or the 'grain' within the voice as Barthes put it, was nothing to do with superficial representations of feelings, but was where – at a deeper level – 'melody really works at the language' of the song, it was 'the body in the voice as it sings'. Anything lacking this 'grain', might have a perfectly respectable semantic and lyrical structure in the formal sense, but it would lack any 'signifying weight' and nothing in it could 'sway us to jouissance'. Such grainless music – mass 'good' music, as heard on records and the radio – has been 'flattened out into perfection' in terms of formal technique and production values, and as such fits well with 'the demands of an average culture':

> Such a culture, defined by the growth of the number of listeners and the disappearance of practitioners (no more amateurs), wants art, wants music, provided they be clear, that they 'translate' an emotion and represent a signified (the 'meaning' of a poem); an art that inoculates pleasure (by reducing it to a known coded emotion) and reconciles the subject to what in music *can be said*: what is said about it, predicatively, by Institution, Criticism, Opinion. (1977: 185)

Although Barthes' preferred focus was classical music, the distinction between music with 'grain' (and hence significance) and that without, was one which he claimed could be extended to popular music – 'some popular singers have a "grain" while others, however famous, do not' – and to instrumental performances, where 'grain' was to be found emanating from the bodily effort of the musician. Indeed, the notion of *performed* music, as opposed to *heard* music, was central to his critique. The music one performs is different, he claimed, to the music one hears: when one is performing, hearing is only ratifying the bodily performance, in which the *body* is not so much 'transmitting', but actually doing the important work of inscribing, making sound and meaning in itself (1997: 149–50). Seen in this light, the music we *listen to* rather than perform, whether in the audience at a concert, on a CD at home, or indeed on the radio in the car, lacks the important physical process of performance. It is 'passive, receptive music, sound music' produced by technicians on our behalf. 'The "technician" of music relieves the listener of all activity, even by procuration, and abolishes in the sphere of music the very notion of *doing*' (1977: 150). Some music, however – Beethoven is adduced here – even though performed by others, has within itself 'something inaudible', that allows the listener to move beyond mere 'receiving' but to inscribe the work anew, thus restoring to listeners something of the role of practical performers, in which they actually 'operate' the music:

> In this way may be rediscovered . . . a certain *musica practica*. What is the use of composing if it is to confine the product within the precinct of the concert or the solitude of listening to the radio? To compose, at least by propensity, is *to give to do*, not to give to hear but to give to write. (1977: 153)

Implicitly, Barthes critique would argue for radio's role to be seen as a malign mediation of music. It casts radio listeners in the role of passive 'hearers' of music, and, as a *mass* medium, radio responds to the demands of an 'average' culture in which the 'erotic' pleasures of music and songs possessing 'grain' are displaced by a diet of technically perfect, flattened out music which pleases the multitude but rarely arouses it. This reading is not without real echoes in the contemporary radio environment. Take the example of one musician from New Zealand, who complains that FM radio in his country is:

> full of shiny things that whistle and hiss at you while displaying their perfectly rounded . . . bass frequencies and smooth-as-silk mid-frequencies. These 'shiny beats' bear little resemblance to a human being singing a heartfelt song. (Chris Knox. Quoted in Pickering and Shuker 1993: 35–6)

It is a commonplace of current radio criticism that music radio output is not only sometimes biased towards the more polished and melodic records of the music industry but also is bland and unchallenging as a whole. Certainly, we saw in chapter 1 that there are real economic imperatives behind a certain homogenizing of output. What is more, within that output records are coded by radio programmers into various 'emotive' categories that Barthes would recognize and condemn. The music-programming software *Selector*, for example, allows each song to be categorized under, say, five 'mood' codes, ranging from something like 'very sad/very dark' to 'very happy/very bright': programmers are advised to schedule 'very dark' records very sparingly. And, as I try to argue more fully in the next chapter, in evaluating the relationship between music radio and popular music tastes, much music radio can be seen to reinforce the success of 'mainstream' sounds – well-produced, melodic and familiar, and, one could argue, 'flattened out into perfection' – at the expense of more demanding and innovative 'specialist' forms.

These distinctions, between familiar and highly polished main-stream pop on the one hand and more jarring forms of specialist music on the other, may not correspond precisely with Barthes' notion of music with-or-without 'grain', but radio's programming of music certainly makes an implicit distinction between music that is expected to arouse and that which is expected to reassure. Take for example the usual distinction in music radio output between the popular 'pop' of daytime, and the more elevated, 'progressive' rock of the evening schedules. It is a distinction which usually prompts parallels between notions of 'high' and 'low' culture, and which also implies that whatever is not superficially expressive (pop) must be in some sense cold and intellectual (even if in some *musical* sense 'superior'). In reality, very little 'specialist' music on the radio is 'prog-rock', art-school music of the sort which Barnard (1989) described as characterizing music radio's evening fare in the 1970s and 1980s. If found at all, it is much more likely to be drawn from sub-genres such as dance or rap, where the dominant ethic is for *less*-produced, street-inspired and harder-edged music produced not by polished technicians with a cool intellectual interest in musical form but by semi-trained '*actors* of music' (as Barthes would call them), creating sounds which are best described as 'raw': music, one could argue, with 'grain' in its voice.

From this viewpoint, the broad distinction we make between the daytime and evening output of music radio is probably better inter-preted, not so much as conveying simply 'hierarchies' of taste, but rather as reflecting a need to 'smooth out' the daytime output by banishing most music with any hint of 'grain' to the evening fringes of the schedule. A playlist allows station managers to reduce the element of risk entailed in leaving individual DJs and producers to select records, thus ensuring a proper consistency of output, an output that – to use Barthes' phrase again – is apparently 'flattened out into perfection'. And as mainstream pop music records become progressively 'better' produced for the global markets, and as radio stations become more finely attuned to what will or will not offend their audiences, any *jouissance*, any music with 'grain', will become more definitively located in the margins of radio output.

Radio, though, does not make a *wholesale* abolition of arousing music in favour of reassuring forms. Rather, it seeks to combine various musical textures in patterns designed to fit with its own *temporal* concerns. Scheduling is not simply a matter of dividing a station's output into 'daytime' and 'evening', but an infinitely more complex process of positioning chosen records over the course of each quarter of an hour, each hour, 'daypart', day and week. And central to this scheduling is the notion of establishing patterns and rhythms, in which the mood, energy and tempo of programmes are varied quite deliberately over time through the records and jingles broadcast. Garner (1990) looked at the arrangement over time of records played during the course of a single programme on the daily schedules, in this case the music-led breakfast show. He asserted that in the programme, the 'real text' is not the individual piece of music, interpreted through its lyrics or style, but 'the clock on the studio wall':

> Records acquire a wholly distinct, complex meaning when broadcast. The precise time of broadcast of a record on a breakfast show, what precedes and follows it, and how it is introduced, is of potentially greater significance than the song's lyrics. (1990: 193–4)

In other words, the way in which music is scheduled *over time* is what creates meanings for the listener. The positioning of records at certain regular times of the show reflects the morning rhythms of preparation for leaving for work or delivering children to school. Familiar 'oldie' records crop up almost routinely after each news bulletin, when 'the listener's need for reassurance' is greatest, and elsewhere 'they function as a statement of reassurance at the crucial time when many are preparing to leave home for work' (1990: 200). The appearance of a familiar record – if not an 'oldie', then certainly a hit – is in this sense a sign of nervousness on the part of programmers that their audience is at its most sensitive and potentially disloyal: it explains why, for example, BBC Radio 1 recently described as 'Radio 1 Anthems' those records which are most instantly associated with the station, which are already familiar and successful, and which, not by chance, are apt to appear after most news bulletins. AM stations, as we know, are likely to have an older and more conservative audience profile than FM stations, and, as Garner observes, such stations 'do not have to decide when a record will be least disturbing. For their target audience, the 35–54 year-olds, every musical sound offers a potentially familiar environment' (1990: 200). It is this familiarity with the music, as much as the *emotive* personality of the DJ, that leads to the frequent habit of records either not being identified at all, or at most being identified by the artist's name rather than by the song title: the music is a *known* quality, and presented as such to reassure the blurry eyed listener.

Yet, at the same time, the *overall* tempo of breakfast radio is upbeat:

> British breakfast shows . . . transmit a contradictory message: it's nice to lie-in and share an on-air joke, but we must all get up and get on with it. . . . The beat of the familiar tune that thunders in over an

early-morning joke is both the driving beat of a new day demanding our attention, and the emotional consolation that this repetition, after all, is what we know. The effect is that of a powerful ritual, exorcising the demon of objection to work by consoling at the same time as being rhythmically cajoling. (Garner 1990: 201)

One could argue here that the music being heard on the morning radio show is not 'passive' music as Barthes might have argued, but structured over time in a way which gives *the programme itself* a compositional quality – and a quality in which, to relocate Barthes' phrase, the musical *flow* 'gives to do': the listener is 'cajoled', *engaged*, by the music-within-the-clock to get up and get on. This temporal significance applies across programmes at all times of the day and week, and to jingles and other incidental music on the radio. Computerized programming routines, like those embodied in *Selector*, are based on the assumption that sudden leaps up or down in tempo, energy, texture or mood, are to be avoided in favour of a more measured flow. One 'rule' – and the whole system is based on rules – might be, for example, that a record with a slow tempo at the start and a slow tempo at its end should not be followed by another record with an identical tempo at both the start and the end, or by a record with a fast tempo at its start: instead, it should be followed by a record with a slow or medium tempo at the start, whatever the end tempo. In other words – radical leaps in tempo are avoided in favour of smaller steps up or down. Beyond that, it might be a rule that no three records in a row would normally be permitted to have a total mood 'score' of more than 11 ('very up') or less than 7 ('down'), and that records should never jump up or down by a value of more than 3 (for example, by going from a record categorized as '5: Very Up' to one categorized as '1: Very Down', as opposed to a more acceptable '3: Medium'). New records, whatever their tempo, mood, energy or texture, are usually 'hammocked', that is positioned with very familiar records either side, to ensure that the musical serendipity provided by radio programmers is always within safely framed limits. Other computer software similar to *Selector* can ensure that jingles are similarly characterized and similarly scheduled, so that beyond their function as brand advertisements for the station itself, they act as musical stepping stones or gear changes to assist the musical flow. They vary stylistically within each programme to enable presenters to effect instant changes of mood – enabling presenters to shift between programme items ranging across subjects and treatments of contrasting emotions. And they vary at different times of the day, so that careful scheduling can establish an appropriate mood – getting on, mellowing out – by varying the tempo, pace and instrumentation of the theme from morning to afternoon to evening. As such, they can be seen as a kind of 'aural punctuation' in musical form, like commas and full-stops, which are taken much for granted by the listener but are essential building blocks for the programme maker.

Such conventions in music programming all suggest that the primary concern of scheduling is not just to highlight the most popular records for the target audience but to ensure that the ebb and flow of mood, tempo, energy and texture is almost always gradual, rather than jarring. In this way, whole programmes and whole sections of the broadcasting day possess a predetermined rhythm. And the rhythm is – on the whole – a reassuring one. It provides peaks and troughs of emotional intensity in quite precisely measured doses, to accompany us through the peaks and troughs of our daily routines. Music, as Shingler and Wieringa observe, 'motivates' – not just us, but the radio text itself, by which we mean the unfolding rhythms of the output over time. It:

> sets radio in motion, charts its rises and falls, and moves it on to something new. Its key function is to stimulate and maintain momentum. The moment radio stops, it ceases to exist. Music, above all else, keeps it flowing. (1998: 70)

It is possible to take this temporal approach one stage further, and argue, as Glenn Gould has done, that even those radio programmes concerned more with speech than with music can be heard to be constructed along very similar compositional lines to music itself. Gould, though first a musician, also made features for Canadian radio in the 1960s. In discussing two of them, *The Idea of North* and *The Latecomers*, he refers to a technique in which he overlaid the voices of certain interviewees, so that they were speaking simultaneously at various points, and – significantly – describes it as 'contrapuntal'; he also makes an analogy between the multi-layering of sounds in his radio features and the musical form of the fugue (Page 1990: 376, 382–3). In discussing how he constructed one particular 'scene' in *The Latecomers*, Gould talks in clear musical terms:

> The scene would become an ABA structure – ternary form, as one would think of it in music. . . . In my mind, all of the scenes in 'North', let's say, or 'The Latecomers', have shapes which are at least conditioned by musical perceptions. (1990: 378–9)

Gould accepts that there are limits to such musical analogies in radio. In fact, his main aesthetic concern was *texture* as much as tempo, and he talks more of different sound 'perspectives' in a given scene than about the rhythm of the programme as a whole. Nevertheless, his concern for musical form suggests ways in which the tendency to interpret radio in the language of visual metaphor – what Beck (1998) has called the 'oculocentrist' tendency of radio criticism – can be reinterpreted in ways that move the debate beyond sound, or 'aurality' per se, to encompass the way in which meanings emerge through the composed flow of music, voices and sounds *over time*. Music on the radio can therefore be seen to carry more than associative, cultural meanings, where particular songs charge listeners with different emotional currents: it also provides a metaphor for the composition of radio programming as a whole, in which – sometimes carefully and artistically, sometimes mechanically through computerized scheduling – further meaning is attached by the precise temporal positioning of each sound. This takes us some way further than Barthes would have allowed, with his implicit view of radio music as passive, unperformed and thus barely of significance. It may be that much of the music we hear on our radio sets is bland and predictable and the overall effect is soothing, but we can also build a picture of radio in which music – taken as a building block, and re-arranged by the medium into a new, larger composition, *performed* by the schedulers and the DJs, and which unfolds over time – is central to radio's task of weaving itself into the currents of our daily lives.

Radio and modernity: time, place and 'communicative capacity'

Throughout this discussion of talk and music on radio, I have frequently touched on two underlying themes which now deserve more direct examination: time and place. Researchers have hinted at some of the ways in which the physical distances between broadcasters and listeners are tackled in order to establish feelings of intimacy with the medium – the 'simulating co-presence' that Montgomery talks of, for instance, or the sense of community engendered by the medium more generally that we saw in our discussion of radio listening in chapter 3. This suggests that creating a *sense of place* is one recurring theme of radio's meaningfulness in modern life. And as well as a sense of place, there is also our sense of *space* to be considered: that in transmitting its signals over many hundreds of miles, and in allowing us in our domestic lives to be 'connected' to events and people beyond physical reach, radio somehow transforms our sense of space *between* different places. Many discussions also hinted at the central role in producing meaningfulness, not so much of individual programmes (or elements of programmes), but of the longer patterns of radio output over time – the way in which the time at which a record is played is perhaps more significant than the lyrics it contains, or the way in which listeners come to associate particular shows and styles of output with particular times of day. This suggests that a second recurring theme should be the ways in which radio's *temporal rhythms* – its narrative structures, hourly cycles and daily and weekly schedules – connect with the temporal rhythms of our everyday lives. In viewing radio from the twin perspectives of 'time' and of 'place', we do not necessarily escape the contradictions of the medium – how in one sense it may contribute (along with other mass media) to the much discussed phenomenon of social alienation, and how in other ways it may, to use Scannell's phrase again, 'rekindle' social life. Even so, without offering a unifying 'theory' of radio, I will make some attempt to explore what may underlie these paradoxes and relate them to some of the concepts of modernity – the patterns of contemporary life – that have been applied to the media more generally. I propose to do this through developing the notion of radio's 'communicative capacity'.

Time

In arguing that radio's real 'text' is the 'clock on the studio wall', Garner (1990) was suggesting that the individual elements making up a radio programme only become fully meaningful when heard in their precise temporal context. We can extend this further. Radio is, to state a truism, a time-based medium. Its texts – its programmes – emerge in a linear flow of time, whether measured in seconds (as in commercials or jingles), hours (individual radio shows), or even weeks (in the case of series or whole advertising campaigns). Indeed, as Crisell reminds us, whereas television can deliver its messages pictorially across the space of the television screen as well as over time, radio has *only* the passage of time in which to do its work (1994: 5–6). A programme's identity, although clearly shaped by the voice of its presenter and the choice of its music, is therefore also to be found in the way it orders its content, say, for example, in the course of each hour. Morning programmes, broadcast when most listeners want to 'get up and get on', arrange their content in a relatively hectic narrative of many short pieces of speech and music; early-afternoon programmes deliberately achieve a more relaxed tempo through fewer and longer segments of sound. Producers, as we saw in chapter 2, construct radio programmes on the basis of a 'clock format': a recurring pattern of sounds and themes arranged in a certain order each hour, with news bulletins, weather reports, sports news and phone-in features at certain fixed times. A programme's clock format is a useful template for producers, but it is also founded on the needs of listeners, who cannot choose the order in which they hear radio, and can only pick and choose what to hear by associating certain programme elements with certain times of the day, and tuning in at the times which allow them to catch them. Of course, no-one can tune in at exactly the right moment, and broadcasters wish to keep their audiences listening for as long as possible. So the clock format is not enough: the 'messages' are, as we know, evanescent, and the past and future are always intangible, and there needs therefore to be a constant 'signposting' back and forwards, with listeners being reminded incessantly about who is talking and what they are talking about, or what the station is that they are listening to, and what is about to happen, in both the immediate and more distant future. This aural signposting is designed to enable listeners to get their bearings quickly, but its net effect is also to create a sense in which the narrative, though recurring and familiar, is also evolving and never-ending – that something worthwhile (whether a chance to win a dream holiday or the chance to hear the latest single by a particular band) could be missed by turning off. The various means by which radio establishes the beginnings and endings of programmes – verbal motifs, jingles, silence and so on – have been described as 'frame' conventions (Goffman 1980: 162–5) or 'boundary rituals' (Fiske and Hartley 1978: 166–7). But in fact, very few radio stations still offer discrete programmes of contrasting genres, preferring longer 'sequence' shows of two or three hours and even then preferring to propel listeners as swiftly and unobtrusively as possible from one programme to the next. Frame conventions and boundary rituals undoubtedly exist, so that, for example, we know from the short 'stab' of a particular jingle that a news bulletin has ended; but framing is rarely expressed in a way which provides an opportunity for listeners to switch off or change stations – they must be encouraged to stay.

In studies of television, the concept of 'flow' has been used to explain the way in which the medium is experienced by viewers, not so much as individual programmes but as a sequence of programmes. Raymond Williams (1974) pointed out that we tend to say we're 'watching television' rather than watching a *particular* TV programme: it is an indication of the way in which dramas, news, adverts and trails – genres which, though different, often imitate each other in form, and which collide with barely marked boundaries between them – are experienced in one sitting as a single flow. Several authors have suggested that this flow should be understood, not as a smooth uninterrupted process, but an essentially discontinuous and fragmented one. Ellis (1982) describes how television's continuity is punctuated by adverts and trails, and how each individual programme is in turn composed of smaller (and often unrelated) building blocks. As Abercrombie makes clear, 'Williams's flow actually takes place across groups of segments' (1996: 16). Such flow is fractured further, as viewers usually change channels many times in the course of an evening's viewing: through zapping, each viewer in effect composes his or her own unique 'flow' of images, sounds and feelings.

Are there parallels in radio? Certainly, listeners rarely 'tune in' for particular programmes: as we noted in chapter 3, they listen *to the radio*, just as Williams' viewers *watch television*. There is a subtle difference, however. Since radio programme schedules are listed less prominently than television schedules in the press, and retuning a radio set has traditionally been more difficult than changing channels on television, listening to the radio is generally a much less promiscuous affair than watching television: listeners do not 'zap' from one station to another in the way they might flick through the channels on television. The 'flow' of sounds experienced by listeners to radio is therefore usually composed of the more coherent and *predetermined* flow of a single station for the entire duration of any one listening session. This may not always be the case in the near future. We saw in chapter 1 how technological developments – the arrival of push-button digital radio sets – will soon allow what one broadcaster described as new and 'scary' levels of listener promiscuity. We also saw that the technology of audio on-demand creates the possibility of listeners constructing their own schedules – their own unique flow – of programmes. Yet for the time being at least, listeners to radio are less able to subvert a given radio station's own constructed pattern of output over time, and they either accept the schedule of programming offered or switch off altogether.

Even so, while radio's flow is *less* fragmented than that of television's because it is habitually experienced through just one station at a time (rather than many channels), it is simultaneously *more* fragmented than television flow because of the intrinsically more segmented nature of even a single station's output. If radio broadcasts are highly formatted, programme segments are much smaller and more rapid in succession than those that television usually offers. Recall the discussion in chapter 2 of the 'acoustic beads' which Crisell describes as constituting the building blocks of programme making. In fact, he makes explicit a comparison with Ellis' 'segmentation' concept:

> Commercial radio output typically consists of a string of acoustic beads, a sequence of records interspersed with commercial breaks, presenter's talk, news, weather information and so on – each 'bead' of

approximately similar length to the others and lasting no more than a few moments. For this kind of output I shall borrow the term 'segmentation' which has been coined in relation to television programming (Ellis 1982: 116–26). It is true that Ellis sees almost all broadcast output as segmented – ultimately divisible into 'bites' consisting of a scene in a play, an advert, a statement from an interviewee, and so on: but the term seems particularly useful here because the segments which make up talk and music sequences on the radio are much more apparent, more discrete and detachable, than those which co-operate in a 'built' programme such as a play or documentary. To a far greater extent they can be added, subtracted or reordered without discernible damage to the whole. (1994: 72)

Compare this with Kaplan's interpretation of MTV – a music-television channel striking for its adoption of an essentially *radio*-based temporal rhythm:

> The channel hypnotizes more than others because it consists of a series of extremely short (four minutes or less) texts that maintain us in an excited state of expectation. The 'coming up next' mechanism that is the staple of all serials is an intrinsic aspect of the minute-by-minute MTV watching. We are trapped by the constant hope that the next video will finally satisfy and, lured by the seductive promise of immediate plenitude, we keep endlessly consuming the short texts. MTV thus carries to an extreme a phenomenon that characterizes most of television. (1987: 4)

MTV might be viewed as 'extreme' in the context of television, but its 'extremely short texts' and 'coming up next mechanism' for enticing the viewer to keep watching is directly comparable to the *bulk* of mainstream radio's output, with its 'acoustic beads' and constant signposting. If so, the concept of flow is even more pertinent in studying radio than it has been for analysing television, though with one important qualification: since radio flow is not quite as fractured across several channels in the way that television flow tends to be, its precise tempo and pattern, along with its content, apparently lies more under the control of the broadcasters themselves than with the listeners.

Higgins and Moss, as we noted earlier, see great ideological significance in this ability of broadcasters to control the flow of sounds over periods of time. Their studies of Australian radio suggested that the apparent haphazardness with which seemingly disparate snippets of news, commercials, personal narratives, songs and comments come together on radio conceals a quite deliberate 'sequence of signs and images whose purpose is to transmit certain cultural messages' (1982: 33). It is not the individual elements of programming which carry meaning so much as their coalescence into a unified message through the planned use of a recurrent temporal pattern: callers' personal narratives around the theme of life-as-being-tough being *followed* by – and *overwhelmed* by – the brash positivism of commercials offering a better future (1982: 37). Higgins and Moss' use of the concept of flow raises a question here, though: why should radio listeners be quite so passively accepting of the consumerist ideology with which they identify? Berland finds one possible answer in the tempo of radio output itself. Radio, she argues, is not a sequence of discontinuous items but a 'motivated' flow of rapid and predictable items in a continuous sequence. The rapidity of the flow is as 'carefully managed' as the predictability of its pattern, and it creates a 'continuous rhythm of sound . . . more powerful than any single item enveloped in its progression'. In this way, radio teaches us 'addiction and forgetfulness': it induces – is *intended* to induce – passive listening, a form of listening which, precisely because it is passive, is accepting and hence vulnerable to any form of persuasion. Listeners, in effect, are simply not given the time to stop and think, because the 'text' they are 'reading' is fast-moving, continuous and – unless one switches off completely – unstoppable (1993b: 210–11).

The issue of time itself is actually taken one stage further by Berland. She argues that mainstream music radio is actively reconstructing – and, in particular, *quickening* – both the rhythms of our daily lives and our sense of historical change. She makes the point that if a station wished to change format, from for example, MOR (Middle of the Road) to CHR (Contemporary Hit Radio), it would – among other changes, such as a brisker presentation style – adopt a smaller playlist with a higher weekly rotation and faster turnover of hits:

> Like the radio schedule itself, with its strict markers of the hour, its subtly clocked rotation of current and past hits, its advanced promotion of a new release, the music playlist functions as a kind of meta-language of time. The playlist offers a grammar of temporality which draws in the listener and produces him or her (economically, as a commodity; experientially, as a listener) as a member of a stylistic community defined, more and more, in inexorably temporal terms, rather than in relation to geographic or more explicitly substantive identification – assembled that is, in terms of the preferred speed and rate of musical consumption. (1993a: 113–14)

In mainstream music radio, Berland suggests, time is 'speeded-up and broken into contemporaneous moments'; radio marks historical time through music, and where its music is turned-over more rapidly, it 'creates a new sense of time, not directly parallel to previous kinds' (1993a: 114).

Radio's relationship with time, and specifically with the rhythms of our daily and weekly lives, has been a central concern of Scannell's analysis of radio (1988, 1996). Here, though, the power relationship between broadcasters and audiences is more evenly balanced, with radio output seen to have a much more sensitive relationship with the pre-existing rhythms of modern life. I mentioned in chapter 3 Scannell's suggestion that broadcasters know their output must adapt itself to, and seek to enter into, the contexts in which it is being heard. These everyday contexts are defined largely by our domestic timetables, the humdrum activities we perform at given moments in the day – getting up, preparing ourselves for work, doing the housework, getting ready for bed, and so on. Radio does not just adapt to these routines and structure its output accordingly across the daily schedule, it also helps *over time* to 'thematize' our days. By marking off each *part* of the day as somehow different – 'breakfast time', 'drive time' – and by marking off each day *as a whole* as a *new* day with fresh events and topics to be discussed (and yet somehow also a day rather like any other), *radio* time chimes with *our* time. Or, as Scannell himself puts it, 'Broadcasting, whose medium is time, articulates our sense of time' (1996: 148–52).

It is also the familiarity of certain patterns of radio output *over time*, that helps accumulate a particular programme's identity – an identity defined above all by its recurrent part in our daily lives. We take for granted the daily presence of shows like the *Today* programme on BBC Radio 4, or Radio 1's *Breakfast Show*, or K-Rock's *Howard Stern Show*, because over time we have come to trust that they will be there and to understand what they will entail. In radio advertising too, commercials are rarely one-offs. Campaigns are based on a given number of 'Opportunities to Hear' ('OTHs') over a period of several weeks: only *over time* will the listener 'get' the message (RAB 1998a, 1998b). If this is so, then formats and schedules are not just tools of production – as we viewed them in chapter 2 – or ways of bending to the listeners' own demands and tastes – as we viewed them in chapter 3 – but also devices which over time make radio *itself* an ordinary, routine part of our lives:

> A single programme has no identity. . . . For output to have the regular, familiar routine character that it has, seriality is crucial. . . . The net effect of all these techniques is cumulative. In and through time programme output, in all its parts and as a whole, takes on a settled, familiar, known and taken-for-granted character. (Scannell 1996: 10–11)

So: it is not *just* that radio takes the 'stuff of ordinary life' to make 'public, communicable, pleasurable' programmes out of it and 'revalue' private life by bringing it into the public domain. It is also a matter of time – the way this ordinary everyday experience unfolds *temporally* in a way that parallels the 'endless continuum of day-to-day life' (Scannell 1988b: 19). Take radio soap operas, where time in the fictional world invariably runs in precise parallel with the real world: if it is Tuesday in *The Archers* it is usually Tuesday in the real world. And if so:

> it follows that the lifetime of . . . listeners unfolds at the same rate as the lives of the characters in the story. Thus one stands in the same temporal relation to them as one does to one's own family, relatives, friends and everyday acquaintances. (Scannell 1996: 159)

Time, then, and the familiarity engendered over time, is one of the foundations upon which radio's intimacy is built. And not just its intimacy, but its sociability too. Recall Douglas' idea in chapter 3, that it is the *simultaneity* of the listening experience which turns individual listeners into communities of listeners: we rarely tape a radio programme in the way that we might record a favourite television programme – so, like everyone else, we have to be listening *at the time* to catch a particular programme. And if we are listening at the same time, that means that we have something in common: our lives stand in the same temporal relation to other listeners as much as they stand in the same temporal relationship to the programmes we hear.

So: radio time 'chimes' with our time in a way that generates intimacy and sociability. Yet 'our time' is itself influenced by 'radio time'. Influenced a great deal, Berland implies, since we often listen to radio stations which mark us off by our 'preferred speed and rate of musical consumption', which generally quicken the pace of our lives and threaten to overwhelm us with the unceasing torrent of their output. Influenced a little less, Scannell implies, if only because radio output has to accommodate itself to the domestic routines within which it is consumed. This is not an unbridgeable gulf in interpretation. Scannell certainly acknowledges that radio has helped us 'thematize' our daily lives by making us aware of what others are doing and *when* each day. This picks up a thread from our earlier discussion of audiences in chapter 3, where I suggested that radio might well be gratifying needs which it has in some sense helped to create. Radio, then, does not just work to time, it also mediates our sense of it. Or, rather, our sense*s* of it. For we must also remember that the fragmentation of radio listening into tighter niche markets means that the 'simultaneity' of radio which Douglas sees as central to its sociable dimension is experienced in ever smaller communities nowadays. We do not have to construct a grand theory of a fractured, alienated society in order to recognize that we do not all live our lives at the same pace and to the same daily pattern, and that different radio stations now offer us several different temporal rhythms with which to live our lives.

Place

Let us turn now to radio's sense of place. Those working as radio producers are frequently urged to use sound to 'take' the listeners to a particular place: they assemble location recordings of aural 'actuality' into atmospheric 'soundscapes' that evoke certain locales. These soundscapes, as Crisell and Shingler and Wieringa remind us, are not accurate reflections of the sounds of the world, but clearly selective and stylized. Nevertheless, the urge to create this sense of place is common, not just to radio drama or features, but also to radio news, and much of the talk scattered through music radio. It is the same urge to 'take' listeners out of their real listening environments that prompts so many outside broadcasts, at concerts, music festivals, sports events, ceremonies, public rallies and so on: they have the virtue of presenting radio stations as not being isolated from the world beyond their studios, and they are presented simultaneously to listeners as a chance for them to take part in an event that they might never be able to attend in person. Television, of course, does much the same, so that we can say that broadcasting as a whole offers some form of window on the world, some access to the ongoing public life that takes place beyond the domestic environments in which we watch TV and listen to the radio. If so, we can argue that while broadcasters use the technology of transmission and networking to send their signals across ever larger distances – 'shrinking' global space – conversely, listeners can use broadcasting to *expand* their horizons.

These horizons, though, are not always expanded in entirely uncomplicated ways. For one thing, an individual item on the radio might seek to create a particular sense of place when dealing with a particular story, but the radio 'text' as a whole is made up of many items – a flow of many different senses-of-place. Format radio gives us, say, a record by an American artist followed by a news report from the Balkans, some sports commentary from Europe and a travel bulletin from the nearest town. As Berland reminds us, radio joins together 'geographically and philosophically unrelated items' in new juxtapositions – it literally splits 'sound from source' (1993b: 210).

All this juxtapositioning takes place in a public 'space' – but a space nevertheless defined by broadcasters rather more than by listeners. Brand and Scannell, in their study of the Tony Blackburn show, suggested the programme's identity lay precisely in its ability to straddle the public institutional space from which the radio presenter speaks and the private, domestic or work spaces from which callers speak. Yet to 'enter' the studio as a caller is 'to cross a threshold, to enter a social environment that creates its own occasions, discursive and performative rules and conventions' (1991: 222–3): all listeners are entitled to enter, but they are there to supply – to co-produce – a pretty strictly defined sense of 'fun' (or, in the case of current affairs phone-ins, 'news'). The public space offered to listeners by radio is therefore one with strictly limited horizons, even if listeners accept that and collude with it in order to simply pass the time in an entertaining way. Ultimately, implies Scannell, if such *sociability* has been achieved, then broadcasting has done its work.

Sociability is, here, a *virtual* coming together – a coming together of listeners with broadcasters, callers and other listeners, in which other people, other cultures, other musics, are 'revealed' through broadcasting. As such, it is at the heart of radio's ability to affirm our sense of place in the world in human terms, and underlies all the medium's claims to a special form of intimacy. But what sort of 'sociability' does radio actually present to us? We know that listeners feel 'close' to *presenters* with whom they are allowed to become familiar. But the overriding characteristic of radio seems to be its ability to make us aware of *other listeners*. Montgomery's study of 'Our Tune', and both Hobson's and Coward's studies of the relationships forged through listening to DJ's, return us time and time again to radio presenting the audience back to itself: we are spoken to as individuals and the personal crises of individuals are described, but a community of shared interests is invoked, 'not the family, or the neighbourhood, or even the nation as such, but rather the radio audience itself' (Montgomery 1991: 175–6).

This radio audience is often defined as specifically tied to a place, it is *local* – and indeed radio, as we saw in chapter 1, is much more highly localized than television. But we also know that the audience definition is constantly shifting, not just between stations but also moment-by-moment within a single station's output: sometimes it is defined by musical taste, at other times by age, by occupation, even by star sign. These definitions promise to draw us out of our geographical and domestic isolation, and offer us membership of new communities of *interest* much less tied to geographical place. Yet, as we also know from our survey of the radio industry in chapter 1, audiences are being packaged into ever smaller 'fragmented' interest groups, and globalization – which the media contribute to and reflect

– can simultaneously make this enlarged world a flatter, more homogenized, one: the news agenda, the music we hear, and the style of programming we hear it packaged in, is everywhere superficially different but almost everywhere essentially the same. This makes the sense of place and community engendered by radio a rather contradictory affair.

Take three examples, drawn in turn from southern Africa, Western Australia and North America. Scannell (1997) looked at patterns of radio listening in Zimbabwe, and showed how, even though many more people listened to the state-broadcaster's 'Radio 2' station than to the more international, Afropop-dominated 'Radio 3', they were poorer and there was something of a stigma attached to it:

> The station [Radio 2] was 'weird', 'not modern', 'country stuff', 'African'. I was told by a friend that some people would switch off Radio 2 before visitors or neighbours came in, so as not to be found listening to the station. (1997: 10–11)

The two stations, both ostensibly serving a national audience, clearly catered for two different musical 'taste publics', but it is noticeable that ZBC's Radio 2 lacked the aspirational quality that attached to its Radio 3. A similar 'pull' towards urban life was detected in Green's study of broadcasting in the Western Australian outback (1998). Here, until the advent of commercial television via Intelsat in 1986, many isolated farmsteads had no television or radio services at all, while other communities received only public-service broadcasts supplied by the Australian Broadcasting Corporation (ABC) – broadcasts which suffered from an image as 'worthy but dull'. Green's study found that, without the adverts – and the glamour, fashion, gossip, music and style that such adverts embodied – listeners felt excluded from membership of a common, popular, *consumerist* culture. Some listeners who took occasional trips to Perth began to make illegal cassette recordings of programmes on 96FM – the city's main commercial pop station – to be brought back for endless replaying once home in the outback. Many of those replying to questionnaires distributed by Green were adamant that what they really wanted from their 'local' radio or television was 'entry' to the cosmopolitan, consumerist lifestyle enjoyed by those living in Perth. In the short term, this could only be achieved by travelling long distances, and capturing on tape the sleek, polished output of someone else's radio station.

One predictable *longer-term* solution to these listeners' demands would no doubt be for their 'local' service to adopt a more 'sophisticated' – that is, 'urban' – style for itself. We saw in chapter 1 how, by repackaging syndicated material beamed across whole networks, many radio stations are becoming the 'localizers' of national or even international content. What's more, as Berland points out in one of her studies of Canadian radio (1993a), where there is a particularly big urban centre its stations seem to act as 'magnets' to listeners in outlying smaller towns. And since these magnet stations are increasingly likely to belong to a branded chain, they are also quite likely to have tighter formats playing a narrower range of mostly nationally and internationally distributed music than their small town competitors; they are likely to belong to a branded chain. In this way, the dominant means by which urban radio formats its own output 'delocalizes' and 'recentralizes' space. Berland therefore draws a parallel with Harold Innis's original thesis about how 'space-binding' media, in permitting more rapid dissemination of information across ever larger spaces, also 'erode local memory and the self-determination of peripheral groups' (Berland 1993a: 111).

What makes radio different to television here is what Berland calls the 'psychic investment' radio listeners – unlike television viewers – make in 'local space', despite its underlying 'recentralizing' tendencies. 'People's feelings about community, about territory, work and weekends, roads and traffic, memory and play, and what might be happening across town' are seized by radio so that it can 'map our symbolic and social environment'. Radio therefore distinguishes itself from television through 'highly conventional and elaborated strategies of representation' – strategies which actively draw attention to the radio station as a live and local entity – which provide a local 'feel' that attracts both listeners and advertisers in the face of competition from television.

> In this context the DJ serves to personalize and thus locate the station as more than an abstract mediation of records, advertisers and listeners. DJs are increasingly disempowered in terms of programming, and make fewer and fewer decisions about music and other content. But it falls to the DJ's voice to provide an index of radio as a live and local medium, to provide immediate evidence of the efficacy of its listeners' desires. It is through that voice that the community hears itself constituted, through that voice that radio assumes authorship of the community, woven into itself through its jokes, its advertisements, its gossip, all represented, recurringly and powerfully, as the map of local life. (1993a: 116)

Radio, then, seems to offer us a more Janus-faced text than television: in spatial terms, at least, it appears to be 'omnisciently "local" without arising from or contributing to local cultures' (1993a: 112). This is where radio provides a particularly striking variation on the broader debate about globalization. It has been transnational in scope for much longer than other electronic media, and it has contributed heavily to the widespread cultural diffusion of Anglo-American pop music. However, through various forms of local stations, micro radio, pirates, and special-interest community stations, commentators suggest that it 'has also been an important instrument of localism' (Held et al. 1999: 351). Yet if Berland is right, this localism is often illusory. Or to put it another way, it gives a highly local 'feel' to a 'text' which, despite its frequent concern with particular soundscapes, is in many respects as a whole largely place-*less*. Radio, as Fairchild concludes, is now more than ever 'deterritorialized' (1999).

'Communicative capacity'

This comes across as a rather more pessimistic conclusion than Scannell's vision of a medium which 'rekindles the life and fire of the world' (1996: 164–5). But they are not irreconcilable views. Berland herself acknowledges radio's central paradox in a passage I have already drawn upon in the first chapter, but which bears repeating here:

> It is a space-binding medium, ensuring the rapid, broad distribution of changing texts without restriction to an originary space or a cultural elite. On the other hand, it is aural, vernacular, immediate, transitory; its composite stream of music and speech, including local (if usually one-way) communication, has the capacity to nourish local identity and oral history, and to render these dynamic through contact with other spaces and cultures. This capacity for mediating the local with the new defines its styles of talk and construction of station identity. (1993: 112)

The important phrase here is *capacity*. Radio has certain capabilities, but they are not always exercised. Perhaps then radio is not communicative as such, it merely has what I shall call 'communicative capacity' – a capacity only sometimes fulfilled. What do I mean by this? We know it is a much more varied phenomenon than television, scattered more widely, and adopting a wider range of forms, from pirate, underground and community stations through to local, national and international stations, and networked chains, some being commercial, others public service. It should be no surprise, therefore, if radio fulfils its communicative capacity in different ways and with varying degrees of success: no single, unifying theory can accommodate its range. Beck (1998) has remarked on radio's essential 'hybridity' – its ability to adapt and change, sometimes drawing on the forms of other mass media like television, at other times exhibiting a fully deployed range of 'radiogenic' features. Even so, some underlying patterns can be discerned. I argued in chapters 1 and 2 that the broad distinction between commercial radio and public-service radio remains meaningful, and if this is so it must manifest itself in the radio text as much as in the structures of the industry. It is significant that, for example, while Scannell and Montgomery – who can perhaps both be described as 'optimists' over radio's communicative powers – focus on case studies drawn from the public-service sector, Higgins and Moss address *commercial* radio, and Berland's focus is quite specifically *music* radio stations in the commercial sector. This is not to suggest that public-service radio everywhere and always nourishes a constructive relationship between its different audiences while commercial radio does not. But it may be that the commercial or public-service status of a radio station does affect the extent to which its communicative capacity is reached.

Rothenbuhler (1996) even argues that commercial radio, on the American model at least, is best understood as lacking any communicative goals *at all*. It communicates, but only as a means to non-communicative (in this case economic) ends; it cares little about the messages it transmits so long as the audience is there to bring in advertising revenue. Rothenbuhler starts by accepting the definition of communication as an act meaningfully orientated to others. There are four elements to this: communicators must have

- A purpose for communication;
- Some idea to express;
- Some means to express it;
- Someone to whom to express it.

Communicating successfully 'requires artful expression adapted to the purpose, the idea, the medium, and the audience' (1996: 130). We normally expect communication to follow rules of 'quantity and quality' – in other words, we expect each other to say neither more nor less than is needed and to say what is relevant and true (Grice 1989). But where communication becomes an instrument for a non-communicative purpose – to make money, rather than to educate, inform or entertain for its own sake – any 'message purpose' becomes subordinate to the 'money purpose':

> If we think of radio stations as trying to communicate with their audiences, as really trying to say something, then changes in format, such as from country to oldies or from rock to all talk, make no sense. They

are irrational changes of mind. That is because these communicators
are not communicators in the normative sense; they are instrumental
communicators, and, as such, their expression is not substantively but
instrumentally motivated. They will say anything if it will likely make
money. . . . In addition to having chosen their medium without regard
for any communicative purpose . . . [they] have done so without any
act of invention, that is without any thought of anything to say. . . .
When business people choose the radio for business reasons, they
also choose a medium of expression, but not for expressive reasons.
(Rothenbuhler 1996: 132–3).

In this interpretation, when disc jockeys prattle and news bulletins
stick to their full duration on a 'quiet' news day, it is because *they
have nothing to say but still need to say something*: the station must go
on broadcasting, because there will always be people within reach of
a station's signal who just might be converted into a commercial
audience of potential consumers. To have to have something to say
24 hours a day – even if it is rather banal – is what drives radio stations towards tight formats based on crude audience typifications:
they provide decision-making rules which avoid the near-impossible
information-processing task of rapid 'message making', deciding
every few minutes who out of the universe of people may be listening and what records, out of the universe of music, should be played
to them (1996: 135).

This picture of commercial 'format' radio as a medium stripped
of real expressive content contrasts quite starkly, at first sight, with
the avowed communicative intention of public-service radio. The
public-service ethic of broadcasting, as embodied in Reith's BBC,
has historically presented radio as a medium which treats listeners,
not so much as consumers but as rational social beings immersed in
a 'public sphere' of free and rational exchange of reasoned opinion.
Put like this, such a contrast could explain the fundamental contradictions we have explored through this chapter: alienating tendencies
emerging from an exploitative commercial sector, and more nurturing forms of communication emerging from the public service. But
it is not quite the case that we are observing two distinct models of
radio communication, one commercial – and typified by Rothenbuhler's North American model – another public service – and
typified by a Reithian-shaped BBC of noble educative, informative,
intentions. Tolson (1991) reminds us that the search for relaxed,
audience-friendly styles of address in the mass media predates commercialization, and that even public-service operators like the BBC
have long communicated within a 'populist', rather than a 'paternalist' public sphere – a modern public sphere, capable of containing
everyday language, placing events and entertainments in a common

public domain, and interconnecting the public and private worlds (Tolson 1991: 195–7). Tolson argues that while there is no single 'communicative ethos', the distinction is therefore not between 'paternalist' (public-service) models and 'populist' (commercial) models, but between two contradictory forces within broadcasting's modern public sphere: a vacillation between 'its two demands for information and entertainment' (1991: 197).

I would argue that, in the specific case of radio, we need to put it slightly differently. Berland wrote of the paradox of radio being a 'space-binding' medium which can nourish local identity through contact with other spaces and cultures, but a medium too where formats – in industrializing both its relations of production and its temporal language – squeeze out its 'vernacular, immediate, transitory' qualities (1993a: 112). In other words, where radio is most heavily formatted, the freedom for truly communicative radio – in Berland's words, radio that renders local identities 'dynamic' – is constrained, diminished. Almost all mainstream radio is now format radio to a greater or lesser extent – broadcasting now cares too much about market share and audience size to be otherwise. But it remains true that commercial radio has a *greater* vested interest in formats than public-service radio, so that to some extent our earlier contrast between commercial and public-service models of communication holds true: commercial radio is more formatted than public-service radio, and as the commercial sector grows so too does the dominance of format radio. Rothenbuhler puts the consequences somewhat brutally:

> Over time, commercial interests displace communicative interests, and meaning and aesthetics become subordinate to commercial exploitation. Commercial radio, then, short of giving up its commercial nature, can only damage radio as a system of communication. (1996: 139)

The vision is apocalyptic, but perhaps more applicable to the mainstream of radio than to radio as a whole. At the end of chapter 1, I argued that the nature of radio still allows for at least some renewal and diversity in the margins of the industry. Low costs, new channels of distribution, and a more individualized production process than is the case in television still allow some creative room for manoeuvre in fulfilling the medium's communicative capacity. Radio, then, is not – or at least, not *yet* – devoid of meaning. What is more, its role in changing our sense of place and of time raises wider issues of social identity:

> as our sense of the past becomes increasingly dependent on mediated symbolic forms, and as our sense of place within it becomes increas-

ingly nourished by media products, so too our sense of the groups and communities with which we share a common path through time and space, a common origin and a common fate, is altered: we feel ourselves to belong to groups and communities which are constituted in part through the media. (Thompson 1995: 35)

The media in general, then, are not simply involved in reporting on a social world which would, as it were continue very much the same without them. Rather, 'the media are actively involved in constituting the social world' (1995: 117). If the radio medium, devoid as it may be of much of its communicative capacity, still helps to define the contours of our social lives, our next task must be to assess the *kinds* of cultures it helps reproduce.

5

Culture

This chapter tries to examine radio's role within popular culture in three main areas. The first is in the area of democratic life, and specifically the way in which radio lives up to its reputation as a medium of information and discussion. The second is in the more diffuse area of identity – how radio might nurture, or destroy, people's sense of 'belonging'; 'belonging' to communities that can be defined, for example by ethnicity, language, place or even by patterns of consumption. The third area has a more specific focus: the way in which radio might shape trends in popular music. One recurring theme is the sense in which the greater interconnectedness of the world's media industries brings with it a greater degree of cultural homogenization at a global level. We have also seen in previous chapters, however, that as well as homogenization, there is a parallel process of 'fragmentation', in which audiences are apparently being split into ever more tightly defined niches. These two trends raise an important question: is radio reinforcing cultural differences, or eroding them? The question is usually addressed in relation to notions of cultural imperialism – and specifically the global spread of American culture at the expense of indigenous ones. This is clearly relevant to radio, as the medium is very much the global purveyor of both American music and American formatting conventions. Yet, as has been pointed out, 'many forms of culture in the world today are, to varying extents, *hybrid cultures* in which different values, beliefs and practices have become deeply entwined' (Thompson 1995: 170). Encounters between different cultures can be invigorating. But if this is to happen these different cultures have to become in some sense visible or audible to each other. Our task, then, is to examine the *ways* in which radio is able to make this happen by exposing audiences to different ideas, and sounds and lifestyles. And the essential question is this: does radio, rather than introducing its listeners to new experiences, erect barriers which keep these experiences at bay? That, of course, raises a further question: erecting barriers might protect threatened ideas and ways of life from extinction, but if cultural encounters can be 'invigorating' might this 'protectionism' be at the price of cultural stasis?

Radio and democratic culture

It is inarguable that the media as a whole play a central role in defining democratic life. 'Democracy', argues McChesney, 'requires that there be an effective system of political communication, broadly construed, that informs and engages the citizenry, drawing people meaningfully into the polity' (1997: 5). How does radio, in particular, measure up to this demanding role?

Certainly, it imbues itself with an *aura* of democracy. It does this, firstly, through its institutional posturing. In its use of the very term radio *station*, it conjures notions of accessibility – we saw in the previous chapter how the medium makes great 'psychic investment' in its localness, through its insinuation with local communities, places and events. In a broader geographical sphere, a public-service broadcaster like the BBC talks of 'nation speaking unto nation', where broadcasting allows a community – whether regional, national or global in scope – to be informed about *itself*.

Radio assumes an aura of democracy, secondly, through the self-conscious use on air of language soaked in demotic values: stations and programmes are the 'voice' of the people, where they 'talkback' to those in positions of influence and power. The German playwright Bertolt Brecht once argued against radio being a channel through which homes passively received information and entertainment: if listeners could transmit as well as receive, he argued, then they would become producers of radio as well as consumers, and it would become a truly public, two-way form of communication (1932). The contemporary radio phone-in programme, built on the ability of listeners to use their telephones to become contributors, at least momentarily, certainly now allows radio to advertise itself to the world as a democratic, reciprocal, *two-way* medium on a large scale – a claim easily enhanced with the rapid adoption of email and Internet discussion forums as a tool of audience involvement.

The third way in which radio presents itself as a democratic medium is through the opportunities it provides for direct participation in its own production. We know that much mainstream radio is professionally produced and owned by large corporations. But we also know that radio is a remarkably *cheap* medium to produce, and, although profitability may be elusive, the relatively low cost of entry makes radio dramatically more accessible than television as a tool of community action. This makes radio, at least in theory, the medium of the more marginalized and disenfranchised sections of the community, as much as of the large corporation or the state: community and neighbourhood stations, pirates, 'free-radio' stations and various forms of clandestine radio, are phenomena with only very rare parallels in the global ecology of television.

We can say, then, that all radio adopts the language of democracy. It also employs the rhetoric of two apparently different democratic functions: one in which it claims to 'mediate' the views of the listeners on their behalf, thus carving out some form of institutionalized 'public sphere' of opinion and debate, and a second in which it claims to be an 'alternative' medium representing, not just the voice, but also the active participation of those incapable of expression through other media or public forums. In reality, of course, these functions are often conflated, and sometimes subverted altogether. For alongside the rhetoric of radio's democratic value lies an equally lively, but more dystopian discourse: the rhetoric of radio's powers of mass manipulation through propaganda, or of its tendency to trivialize important political and social issues through its simplistic and fleeting attentions.

The tradition of radio as both the agent of crude propaganda and, simultaneously, the chosen medium of alternative voices, is probably at its strongest in the developing world. High in the mountains of Bolivia, for example, communities of tin-miners have long run a network of small, self-owned and self-controlled radio stations. In his study of these miners' radio stations, O'Connor (1990) identified their role in creating a culture of resistance to the authoritarian tendencies of the central government. In 'normal' times of relative democratic openness, the stations would act as a cultural link between the miners union and its members, broadcasting concerts, live music and poetry, community news, comedies and political satires; in times of military rule, the stations formed a network of resistance. O'Connor suggests that radio was the ideal medium for this political expression: it reached – and therefore held together – extremely isolated communities in a way that newspapers could never do; it suited the oral – and often illiterate – culture of the mining communities, very often speaking their indigenous languages (such as Aymara and Quechua); and finally, not only were radio receivers affordable in most homes and perfectly usable beyond the reach of mains electricity, but the technology of *transmitting* was easily learned by amateurs and relatively cheap to buy and maintain. It was, O'Connor argues, no coincidence that when the Bolivian regime wished to undercut the stations' effectiveness in uniting the miners, it distributed television sets on very easy payment terms and helped foster a boom in commercial media retransmitting programmes from Brazil, Mexico and Venezuela.

The example of the Bolivian tin-miners' stations neatly illustrates the two fundamental reasons for radio having a greater impact than either television or the press in much of the developing world: first, its oral nature, which overcomes widespread illiteracy; and secondly, its technical and economic accessibility as a medium of participation. The impact of its oral nature is visible in rural Africa, just as much as in Latin America, where newspapers are also rarely distributed widely and where many more households own radio receivers than TV sets. Radio, indeed, has long been promoted by UNESCO and other international aid agencies as a tool of development, and observers have noted its ubiquity in the social landscape of Africa, with people spending long periods of time in the fields and in cars with receivers 'stuck to their ear', or carried through public spaces on shoulders, or even amplified throughout entire neighbourhoods (Chrétien et al. 1995: 74; Kellow and Steeves 1998; Hamm 1995a). It was in these circumstances that a radio soap opera, *Gueza Mwendo*, was recently listened to in Tanzania by some six million people every week. It told the story of Mashaka the truck-driver, who 'spends most of his time on the roads of east Africa, rarely sees his wife and has a girlfriend in every town': it is also the story of his deteriorating health through the onset of AIDS. Tanzania, like much of Africa, has a strong tradition of education through story-telling, and it comes as no surprise that one survey suggested that three-quarters of the population seemed to have been made aware of AIDS, and its prevention, through radio programmes like *Gueza Mwendo* (Gough 1999).

Radio's second fundamental characteristic in this discussion of democratic culture – its technical and economic accessibility – is manifested in countless examples beyond the Bolivian mountains of community-owned and community-run stations. These at least provide the *opportunity* for self-expression in the face of dominant political or cultural forces: stations for native American Indians in Alaska, South Dakota and central America, for the urban poor living in the heart of western capitalism in the case of WLIB-AM in New York City's East Harlem district, or for overtly radical political voices in the case of KPFA-FM in Berkeley, California (Stavitsky 1993; Schulman 1988). Such stations may not be profitable, but are still sustainable because of their ability to run on a combination of cheap equipment and free, voluntary labour.

Radio's role as a channel for partisan political voices reaches its most direct expression in so-called 'clandestine' stations, which operate entirely underground to broadcast the views of revolutionary or counter-revolutionary groups (Soley and Nichols 1987; Soley 1993). In his surveys of what he calls the 'dark side of the spectrum', Soley identifies several hundred clandestine stations operating across the globe in the early 1990s:

> All that's required to operate a clandestine radio station in support or opposition of one cause or another is a transmitter, a message and the hope that someone will listen. . . . And because radio can reach all segments of society regardless of education or socioeconomic class, clandestine messages [through radio] will continue to be the preferred medium for groups seeking to express their views or to foment revolution, liberation or rebellion. (1993: 130, 138)

Significantly, clandestine radio has not just outlived the Cold War, but even proliferated through the 1990s. This, Soley argues, is 'perhaps one manifestation of unleashed nationalism and demands for political democracy' in an era where US–Soviet tensions have been replaced, not by openness, but by new outbreaks of regional and ethnic strife. In the past decade, for example, there have been numerous clandestine stations in Africa, such as the radio of the Sudanese People's Liberation Army (Radio SPLA), Radio Fidelité in Algeria, and those operated by the various warlords of Somalia; about the same number have been operating in Asia – such as one excoriating the military regime in Burma – and yet more have appeared in the former Soviet states of Central Asia (1993: 138).

There is, then, a vigorous tradition of radio as an 'alternative' medium of expression. What counts, of course, is whether or not these channels of communication are always entirely convincing examples of grassroots democracy rather than covert political action, and whether they even achieve their aim of a more widely drawn and more participatory public sphere of debate. The evidence is rather mixed. Certainly, O'Connor argues, the tin-miners' stations of Bolivia helped foster a collective culture of resistance in the face of an undemocratic regime. Similarly, a socially owned radio station like B92 in Belgrade provided 'the only source of alternative information in and from Serbia' as Slobodan Milosevic's regime progressively stifled opposition to his regime and achieved effective censorship of all domestic *television* news output in the late 1990s (Matic 1999a). Yet in both the Bolivian and Serbian examples, the fate of the stations is also significant. O'Connor traces how, in time, the Bolivian stations were exposed to frequent internal divisions:

> The staff was changed each time a different political faction gained control of the local union. . . . These kinds of difficulties generally prevented the miners from making long-term plans or developing a coherent philosophy of alternative broadcasting. (1990: 106)

These sorts of 'internal' difficulties in establishing 'democratic radio' have been examined closely by Hochheimer (1993). He suggests that issues of power and control frequently disturb the good intentions of those participating in station life, and he identifies several recurring problems. Three, in particular, are overarching:

- First, it is not always established clearly who is serving whom: small stations in culturally homogeneous areas may successfully act as channels for community members to share information and ideas between themselves – they are 'of' the community, not just 'for' the community – but more culturally mixed areas, with larger populations, make it difficult to identify and serve all sections of the community fairly: which are the legitimate voices to be heard and how much gatekeeping does there need to be?
- Secondly, the precise degree of community participation in the production of programmes can bring problems: the most committed and active can become entrenched, while others, who are perhaps less articulate and with less physical access to the station or with less free time, can become marginalized.
- Thirdly, there are emotional, economic and cultural restraints on collective enterprise: stations may reject formal structures, with clear job demarcation, wide variations in pay, and streamlined decision-making, but their preferred model of task-sharing and collective decision-making is both time-consuming and emotionally draining for those involved (1993: 475–81).

Hochheimer quotes Rothschild-Whitt (1979) in concluding that the media 'can only be as democratic, free and pluralistic as the society within which they exist' – a society which is of course largely capitalist and laissez-faire:

> It is very difficult to sustain collectivist personalities. It is asking, in effect, that people shift gears, that they learn to act one way inside their collective, and another way outside. In this sense, the difficulty of creating and sustaining collectivist attributes and behaviour patterns results from a cultural disjuncture. It derives from the fact that alter-

native work organizations are as yet isolated examples of collectivism in an otherwise capitalist-bureaucratic context. (1979: 522)

Given this 'cultural disjuncture', it comes as no surprise that the story of many community-led, participatory or 'alternative' radio stations is the story of steady professionalization – and with it a real or perceived loss of legitimacy 'in the ears of its audience and supporters' (Hochheimer 1993: 481). Stavitsky traces the example of Pacifica's KPFA at Berkeley, California, founded in 1949 'to promote peace, social justice, the labour movement and the arts' (1993: 87). Within an eclectic mix of programmes, it provided a regular channel of expression for opponents of US action in the Korean War and supporters of legalising cannabis. By the early 1990s, though, its manager had cancelled much of the volunteer programming in favour of 'a more uniform, professionally produced format of music and public affairs that includes national news programmes beamed in from the company's headquarters; the station had also moved out of a converted flat and into a 'state-of-the-art $3.5-million facility' (Stavitsky 1993: 87–8). Unsurprisingly, dissident volunteers and listeners have attacked the station as undemocratic and insensitive to multiculturalism, and have warned of the 'NPR-ization' of KPFA – a reference to complaints that National Public Radio has lost its alternative edge and 'joined the media mainstream' (1993: 88). Changes at KPFA reached their logical conclusion in the summer of 1999, with a full-scale clear-out of long-standing staff to reflect changes in programming ordered by the station's owners.

If stations such as those run by Bolivian tin-miners or America's counter-culture activists steadily lost their 'participatory' character, what then was the fate of Belgrade's B92? Although it survived as an independent voice within Serbia during the early days of NATO's aerial bombing in 1999, partly by resorting to Internet-only programming when its transmitter was seized, it was taken over by an organization loyal to the Milosevic regime which proceeded to broadcast *pro*-government views, *but still under the name of B92* (Matic 1999b). This phenomenon, in which a station can entirely mislead listeners about its sponsorship and purpose, is typical, Soley argues, of most clandestine stations across the world. He draws a distinction between 'grey' and 'black' radio stations. 'Grey' stations are attributed to indigenous dissident groups, but are in fact sponsored by outside governments or their intelligence agencies. Two examples of grey stations, among the many, include 'Radio España Independiente', which called itself 'the Pyrenees radio station' but was in fact Soviet-backed and Soviet-based, and the 'Voice of the Iraqi People', broadcasting anti-Saddam Hussein propaganda from Saudi Arabia and with US backing during the Gulf War. 'Black' stations are similarly sponsored, but masquerade as those of the enemy: during the Vietnam war, for example, the CIA ran a station which claimed to be 'Liberation Radio', the Viet Cong's grey station (Soley 1993: 129–37).

So: 'participatory' radio – whether of the open community-kind or of the more clandestine-kind – is very often not quite as 'alternative' as it might at first appear. The central question, though, is what *quantity* and what *quality* of political debate or action does it actually foster? Is it a marginal phenomenon, or does it have real cultural impact? One piece of evidence is provided by Manaev (1991), who examined the ideological influence on Soviet youth of listening to western radio stations such as Radio Liberty, Radio Free Europe and the BBC World Service – stations which Soley would classify as 'white' because they are open about their location and sponsorship, but which should clearly be regarded as 'alternative' in the context of Soviet life in the very early days of glasnost and perestroika. In one survey, Manaev discovered that more than 80 per cent of young people listened to western radio. Most of these listeners went on to discuss the programmes with friends and colleagues, and those who listened most were most likely to change their opinions on political issues. A spiral of change was created:

> Contact with a source itself often leads to an increase in radio listening; the listener's initial interest widens from musical programs to information and propaganda. In turn, higher levels of radio listening, including more information consumption and growing interest, stimulate the listener's desire to share impressions with persons of the same age as well as to work out a group opinion based on new facts and opinions, which gradually increase in number. . . . Group discussions strengthen and increase the listener's initial interest in and positive attitude toward the programs and their content; often these discussions lead to listeners changing their opinion. . . . A modified opinion requires new supporting arguments, so searching for those arguments makes information consumption more active and purposeful. In other words, the process by which Western radio gains influence escalates.
> (Soley 1993: 77)

This escalating influence may account for the effectiveness of stations like the US-sponsored 'Voice of the Iraqi People' in helping to ignite internal rebellion against Saddam Hussein's regime at the tail end of the Gulf War. Soley suggests the rebellion was evidence of widespread listenership among northern Kurds and southern Shi-ites. Yet, as Soley also notes, one of the station's operators has since regretted his influence, since he felt he had encouraged a rebellion subsequently unsupported by outside military help (1993: 136). The radio broadcasts, in a sense, had been *too* effective. It reveals, Manaev would suggest, an inherent risk in the sudden provision of previously unmet 'informational and sociocultural needs and interests': the tendency towards wholesale acceptance of new opinions, combined perhaps with an exaggerated distrust of the old, established media (1991: 72).

Manaev suggests that listeners can be alert to these dangers, because they easily distinguish credible programmes from the incredible: in his surveys, where programmes were heard to contain open apologias for the Western way of life or poorly supported criticisms of Soviet life, listeners were repelled (1991: 89). Given this, he concludes, western radio broadcasts were a 'democratizing' force in the last days of the Soviet Union. The problem here, though, is that credibility and truth – and the most constructive social *responses* to what is perceived to be the truth – are much more difficult to measure for those listeners most unused to a plurality of viewpoints or the nature of consensus building. In these circumstances, if Manaev's theory of 'escalating influence' holds true, radio is just as likely to be an instrument of terror as a force for democratization.

Perhaps the most traumatic example of an 'escalating influence' in the service of terror, rather than democracy, is the so-called 'genocide broadcasts' in Rwanda, which have been studied by Kellow and Steeves (1998). Their analysis suggests radio broadcasts by 'Radio-Télévision Libre des Milles Collines' (RTLM) helped rouse civilian Hutus in the country to the mass slaughter of up to 1 million of their Tutsi neighbours in 1994. Kellow and Steeves show how the radio broadcasts used an ethnic framework to report what was essentially a political struggle. Through alarming and misleading information, they amounted to an incendiary 'kill-or-be-killed' message, which spread fear, rumour and panic (see box 5.1).

Kellow and Steeves suggest that the particular development of radio in Africa had laid the foundations for this mass effect: strong oral traditions and widespread illiteracy meant that radio was quickly seen by political leaders as a powerful kind of 'political megaphone' in their service (Bourgault 1995: 80), and listeners often conceived radio as literally 'the government itself speaking' (Hachten 1974: 396). Moreover, some African countries had strong traditions of hierarchy and authoritarianism (undoubtedly exacerbated in Rwanda's case by successive German and Belgian colonial habits of stratifying their administration on largely artificial ethnic lines), so that blind obedience to the orders of official voices on the radio was highly likely:

> In other words, the government used radio and other media as agenda-setting and framing tools. Rwandans became increasingly dependent

Box 5.1   The Rwandan Genocide broadcasts

Kellow and Steeves (1998) analyzed several excerpts from the radio broadcasts of the Rwandan government-controlled Radio-Télévision Libre des Mille Collines (RTLM), to assess their role in the mass-killings which swept the country in 1994. The broadcasts often appeared to be using 'a technique of reversal to encourage genocide. The station encouraged Hutu hatred and slaughter of the Tutsis by talking about Tutsi hate of the Hutus' (1998: 119).

The following extract is from a broadcast on the morning of April 6 1994. It was a 'dialogue' supposedly between two Tutsis, performed as a song:

– The truth resists all ordeals, even the ordeal of fire. I talk to people who understand. Me, I hate Hutus. Me, I hate Hutus. Me, I hate Hutus who become Tutsis.
– What are you saying, Mutawa?
– Let me say it. I'm getting things off my chest. I'm going to tell you why I do hate them. Me, I hate the Hutus. I hate their 'Hutuness,' which makes them want to be our equals.
– Here, I agree with you.
– Me, I hate the Hutus. They're very arrogant with each other. The one who becomes important despises the other Hutus even though they are the same. Me, I hate the Hutus. The greedy Hutus [take everything, give nothing], and they ignore me. They like to live as slaves, and practice slavery amongst themselves.
– Can we blame you for that [hating them]?
– How lucky we are that there are not many here who want to be our equals.

(Reporters Sans Frontieres. Morning radio broadcast and commentary from Radio Libre des Mille Collines, Kigali, Rwanda. Transcription by Herve Deguine and Ivan Duroy; Siegfried Praille, Trans. Available: http://www.intac.com/PubService/rwanda/RTLM/tranduction.html)

Source: Kellow and Steeves 1998: 119

on radio for information about government, especially given their limited literacy and foreign language skills, and a dearth of alternative information sources. The war years beginning in 1990 intensified the government's, and opposition's, use of media, and transformed media into macro-agenda-setting tools with an agenda of ethnic hatred. . . . The propaganda relayed by the media was unrelenting and convincing during the years preceding the massacres. Thus psychological conditions for collective reaction effects were put in place. (Kellow and Steeves 1998: 115–17)

Kellow and Steeves attempt some interesting parallels between the Rwandan genocide broadcasts and the widespread panic which apparently resulted from Orson Welles' *War of the Worlds* radio drama broadcast in the USA in 1938. They identify four points of similarity between their own analysis and that of Cantril (1940), who had examined reaction to the Welles' drama:

- The nature of public confidence in the medium of radio. *War of the Worlds* was transmitted at a time when radio had replaced newspapers as the primary, and most reliable, source of news in American public opinion; the Rwandan genocide broadcasts reached a population highly dependent on radio and uncritical of its credibility.
- The degree of political instability. Just as the USA faced political and economic instability resulting from the Depression and the threat of war in 1938, Rwanda in 1994 faced a fractious political struggle for control of government which had polarized ethnic loyalties and harmed the country's fragile economy.
- The technical proficiency of the broadcasts. Welles' use of technically convincing realism – aping radio news conventions such as on-the-spot reporting, interviewing 'experts' and references to real place names – was, Cantril argues, central to the drama's ability to be credible. RTLM broadcasts in Rwanda were similarly well executed, referring to well-known historical events and religious beliefs and reporting massacres at specific locations and times.
- The social situations in which they were heard. Cantril reported that many American listeners in 1938 had tuned in to the drama as a result of the contagion of fear and excitement of people who had quickly called one another; Kellow and Steeves point out that group listening was common in Rwanda, as in much of Africa, so that 'people had each other to ignite fear and to corroborate their opinions, judgements and reactions' (Kellow and Steeves 1998: 124–5; Lewis and Booth 1989: 170).

Many of these parallels draw on broader concepts of so-called media 'effects' – such as those theories examining 'dependency' and 'collective reaction'. These were examined more directly in chapter 3, in the context of radio listening generally. There, I suggested that, although still valid, such perspectives may underestimate the ability of different listeners to interpret programmes in a variety of unpredictable – and unmanaged – ways. It is also worth pointing out that it is quite possible to interpret the reaction to the *War of the Worlds* broadcast as an indication, not of mass hysteria so much as how radio had become a taken-for-granted and *trusted* institution in daily life for most Americans. Parallels between Welles' programme and the genocide broadcasts may therefore be somewhat stretched. Here, though, we can nevertheless conclude that, whatever the broader implications of Kellow and Steeves' analysis of Rwandan radio, it certainly offers a *prime facie* challenge to the familiar rhetoric over radio's democratic nature. It reminds us that, although radio can be credibly presented as an 'alternative' channel of expression for communities too poor or unskilled to operate television, or too illiterate and widely scattered to read newspapers, an *overdependence* on the medium brings its own dangers – particularly where audiences are unused to weighing-up for themselves the value of the widely diverse opinions to which they may be exposed. We also need to remember Hochheimer's warnings over the inherent difficulties faced by 'participatory' radio stations: that the entrenchment of some sections of a community at the expense of others, as well as a drift towards professionalization, can lead to a steady loss in a station's credibility as a credible channel for grassroots opinion.

Radio, of course, does not have to be 'participatory' in order to claim its democratic credentials. In writing of the 'cultural disjuncture' between the collectivist ethic of much community radio and the individualism and commercialism of wider society, Hochheimer underlines its relatively marginal status across much of the globe. 'Mainstream' radio – professionally produced and run by commercial or public-service corporations – dominates the developed world, and large parts of the developing world such as Brazil, south-east Asia and eastern Europe. As we know, it frequently claims to be a 'window on the world' – implying a democratic function in simply 'informing the citizenry' of events around them. More than that, though, its professionalized character means it takes upon itself the task of *interpreting* these events *on behalf* of its listeners. We saw in the last chapter how some analyses suggest that in *mediating* the world in this way radio constructs a 'pseudo-reality' through the filter of a dominant ideology of consumerism (Higgins and Moss 1982, 1984), and that at the very least, phone-in hosts 'formulate' the meaning of calls in a way which pares down the range of interpretation of events open to listeners (Hutchby 1991). Yet talk-show hosts such as the American radio-presenter Diane Rehm are adamant that the medium still acts as an 'electronic backyard fence' in which views are freely exchanged in a public forum (1993: 64–5). We need, then, to test the degree to which ideas and opinions mediated by mainstream – as opposed to directly 'participatory' – radio, can be a democratizing force. Specifically: does contemporary 'talk-radio' – which is perhaps the loudest voice in advocating radio's democratic credentials – meet McChesney's requirement for a system of political communication 'broadly construed, that informs and engages'?

American talk-radio, a genre epitomised by presenters such as Rush Limbaugh, Howard Stern, Laura Schlesinger and (on NPR) Diane Rehm, is a useful focus in helping to answer this question. Its format – phone-ins from listeners discussing current issues, chaired forcefully by charismatic personalities – is much emulated in the UK, Europe and Australasia; in the USA itself, the combined effect of satellite technology and syndication has been to transform the radio talk-show from a local exchange of parochial concerns into a national forum of debate with a reputation for changing the course of political life. The most successful radio hosts, for example, are now syndicated to something between 500 and 1,000 radio stations across the country. According to Rehm, what listeners to these programmes gain is 'individual empowerment':

> Talk radio is . . . a provocative and even dangerous medium, capable of representing an extreme form of democracy that gives voice and weight to every idea without stifling or censoring. . . . In offering a forum for ideas and the exchange of viewpoints, talk radio contributes to a growing understanding of the complex issues confronting society. . . . People will sort through what may be conflicting ideas and find a way to make sense of the most complicated issues. . . . It is, perhaps, the epitome of participatory democracy in the electronic age. . . . Political leaders and journalists . . . are learning to listen to the voices over the electronic backyard fence. (1993: 64–9)

Howard Stern makes a claim for his show which has clear echoes of Rehm's 'electronic backyard fence': his stated intention is always to 'talk the way guys talk sitting around a bar' (Smith 1998: 77). Rush Limbaugh, who calls himself the 'Doctor of Democracy', stoutly rejects the idea that he sets a political agenda through his show: he is merely validating 'what people were already believing but weren't hearing or reading in the more mainstream media' (1998: 75). Taking these assertions at face value, four closely related democratic claims appear to be being made for these hosts' programmes:

- They expose a wide range of views;
- They help inform the political elite of popular opinion;
- They help improve public understanding of complex issues and events;

■   Lacking their own agenda, they provide a populist counterbalance to a 'mainstream' media characterized by the values of a progressive, liberal elite.

Some light is cast on the validity of the first claim by a study of talk-radio in the American Midwest by Armstrong and Rubin (1989). They suggest that those who call in to talk-radio programmes are 'less mobile and less socially interactive' than the average listener, and that they find the experience lessens their sense of loneliness and anxiety. The fact that the talk-radio conversation is conducted over the telephone, with its lack of visual cues in comparison to face-to-face social encounters or appearing on television, is significant too: it makes it easier to discuss sensitive personal issues or unusual views. Armstrong and Rubin conclude that:

> Talk radio provides callers with an accessible and non-threatening alternative to interpersonal communication . . . callers can compensate for restricted interaction through mediated connection with others. . . . As with the telephone, which offers psychological security and anonymity, talk radio's lack of visual contact may contribute to a caller's relaxation and satisfaction. Callers not only listen in on the conversation but also become participants in a mediated, interpersonal encounter, which is freer from threat and embarrassment than face-to-face interaction. (1989: 89–92)

In this interpretation, it would not be hard to envisage a broad distinction to be made between the performance of guests on television talk-shows as representing a more confident, even exhibitionist, strand of public opinion, and the ability of radio to put into the public domain the voices of a more sizeable but often silent, rather introverted, constituency of opinion. This would justify in some way talk-radio's claim to offer a channel of expression for a somewhat 'dispossessed' community – and indeed Levin quickly noticed that this form of radio was 'the province of proletariat discontent, the only medium easily available to the underclass' (1987: xiii). It has echoes, too, of Scannell's vision of broadcasting which is capable of 'repersonalizing the world' (1996: 165).

A specific example of the way in which such 'hidden' public values revealed by the radio talk-show have been seen to reshape political policy, to inform a political elite apparently out of touch with grassroots feelings, is offered by Page and Tannenbaum (1996). They analysed media coverage of the nomination of Zoe Baird for the post of Attorney General by Bill Clinton when he had just been elected President at the end of 1992. Baird was eventually forced to pull out from the running after being criticized for employing two illegal immigrants for domestic work and failing to pay social security taxes for them at the time. Page and Tannenbaum surveyed newspaper, television and radio discussion in the days following the first mention of her difficulties, and found that while most press and television coverage was slow in alluding to public outrage over events, *radio* talk-shows quickly painted a picture in which many 'ordinary Americans were getting upset about Baird'. While accepting that most callers to radio talk-shows are 'generally quite unrepresentative of the public as a whole' – they are 'mostly men, older, more apt to be retired, more conservative, and more anti-Clinton than the average American' – Page and Tannenbaum argue that 'they voiced the *values* of average Americans more accurately than did the elite consensus of the time' (1996: 45–6). Or, as one opinion piece in the New York Times put it:

> The Baird story is rife with trivialities of the sort that may not amount to a hill of beans in higher Washington but tend to infuriate the masses who telephone talk-radio stations. (Russell Baker, *New York Times*, 16 January 1993. Quoted in Page and Tannenbaum 1996: 42)

Page and Tannenbaum conclude that it was the momentum provided by radio phone-ins, accurately reflecting a 'relatively autonomous popular uprising', which 'overcame the complacency of Washington officials and media elites, changed public discourse, and overturned Baird's sure-thing confirmation' (1996: 44). In this particular instance, they suggest, the Washington elite, encompassing both politicians and press and television commentators, had been blind to popular feelings because their class position was quite different from the majority of American citizens who knew *they* could not afford domestic help or risk avoiding their taxes. It was, they conclude, 'a victory for democracy, a demonstration that, under certain circumstances, unrepresentative surrogate deliberators can be overcome by direct, populistic deliberation' (1996: 51). Other examples of talk-radio's impact on American political events are cited by Smith: among others, she identifies radio talk programmes as 'influential' in stopping congressional pay rises in 1989, in vilifying George Bush over his 1990 tax rises and in helping the Republicans in the 1994 mid-term elections (1998: 74–5).

Radio – or, more specifically, the talk-radio phone-in – is being defined implicitly here as an 'alternative channel' which repairs the democratic deficit of 'mediated public deliberation'. *Direct* deliberation on all matters of public policy is obviously difficult, and most democracies therefore accept that deliberation is, of necessity, mediated through the mass media: professional communicators, speak to and for the public, and act in effect as representatives of the broader citizenry. The space created for the ongoing dialogue among and between citizens and their representatives is what constitutes the essence of the 'public sphere' – that space opened up by the media in which opposing views can contend in the 'marketplace' of ideas and allow the public to reach informed opinions. Page and Tannenbaum's study suggests that this discursive space fails whenever surrogate deliberators are systematically unrepresentative. This danger has long been recognized by broadcasters and theorists of the media (see for instance Garnham 1992: 364–7), though most would argue that the gradual inclusion of the voice of the 'ordinary citizen' in the media – what Scannell calls the 'extension of communicative rights' – has ensured that the 'public sphere' has long been expanded from the narrowly based liberal elite of the public-service ideal to a more broadly based, populist one (Habermas 1989; Scannell 1996). The mass media as a whole have shared the burden of this enterprise, but the talk-radio phone-in can at least stake some claim to having been instrumental in achieving this broader base. Indeed, the ubiquity of the genre would argue for it now being, not so much an 'alternative channel' for communication, as Page and Tannenbaum assert, but a normal part of the contemporary public sphere.

The problem, though, is that populism is not quite the same as democracy. There is no certainty, for instance, that an *expanded*, more populist public sphere is an especially *diverse* one capable of accommodating a 'broadly construed' exchange of ideas, or that more rational voices will prevail over louder ones. The 'articulation' of essentially conservative popular attitudes defines the essence of talk-radio's success in the 1980s and 1990s – a reaction, Levin suggests, to the popular view that the proper order of things had been inverted by progressive liberals in the 1960s and 1970s. Talk-radio voices, he noticed, were 'preoccupied with emasculation' (1987: 27). One consistent preoccupation, above all others perhaps, has been the issue of gender. Douglas points out that, beyond the simple fact of most talk-show hosts and most listeners being men, there also lies a discourse which is invariably about challenging the achievements of feminism – a discourse which revels in defying all liberal sensibilities. In this respect, talk-radio has consistently excluded female perspectives on many social issues (1999: 289–91). Rehm, who as a woman is genuinely something of a rarity in talk-radio, herself admits that 'listeners tend to tune in where their own views are reflected . . . the most difficult task facing the talk-show host is to remain open to all voices' (1993: 67). This difficulty is illustrated vividly by the phenomenon of Rush Limbaugh's so-called 'ditto-heads' – callers to his show who preface their comments with the word 'ditto' to affirm agreement with his, or other callers', previous pronouncements (Lewis 1993).

Such self-fulfilling consensus is assisted by the USA Federal Communication Commission's steady deregulation process: in 1987 it abolished the long-standing 'Fairness Doctrine', henceforth allowing radio stations to broadcast controversial material on political and social issues without having to present opposing points of view (Stavitsky 1993; Smith 1998: 74). A free exchange of a variety of views is a *sine qua non* of a working public sphere, but in a fragmented, segmented radio marketplace liberated from obligations of balance, each programme holds up, not a revealing window on the world through which new ideas and values can be revealed, but a mirror which merely reflects back the listeners' own existence: the programmes are likely to reinforce listeners' existing opinions as much as change them.

Indeed, as Lewis (1993) has shown, a presenter like Limbaugh succeeds precisely *because* he creates a sense of closed community among his listeners and between them and their idol. It is, Lewis argues, the 'art of using radio to connect' – an art adopted by earlier conservative talk-show hosts from the 1930s, such as John Romulus Brinkley, Huey Long and the anti-Semitic Father Charles Coughlin:

> Each of these Limbaugh predecessors had an engaging, almost conspiratorial, way of bringing his audience into league with him. Each gave the listener the sense that, together, they were right-thinking people who would create a better world. Limbaugh's tone is equally conspiratorial. . . . [He] articulates the frustrations of these people far better than they could themselves, offering solutions based on his version of common sense. Limbaugh sounds a single message: Liberals are ruining the country and if we don't stop them, the United States will slide inevitably into fiscal and moral decay. (1993: 57–9)

An individual talk-show, then, cannot always guarantee a wide range of views *within* its own boundaries. But might the radio marketplace as a whole provide diversity *between* different shows and different stations? Talk-radio has been a fast-growing genre in the USA, particularly useful in filling the AM frequencies deserted by music-radio formats, and, Lewis notes, 'no network seems complete without a talk show' (1993: 61). Yet, as we saw in chapter 1, the market as a whole does not offer unlimited variety. About one in every ten radio stations in the USA is Christian – some 1,100 in all – and the majority, according to Stavitsky, are busy 'mobilizing listeners in support of the conservative Christian political and social agenda' (1993: 80–1). Smith estimated that by 1998, about 70 per cent of talk show hosts across the US held 'conservative' views, and that the few liberal or moderate hosts to be heard were typically paired with conservative counterparts: station managers, she showed, argued that 'liberals won't sell because they don't have what it takes to be provocative and entertaining' (1998: 78).

The key word here is 'entertaining'. And when it is applied to political coverage the effect – it is argued – is a perniciously trivializing discourse:

> Across the nation, scores of Limbaugh wannabes sit in radio studios . . . these Rush clones dedicate themselves to bringing out the dark angels of their listeners' nature by taking hot stories and heating them up even further. . . . Talk shows take the trivial and make it substantial. Homosexuals serving in the military is of little consequence when compared with $200 billion deficits and a $4 trillion debt. Yet the lunchtime diner sitting entranced in a Rush room [an area in a cafe set aside for listening to Limbaugh's show], or a trucker heading west out of Amarillo on Interstate 40, or a mother sitting in her kitchen in Rapid City, sipping coffee from her Limbaugh mug, hears little of substance about the debt. What does filter through comes in the form of a slogan. (Lewis 1993: 61)

Lewis implies that the danger to rational political debate lies, not so much with Rush Limbaugh himself, but with the *spread* of a degenerate radio format characterized by the simplistic and distorting discourse of 'shock-jocks'. Beyond the USA, other countries (such as the UK) have maintained a stronger regulatory requirement for the broadly 'balanced' discussion of current affairs, so that the ability of 'jocks' to *shock* is more circumscribed. Nevertheless, the controversial radio talk-show host is now an established feature of the *global* radio environment, and the spread of a trivialized political discourse may be its corollary.

The genre reflects part of what McChesney sees as a wider media phenomenon, a pattern of corporate power which is both *symptom* and *cause* of a democratic deficit. He describes the gradual adoption in America through the twentieth century of a 'professional' journalism of self-proclaimed objectivity:

> It was hardly neutral. On one hand, the commercial requirements for media content to satisfy media owners and advertisers were built implicitly into the professional ideology. . . . On the other hand, corporate activities and the affairs of the wealthy were not subject to the same degree of scrutiny as government practices; the professional codes deemed the affairs of powerful economic actors vastly less newsworthy than the activities of politicians. In this manner 'objective' jour-

nalism effectively internalized corporate capitalism as the natural order for a democracy. . . . The dominant institutional factors have pressed for a decontextualized, depoliticized and conservative journalism. . . . Indeed, in what stands as perhaps the most damning statement one could make about the news media, some studies have suggested that the more a person consumes commercial news, the less capable that person is of understanding politics or public affairs. (1997: 14, 17)

If this is accepted, it paints a bleak portrait of the contribution towards American democratic culture made by the sort of journalism found on US commercial radio stations. But what of public-service radio, and perhaps specifically *British* public-service radio, where journalism has long been characterized by even more vigorous claims to objectivity, neutrality, impartiality and so on? Schlesinger's study of BBC journalists, which I mentioned in chapter 2 in the context of the 'stopwatch culture' of production, reaches conclusions which are barely less sceptical:

News does not select itself, but is rather the product of judgements concerning the social relevance of given events and situations based on assumptions concerning their interest and importance. The 'reality' it portrays is always in at least one sense fundamentally biased, simply in virtue of the inescapable decision to designate an issue or event newsworthy, and then to construct an account of it in a specific framework of interpretation. (1978: 164–5)

Schlesinger suggests that, although impartiality is the 'linchpin' of the BBC's ideology, it is a notion 'saturated with political and philosophical implications' (1978: 163). 'Impartiality', he argues, 'can only have meaning in the context of an existing set of values, and in the case of the BBC the relevant complex of values is that of the "consensus" ' – a consensus defined by one radio reporter at the time as 'middle-class liberalism' (1978: 164–6).

The focus of Schlesinger's study was specifically the BBC's newsroom, and it is now more than twenty years old. Even so, it is significant that the Corporation's current 'Producer Guidelines' issued to staff in *all* areas of factual programming, from news, through to magazines, quizzes and talk-shows, is suffused with almost exactly the same language of impartiality – a notion that, similarly, cannot be taken entirely at face value. This is not necessarily to suggest that radio, whether in the hands of powerful corporate interests or public corporations *consciously* sets out to deceive or manipulate. It is just that, as Schlesinger himself implies, the process of selection in radio journalism is inherently constraining. Take Silverstone's description of the anguish involved in the making of a BBC science documentary – a programme for television, admittedly, but constructed within the same editorial guidelines as any similar radio programme when it comes to sifting through the range of possible contributors and ideas:

> Somehow from these competing claims for attention and inclusion a political position must be constructed. The formal requirement is balance, but of course that cannot be perfect because of the structural constraints which define what can and what cannot be measured in the scales. Indeed, even at this early stage some of the elements, some of the names, those for example which represent the more original or the amateur, eccentric positions in the . . . story, are already about to be excluded. Whatever political position the film finally adopts it must be legitimised by reference to one of a small number of alternatives within our culture, whether they be of the dominant or the acceptably antagonistic . . . too many qualifications, too much grey, will deprive the film of its coherence. (1985: 10, 35)

Issues are most easily discussed – or, more precisely *dramatized* – in terms of dichotomies – a studio discussion with one speaker 'for' a particular position and another 'against', for example: in a non-visual medium like radio especially, too many voices at once can be confusing for a listener. Yet this reliance on polarized views can sometimes involve a gross simplification of complex matters. Many producers are aware of this, but the various constraints placed upon them which we discussed in chapter 2, such as the pressures of time, financial constraints and – perhaps above all – the need to create at least some level of dramatic tension (to make 'compelling', 'good' radio), prove overpowering.

We might conclude, then, that radio's claims to be an instrument of democracy are somewhat inflated. True, it is a pervasive medium, cheap to listen to, and accessibly oral. It is also immeasurably cheaper and more open as a medium of active participation than, say, television. Yet, the public sphere of debate which it constructs is strikingly imperfect – a discursive space where active participation is never easy, the language of argument is often more demagogic than democratic, and where the exigencies of production often lead to trivialization and simplification. Perhaps, though, we should also be a little forgiving. It is easy to place too much of a burden of responsibility upon radio, as with other mass media, for our democratic well being. Radio, is of course, an informational medium, perfectly placed by its liveness and pervasiveness to connect us to contemporary events and debates. But it is also a medium for entertainment, and much of what we regard in radio as there to inform us – the talk-shows, the 'shock-jocks', the phone-ins – is, in truth, very often designed much more

with entertainment in mind: we quite often listen to such programmes to be entertained – as Scannell would say, we quite often
listen to talk *for talk's sake*, for *fun*. Perhaps, then, our expectations
for radio are a little unrealistic.

Radio and identity

One theme implicit in the previous chapter was radio's ability to
extend a community *to itself*. 'Through radio', one American radio
executive asserts, 'you hear what you are'. We might come to know
ourselves through television or the press, but radio – more minutely
segmented than other media – provides a more *precise* reflection of
the fragmented communities of modern societies, whether communities are defined by nationality, ethnicity, sex, or simply by patterns
of consumption and taste. 'Just as we live and work in largely separate social segments, we listen to . . . largely separate segments of
radio' (Powell 1993: 71–6). It is an optimistic vision: not without
some nostalgia for the 'shared common experiences' which characterized the days of very little 'choice' in our listening, but nevertheless inspired by radio's ability to identify and serve a niche market
unbounded by geography, to respond to shifting – and ever more
minutely defined – notions of identity.

Radio's intimate connection with *music* is also important here.
Music, rather than talk, is the main component of most of the world's
radio stations and networks, and music, in and of itself, is undoubtedly a 'central instrument in the construction, definition and redefi-
nition of national identities' – witness the place of national anthems,
Irish folk-music in the pubs of London and New York, and – more
sinisterly – the role of National Socialist songs in reinforcing Nazi
concepts of national purity (Bennett 1997: 21). Indeed, Frith has
suggested that, 'only music seems capable of creating this sort of
spontaneous . . . identity, this kind of personally felt patriotism'
(1987: 141). What is more, this ability of music to help people establish their *sense of place* is crucial in an age of cultural cross-
fertilization and rapid social change. Giddens observes how modernity has produced a phantasmagoric separation of space from place,
with social influences penetrating and shaping places far removed in
space. Music is one way in which individuals and groups of people
seek to culturally 'relocate' themselves in the face of this process
(Bennett 1997: 22).

Radio's status here is ambiguous, though. If it is true that through
radio we *hear what we are*, it is also true that to some extent we *are
what we hear*. 'Taste', Pickering and Shuker argue, 'grows upon that

which it is fed' (1993: 37). The problem, as I suggested in relation to the populist discourses of American talk shows, is that radio offers no certainty that 'taste' is always fed a *balanced* diet. Through the hourly and daily replaying of certain records and certain news stories and the reiteration of certain language and phrases, selected from the huge universe of available music, events and words, radio may exaggerate or even distort certain tastes, or notions of identity, rather than simply reflecting them. The central issue is how to interpret this cultural selectivity. Take for example a radio station's preference in its schedules for mainstream musical acts with global appeal, rather than the indigenous music of its own backyard. Is the station a harmful conduit of homogenization, or an engine of an exciting cultural cross-fertilization? Conversely, when a station, at the level of either the local community or the nation state, chooses to turn its back on the perceived popular tastes of its general listenership and instead select music or talk with a more narrow or untested appeal, is this radio acting as a force for positive cultural leadership, or radio as the mouthpiece for narrow sectional interests (whether liberal or authoritarian)?

The answers to these questions are difficult to discern, not just because they depend on one's own assumptions about radio's precise purpose – is it to cater for existing, known and therefore potentially profitable tastes, or is it to take the risk of interpreting and even *shaping* taste on the listeners' behalf – but also because the boundaries of people's identities are so complex and blurred. We are, for example, defined at different times *and* simultaneously by our membership of a nation-state, a local community, an ethnic group and a set of musical tastes. Radio almost, but not quite entirely, matches this range. While being the local medium par excellence, radio is also able to reach across large spaces, *potentially* threatening place-specific cultures with its homogenized content, *potentially* forging new de-localized communities of interest; it has a history in which nation states often led the way in establishing services, but its *oral* code of communication allows it to tie itself to communities of language which ignore official borders; it betrays a commercial imperative to reach large, high-spending audiences, but it also has a cost structure which creates at least the *possibility* of a community station surviving on the tiniest of audiences. It is, in short, the most adaptable of media in 'finding' its audience. Yet, as we know, a radio station can never quite get to know *all* of its audience members, and it serves purposes other than the purely cultural or symbolic, such as creating the conditions of maximum profit and minimum costs for shareholders. So although Powell claims radio 'mirrors our own fragmentation', it is never guaranteed to be a perfect reflection for us all.

To explore the ways in which these cultural disjunctions unfold through radio, let us look at specific studies, in turn, from Latin America, Australia, China, South Africa, New Zealand and, in a later section, the UK. These examples are not designed to amount to a comparative global study in itself, and still less to define a 'unifying theory' of radio's cultural power. They are merely attempts to draw out some common threads which run through a highly heterogeneous radio landscape. Indeed, I hope to show that the most common thread of all is the *difficulty* radio very often has, despite the claims that it 'mirrors' our identities, to overcome the specific historical, geographical, political or economic limitations within which it operates.

Let us begin, then, in Peru. Here, despite the general assumption that mass media impose cultural homogeneity, Lloréns (1991) has argued that some radio stations have successfully preserved a traditional folk culture – namely that of the Andean highland migrants working in the capital city, Lima. These migrants are geographically detached from their homelands and face a mainstream media in which 'the dominant national culture does not incorporate their cultural expressions in its general cultural practices' (1991: 179). Newspapers, Lloréns notes, have traditionally failed to penetrate the remote highland settlements, and in any case using them demands an uncommon level of literacy; television is both too technically complex and too expensive for them to participate in except as viewers. The migrants have, however, bought airtime on commercial radio stations in the city, to produce what they call 'programas folclóricos', which can also be heard back 'home' in the mountains. The programmes consist of Andean folk-music, Peruvian highland lore and news about migrants' social and cultural activities; they often use the Quechua language, adopt an intimate and homely style, and by appealing so pervasively to highland culture, listenership from other cultural groups is actively – if unconsciously – discouraged. Although station managers began by only offering the migrants slots on the night-time margins of their schedules, there were over 200 folk programmes on Lima radio stations by the late 1980s and they had surpassed the total output of the typical Peruvian urban musical genres of 'chicha' and 'criollo-costeno'. These programmes, Lloréns concludes, were 'no longer a marginal phenomenon in Peruvian radio broadcasting' (1991: 178).

Significantly, each of these programmes was produced by the cultural association of a different migrant group, so that they were intended 'to be heard not by any highland migrant in Lima, nor by all Andean migrants in general, but primarily by those who come from and are identified with the specific region or locality that the association "represents" in Lima'. Many also met their costs through fund-raising events involving listeners, so that 'the overall process becomes a collective cultural activity' (1991: 182–3). The programmes, in other words, avoided the blunt imposition of a uniform Andean culture, and successfully identified and nurtured a whole *series* of popularly recognized cultures through an impressive degree of audience segmentation and participation. There is very little space in this model for cultural cross-fertilization, but, Lloréns argues, the threat of cultural homogenization has been avoided:

> Programas folclóricos may serve as shields against some of the feelings of estrangement and the external pressures of acculturation that rural migrants find in the urban environment. . . . All of this suggests that electronic media can be used – to some extent and given certain conditions – to express non-dominant discourses and to communicate messages constructed and controlled by popular social sectors. (1991: 187)

The success of the Andean migrant's folk programmes rests, however, on a precarious footing. The direct expression of threatened culture appears conditional in some part on the direct *participation* of those concerned without any need for what Lloréns calls 'gifted interpreters of the collective feeling', that is trained professionals (1991: 187). But, as I argued earlier in relation to the tin-miners' stations of Bolivia and elsewhere, there are strong pressures everywhere towards professionalization, even in small community stations.

The sort of problems this creates are well illustrated in Browne's study of aboriginal radio in Australia (1990). He suggests that some aspects of aboriginal culture, such as songs that last for hours or even days, or a desire to have long pauses after receiving information in order to reflect upon it, are inherently ill-suited to the radio medium. However, even though many aborigines distrusted 'European' radio – which had almost totally neglected them until the mid 1970s – it was the only kind they knew: it was therefore very difficult to conceive of how to use radio in new ways, and the first aboriginal practitioners tended to adopt the prevailing rules of programming. Indeed, Browne suggests, 'it is very difficult to totally rethink the possibilities of radio' (1990: 119). Moreover, since many urban aborigines – the first to broadcast and listen to the new stations – were second or even third generation urban-dwellers who had lost contact with tribal traditions, much of their community 'was unlikely to embrace wholeheartedly a radio service that reflected only tribal roots' (1990: 114). The result is that these stations are now characterized by a significant proportion of European or American music, often packaged in familiar western formats, and a political discourse in its news and current affairs that requires 'ability in European interaction styles, good conversational skills' rather than ability in the traditional aboriginal discourse built around periods of reflection (1990: 114, 118). Browne notes that much of the broadcasting is in English, rather than one or other of the 150 or so aboriginal languages. This makes the broadcasts more accessible to a wider audience, but 'probably serves to erode the validity of tribal tradition' (1990: 118).

Browne's study of aboriginal radio in Australia would appear to negate the picture established by Lloréns in Peru. Far from providing an example of 'alternative' communication channels through which separate cultures can be reinforced, Browne suggests that radio appears more as a means by which western media practices and cultures can *extend* their hold over non-western cultures – a version, perhaps, of the broader 'dependency theory' familiar in studies of the global film and television industries. Even so, I would argue that there is a middle ground to be staked out between these two positions. Browne certainly recognizes that in the case of aboriginal radio, we are not witnessing wholesale assimilation but something more complex and unpredictable. For a start, the presence of at least some aboriginal music within programmes that appeal to younger 'European-Australians', has exposed this 'new' genre to serious critical attention and a significant market of record buyers. A second complicating factor is the stations' habit of exchanging programme material, so that according to Browne, listeners have realized 'their problems were not unique and that aborigines dispersed throughout Australia were in certain respects one people' (1990: 114). Finally, Browne notes that the demographic profile of station staff may distance them from assimilation as much as from strong tribal identification:

> Like broadcasters everywhere, the Aborigines who staff broadcast services are not inherently representative of their communities. They may see their jobs as an opportunity for fame within their communities or beyond them, a stepping-stone to a higher position . . . or a means of galvanising community response to situations and feelings that have engaged their personal attention. The broadcast service reflects the interests of individual staff members; it may or may not reflect community tastes, interests and aspirations. (1990: 117)

This conclusion suggests that the ability of radio to be either a shield of alternative cultures or a force for the elimination of them has at least an element of randomness to it. It is, at the very least, partly conditional on the particular personalities of those involved.

But what of those cases where radio's cultural content has been shaped in a more concerted way by more powerful agencies? The cultural effects of state-controlled radio in both Apartheid-era South Africa and the People's Republic of China have been explored by Hamm (1991, 1995b). In China, a senior manager of the Central People's Broadcasting Station (CPBS), describes the organization's role as bearing the responsibility of 'selecting what is best for its audience' (1995b: 276). What it selects is predominantly 'light' music – instrumental arrangements, perhaps drawing on elements of traditional Chinese styles, but with a familiar, melodic 'light orchestral' sound clearly influenced by western orchestral traditions. There is some limited tolerance of pop music drawn from Hong Kong, Taiwan and beyond (which has been labelled generically as 'Pacific Pop'), and of traditional Chinese opera (which has historically drawn audiences from a wide range in the country). Significantly, though, rock music is too associated with individualism, rather than collectivism, to be seen as appropriate, and the music of China's 'national minorities' (such as those living in Inner Mongolia or Tibet) is almost never heard in its original form. Why, asks Hamm, this emphasis on modern light orchestral music, rather than, say, more traditional indigenous forms? He notes Mao's earlier desire for a mass culture 'led only by the culture and ideology of the proletariat', but suggests that there was in fact no 'ready-made' proletarian genre of music to draw upon before Liberation. The need, therefore, was:

> to create a new body of music for the people, drawn from the 'scattered and unsystematic' music of the masses, 'co-ordinated and systematized after careful study' by persons qualified by political and professional training, and then given back to the masses and 'explained and popularized' until they are willing to accept this new product 'as their own'. (1995b: 278)

The adaptation of western models of harmony, intonation and instrumentation was central to this process of 'creation' because western music was taken to be more modern and scientific than 'reactionary' Chinese forms, and 'modern' could therefore be equated with 'revolutionary'. Consequently, the music of China's national minorities is used predominantly as melodic raw material for the country's conservatory-trained composers to make 'light' instrumental arrangements to be broadcast back to the regions. Much of the Pacific Pop is tolerated because, unlike rock, it fits so well stylistically with light music – though again, it is mostly heard in Chinese versions reworked by classically trained composers. This, Hamm argues, is:

music drawn from the masses, then given back to them in 'improved' form. . . . The vast majority of this music draws in some way or other on music of the Chinese people, whether folk, classical, or ethnic, which is then mediated by trained musicians into a more 'correct' form, stylistically neutral and divorced from its original social or ritual context. (1995b: 291–2)

Striking parallels exist with South Africa's radio services during its Apartheid era. There, the South African Broadcasting Corporation (SABC) 'theorised and programmed in accordance with state ideology', though in its case the intention was to exaggerate ethnic differences rather than neutralize them (Hamm 1991). As Hamm points out, black cultural, political and linguistic identity in southern Africa had long been infinitely complex, with community boundaries ever shifting and long-term cultural interaction between neighbouring groups. The Apartheid ideology of 'separate development', however, held that South Africa was really populated by various 'native tribes', each a homogeneous unit with a distinct language and culture, each living within clearly defined geographical boundaries. Right through the 1960s, 1970s and 1980s, the state-controlled media were 'given the task of bringing about general acceptance of this ideologically based mythology, by persuading the entire population that this was the "way things were"' (1991: 152–3). It was a striking embodiment of what Barthes saw as the central function of mythology: 'myth consists in overturning culture into nature or, at least, the social and cultural, the ideological, the historical into the "natural"' (1973: 165).

The SABC's programmes for black listeners were known collectively as Radio Bantu, but they were actually distributed via a series of *separate* FM transmitters, each reaching a precisely targeted geographical area. Music was the main component of the programmes, and all music selected had to relate in some way to the culture of the 'tribal' group at which a given service was aimed: 'there should be something "Zulu" about a piece to be played on Radio Zulu, something "Xhosa" about the music broadcast on Radio Xhosa' and so on (Hamm 1991: 160). Originally, much of the music was traditional tribal music, or choral music, which usefully emphasized the separate identity of each ethnic group and introduced a Christian overlay. But many black listeners looked around them and saw *western* culture as directly associated with economic advantage and cultural superiority. Unsurprisingly, they wanted more western (particularly American) contemporary music. Such popular forms were long resisted as 'morally unacceptable' for those services aimed at the ruling white minority, but since the regime had no particular interest in 'elevating' musical taste among the black majority population, it took no moral stand against pop music on their radio services. Indeed, since Radio Bantu's mission was simply to catch the attention of as many black people as possible in order to persuade them of the 'naturalness' of Separate Development, 'music with a much wider base would *have to be* programmed' (1991: 163; my italics).

The musical style most favoured subsequently by Radio Bantu was jive. This came to be a generic term for a large repertoire of black South African social dance music: it covered both instrumental jive, which, being 'textless', could not undermine state ideology, and vocal jive, which underlined cultural separatism by drawing on the language and traditional music of a given ethnic group. Jive combined traditional African elements with modern instruments and harmonies, and its appeal cut across class lines. It was, in short, the musical genre best placed to secure a mass black listenership in both rural and township communities, and was so fully embraced by the broadcasters that it was sometimes called *msakazo* ('radio music'). Even if such 'radio music' is interpreted as ideologically 'neutral' in itself, it was, Hamm argues, 'selected for its appeal to the largest possible number of listeners within that particular ethnic group, functioning to attract an audience to a radio service whose most important business was selling ideology' (1991: 169). Radio, in this South African context, is then a *generator* rather than simply a *transmitter* of culture. In shaping attitudes over decades, in helping to construct a mythological cultural ecology of tribal *difference* at odds with the real one, the medium 'played a major role' in sustaining Apartheid (1991: 147).

But, as Hamm also points out, the effectiveness of a state-controlled radio service like SABC or the CPBS 'depends largely on the extent to which its programming dominates other components of the musical life of the country – live performances, listening to pre-recorded music, other radio services' (1995b: 271). And in both China and South Africa, this *domination* has been difficult to sustain beyond the 1980s. Certainly, radio, for all the reasons we have already examined – the affordability of radio sets, their battery power overcoming the non-electrified nature of many underdeveloped areas, its portability suiting migrant labour, its oral appeal to under-literate peoples – has been more significant than television in such cultural 'generation'. As early as 1974 in South Africa, nearly 98 per cent of the black population had access to radio and listened to it at least sometimes (1991: 159); when Hamm visited China in 1988, there were about 10 million TV sets in the country, but some 400 million radio receivers (1995b: 300–1). However, one survey in Beijing suggests that by the mid 1990s only a small percentage of the Chinese population was dependent on radio as a major source of their music: films and, above all, cassettes, were already more popular sources. At the same time, a steady decentralization of the state broadcasting network has led to a corresponding decentralization of music programming in large parts of the People's Republic. Radio Shanghai, for instance, has been broadcasting a significant amount of Japanese and western pop, and a poll of its audience in 1988 showed that the American singer Michael Jackson was overwhelmingly the most popular artist. This suggests a substantial disagreement between popular musical tastes and the types of music given most airplay on the remaining state-run 'National Services'. It also reveals that while music may be 'an important site of political struggle' in China, its government 'will find it more difficult now than in the past to control musical taste' (1995b: 301–4).

In South Africa too the attempt to employ radio to reinforce cultural policy has long run into difficulties. South African state radio had clearly been more successful than China in catering to popular musical tastes, but even there almost four out of every ten black South Africans were avoiding Radio Bantu even by the end of the 1970s – usually tuning-in instead to the American and British pop and rock of a commercial station transmitting from Mozambique. Through the 1980s, a whole series of other commercial radio stations came on stream, transmitting from neighbouring countries such as Swaziland. The Apartheid government's policy of Separate Development also became a victim of its own 'success' in creating a series of pseudo-autonomous 'tribal' homelands. Each homeland soon developed its own radio services, and – more sensitive to listeners' tastes – they usually programmed, not so much the music of their own homelands, but British, American and Caribbean pop, or a mix of international hits and the best of South African pop, regardless of its precise 'tribal' background. By the end of the 1980s, then:

> The carefully constructed myth of ethnic separateness perpetuated by the SABC for two decades was challenged by everyday empirical evidence, as radio audiences chose, enjoyed and comprehended music created by persons from other ethnic backgrounds. (Hamm 1991: 171–2)

Both China and South Africa appear to offer examples where international forces, and international *market* forces in particular, have destroyed any attempt to use radio to re-order popular cultural tastes for ideological ends at the level of the nation state. The *de facto* ending of state radio monopolies, the steady diffusion of international music through cassettes and films, and more recently the expanding reach of transnational services delivered by satellite or relayed across syndicated networks, mean that wherever radio stations transmit programming noticeably out of step with popular taste, listeners will vote with their dials or switch off altogether. Choice, in these circumstances, has brought an element of liberation from the prescribed menu of officially approved radio fare.

The theory of 'cultural dependency', however, provides a warning over the price sometimes paid in this transaction. It suggests that one kind of dependency – that based in this instance on state-run radio services – has simply been replaced by another kind of dependency – namely one based on transnational communications empires distributing a globally homogenized (and typically Anglo-American) programme content – material which displaces local and regional content, and in so doing overpowers local cultural identities.

The picture of music radio in New Zealand provided by Pickering and Shuker (1993) reinforces this suggestion – but, additionally, offers some possible ways out for local cultures. Their studies suggest that, in New Zealand at least, most radio stations are addicted to favouring the international musical artist over the locally grown one. New, low-cost music technologies would appear to make localized music production *easier*, but commercial radio stations throughout the country persist in giving negligible attention to local artists: programmers, often hired in from America and Australia, 'consider the marketing of proven foreign material a much safer option' in attracting large audiences (1993: 28). Without significant airplay for indigenous music, recording companies have withdrawn their investment in local talent, and 'the radio programmers can then aver that this has occurred as a result of the lack of quality in local products . . . a classic instance of a self-fulfilling prophecy' (1993: 31). Pickering and Shuker identify a further institutionalized prejudice: radio programmers' apparent preference for technically clean and glossy production standards 'entails a built-in obstacle to the broad circulation of other types of music' produced in African, Latin American or Asian countries. The combined effects are 'culturally negative':

> Since exposure influences taste, and taste can in cultural terms be broadly or narrowly based, the predominance of international hits on FM radio and music TV has broad implications for musical aesthetics . . . when the cultural dietary regime is to a high degree homogeneous, this is likely to engender prejudice to other musical forms and styles not usually encountered in the processes of everyday media consumption. (1993: 37)

Pickering and Shuker suggest that a cultural quota system, much like that in Australia, is the obvious solution: it would, say, require stations to schedule local producis for up to a fifth of their daytime schedules. Such quotas, they recognize, have long been resisted by broadcasters as 'the Orwellian bogey of unbridled state power'. But, they argue, quotas allow the medium to strike a delicate balance between internationalism and localism. Noting the sort of power wielded by global conglomerates that we examined in chapter 1, Pickering and Shuker suggest that 'a healthy music scene cannot flourish either under excessive state control *or* under the corporate control of transnational capitalist enterprises'. On the one hand, excluding foreign material altogether would prevent a particular country's musical practices from being *enriched* by exposure to idioms and styles from elsewhere, on the other hand, the entirely free play of market forces, with radio stations unimpeded by certain principles of balance and cultural responsibility, would inevitably *swamp* indigenous practices, 'threatening musical diversity, the vitality of local music cultures and consumer accessibility to a wide range of transcultural music forms' (1993: 47–8). The aim, Pickering and Shuker suggest, would be to use quotas on radio to help rebalance the forces of localism and internationalization:

> Popular culture in any localized sense is today a hybridization of symbolic forms and practices. . . . [It] is vital that the conditions for such interaction are maintained in any particular region or country of the world. There is no point arguing for these conditions on the basis of static-indigenous conceptions of locally produced popular music. . . . Locally produced music has rarely had the fixity of association with specific contexts which have been key features identified with that paradigm in the past. . . . Any contemporary sense of the local-popular cannot . . . be confined to a specific locality. It may for instance, be annexed by certain geographically dispersed communities of interest as by any more traditionally defined communities of place. (1993: 52)

This, then, takes us towards a possible defining role for radio in its relationship with popular music – and indeed cultural identity in general. If, on the one hand, radio is open to a *controlled range* of music, it becomes a potential agent for the hybridization of music – a potentially invigorating process; if, on the other hand, radio is closed and prejudiced it leads to cultural stasis; if it is too open to the music of the marketplace it leads to cultural domination.

Radio, music and cultural change

Underlying Pickering and Shuker's analysis is an appreciation of radio's role in the *dynamic* aspect of popular musical culture. Radio, since it is a global distributor above all else of music, may often act as an agent of homogenization, but used sensitively its very ability to interpenetrate the local and international dimensions of society means it is a medium at least *capable* of providing 'the conditions of interaction' in the ongoing creation of 'hybridized' symbolic forms and practices. The issue though, as Pickering and Shuker rightly suggest, is how such 'interactive processes' occur, and with what results. Or, to be more specific: given the global dominance of commercial radio forms and internationalized music formats, as well as the highly segmented character of contemporary listening, is there *any* evidence that radio is any longer capable of enriching diversity through such interaction?

Our understanding of radio's ability – or, as more commonly stated, its *in*ability – to encourage musical innovation, is based largely on the disjunction between the needs of radio and the needs of the music industry. Take the record sales charts. Each week, on average, between one- and two-hundred singles are released in the UK. To reach number one, a single would currently have to sell on average some 125,000 copies in a week. Exposure on radio is a crucial prerequisite of sales success on this scale. But a radio station, even if it wished to, would be hard pushed to play more than a fraction of the releases. So a chain of selection processes begins which has a crucial impact on the success of each record. These processes have long been shaped by the assumption, demonstrated by Hennion and Meadel in their study of RTL-Radio Luxembourg that, 'the radio audience and the record-buyers do not coincide and the one is not included with the other' (1986: 286). Their study showed how stations like Radio Luxembourg, with ten million listeners drawn from a wide range of ages and classes, could not select in proportion to record company catalogues – five country records here, three jazz records there, and so on – simply because the radio listenership has tended to be much less specialized than the record market: most records – particularly singles – are bought by teenagers, and the records are produced largely in various musical genres; radio, in contrast, has a listenership much larger and much more diverse. Unsurprisingly, therefore, radio programmers tend to favour the safe and the familiar, and banish more demanding records, creating something of a 'middlebrow' mainstream. The phenomenon resonates through history. Scannell and Cardiff (1991) showed how in the earliest days of broadcasting in Britain, radio uprooted particular and geographically isolated musics and brought them together in 'a strange new abstract unity':

> Because the nature of the medium did not favour one kind of music at the expense of another, and because its social direction was towards

the whole community, the BBC rapidly found itself undertaking the presentation of all forms of music that had any appreciable audience (and some that had none) side by side in a single channel. (1991: 182)

Yet what Scannell and Cardiff called the consequent 'collision' of these various musics and their publics produced, not tolerant and eclectic listeners, but a series of negative responses to some kinds of music in order to affirm preferences over others. Similarly, early BBC radio producers – drawn as they were from the intelligentsia – could not resist treating different music genres as a series of tastes to be arranged in a hierarchy of values (1991: 207). Barnard (1989) has traced how the BBC's subsequent embrace of pop music, with the creation of Radio 1 in 1967, illustrated a continuity of approach with the 1930s: a single channel that dealt with the broad range of music and tastes within its remit by separating output into a daytime 'mainstream' service for the largest and most diverse audiences who disliked extremes and an evening 'specialist' service that provided a platform for more eclectic and demanding genres:

> Just as jazz had always figured on the periphery of the Light Programme schedules, beloved of radio producers yet kept separate from the mainstream almost as an act of deliberate intellectual apartheid, so 'progressive rock' assumed a similar mantle after 1967 . . . instead of seeking to incorporate progressive rock within the daytime schedules – 'I don't believe there is anything at all to be gained from playing it on mainstream radio' (Derek Chinnery [Controller, quoted from *Music Week*, 20 April 1974]) – Radio 1 emphasized its distinction from Top 40 pop by giving it air-time at weekends, in the early evening and . . . late at night. (1991: 54)

In this model, just as with the BBC's National Programme in the 1930s or Radio Luxembourg in the 1980s, a *hierarchy of taste*, in which progressive, trend-setting forms of music were distinguished – and elevated – from more popular styles, was established through the daily scheduling patterns of each station. Specialist musics, representing a series of minority tastes, were equated with evening broadcasting, while more familiar and less demanding musics were served before the larger – and therefore more diverse – daytime audiences. A record might occasionally move from minority appeal among record-buying aficionados to a wider, mass appeal among the broader swathe of listeners. But more often than not, the internal scheduling of a radio station, which tended to be reinforced by the bifurcation of production into distinct specialist and mainstream teams of staff, placed considerable structural barriers between the two markets. There was little room for cultural 'cross-fertilization' between the various strata of popular music.

Since then, of course, the segmentation of radio into niche formats has brought a greater contiguity between the radio listener and the record buyer: the radio listener has become very nearly as specialized a being as the record buyer. Few stations can accommodate the forty year long (and ever-expanding) repertoire of pop and rock as a whole: most target a narrower audience by salami-slicing the genre into smaller epochs or specializing in sub-genres such as jazz, hard-rock, Top-40, country, dance and so on – formats that coincide almost precisely with the catalogue divisions of the record industry itself. Many offer a consistent schedule across twenty-four hours and dispense with any internal distinction between 'specialist' and 'mainstream'.

But market segmentation has created new barriers between the different genres of pop music – this time not *within* a radio station's own schedules, but *between* the various separate stations. Each station presents itself as a consistent and reliable mediator between a specific sub-group of products of the record industry and a specific subgroup of the audience (Barnes 1990). In this arrangement, advertisers searching for a particular audience can be best attracted by a station guaranteeing *predictable* choices about music on air. McCourt and Rothenbuhler, noting how one of the maxims of Top-40 programming is to avoid anything which polarizes listener attitudes ('what you don't play can't hurt you'), observed how computerized scheduling – now ubiquitous in music radio – intensifies this process by diminishing the autonomy of DJs to play their favourites and increasing the speed with which an 'aberrant' song can be eliminated from the schedules. 'The incorporation of computers into radio station's operations', they argue, thus 'contributes to the standardization of music that is played' (1987: 105).

This segmentation of the radio audience into different 'taste publics' each served with a range of music sufficiently narrow to avoid offence, feeds back into the music industry as a whole. Negus (1993) demonstrated how record companies in the USA come to define artists or specific recordings in terms of a particular radio format, and then target appropriate stations. Music that does not fit a specific format will probably receive little or no radio airplay. The only hope for an artist wishing to reach the mainstream – the ultimate prize for the record companies – is to 'cross-over' from one format to another, eventually gaining airplay on Contemporary Hit Radio (CHR) stations and across various neighbouring formats over an ever-expanding chain. But as Negus shows, the difficulty facing such artists lies in the fact that CHR stations, by their very nature, *reflect* success rather more than they create it: programme directors, even if satisfied a new release fits their format, won't playlist it until further convinced of the 'support' it is receiving from the record company *and from other radio stations*. 'Radio airplay is determined in part by radio airplay' (McCourt and Rothenbuhler 1987: 102).

Accordingly, the programmers scan so-called 'tip-sheet' magazines, which provide weekly information on releases, radio airplay and listener responses, while the record companies themselves attempt to influence their decision by placing adverts which consist almost entirely of lists of radio stations that are playing a particular record. The *quality* of data here is crucial, but McCourt and Rothenbuhler, in their study of sales and airplay information provided by point-of-sale technology like Soundscan (1997), suggest it does not always avoid inbuilt distortions. They show that airplay data can be criticized for concentrating on large urban radio stations with short playlists and less willingness to expose new artists, while sales data is biased by concentrating disproportionately on those record stores – chains and so-called 'rack' stores – which 'follow the market' rather than the independent record shops that 'start the market' in terms of selling new and developing talent. Nevertheless, the chart information thus gathered is treated as a key tool in informing corporate decisions on which acts to sign and which records get airplay. Thus, in attempting to manage the uncertainty which is so intrinsic to a creative industry like music, systems like Soundscan may further inhibit the ability of radio stations and record companies to adapt quickly to new grass-roots musical currents.

With so finite an opportunity of attracting the attention of the CHR radio stations, and so many records to promote, there is usually neither the time nor the budget to attempt crossover in the case of newer artists signed to smaller corporations, and 'the vast majority of records remain stuck in their rigid formatted groove' (Negus 1993: 60–1). Significantly, Negus argues, the segmented character of radio permeates the record industry, not just in the marketing of genres separately, but also through the signing of new artists:

> Although A&R staff usually have a large degree of formal autonomy to sign who they choose, in practice they need the support of the radio promotion staff who will be handling the recordings of any act they acquire. When an A&R person finds an act they wish to sign, they are immediately confronted with the promotional staff who want to know what format the artist fits into. (1993: 62)

This cautionary approach to signing new artists is just one aspect of the popular music industry's need to manage uncertainty, discussed by Hirsch in his influential analysis of how cultural organizations process 'fads and fashions' (1990). He positioned radio stations, like other media organizations, as 'institutional gatekeepers' which filter 'raw materials' passing along a chain. At the same time, he recognized that these gatekeepers' decisions were fed back to producers in a way which allowed acceptable styles to be imitated and reproduced on a large scale. Negus offers a subtle variant on this approach, presenting radio stations not so much as 'institutional gatekeepers' but – drawing on Bourdieu – rather as 'cultural intermediaries', standing at the fulcrum of a two-way flow of influence between artists and audiences. Record company and radio station personnel are thus 'constantly contributing to the production of and then reorganizing, circulating and *mediating* the words, sounds and images of popular music to audiences across a range of entertainment media and cultural texts' (1996: 62). Much recent analysis suggests that the segmentation of radio and its reliance on pseudo-scientific data has squeezed uncertainty almost entirely out of this equation: the cultural intermediaries – the music programmers of radio – are mediating in ways that have traded-in responsiveness to new musical trends in exchange for the commercial advantages of predictability and familiarity.

Let us return to our central question, though. What are the wider cultural *effects* of this formatting, and all the 'managing of uncertainty' that drives it? At the very least, it has entrenched what Douglas has called contemporary radio-listening's 'mutually exclusive auditory niches' (1999: 349). Radio is erecting increasingly impermeable barriers between musical genres, and so blocking the 'hybridization' that Pickering and Shuker suggested is precisely what makes musical culture *dynamic*. Even so, we need to ask whether *all* radio programming everywhere inevitably conspires to follow musical taste rather more than to shape it. Recent changes in programming at the UK's most widely listened-to pop-music radio station BBC Radio 1 might suggest that it *is* possible to see a culturally 'interactive process' at work between different 'taste publics'. Radio 1 has long been in a position to re-shape the wider radio and record market if it chose to do so. As a public-service broadcaster, its programming – its gatekeeping behaviour, as we might put it – is less fixed by market obligations to particular audiences or formats than it is for most commercial licensees. Radio 1 could choose to lead, rather than slavishly to follow musical tastes. And if it did so, its effect on the British record and radio industry would not be negligible: with generally the largest audience of any single station in the UK, Radio 1 has long had the power to 'make or break' a record (Negus 1993: 63).

In practice, Radio 1 has traditionally responded to the nuances of shifting public tastes through providing space for specialist genres at the margins of its schedules. Already in the early 1990s, it was 'one of the few stations where a plurality of musics can coexist and where newer sounds can at least get some form of exposure' (1993: 66). Even so, this enduring habit of hiving-off 'difficult' music to the evenings and night-times clearly does little in the way of exposing a *mass* (that is, *daytime*) audience to new and unfamiliar sounds. In the mid 1990s, however, a series of changes in music policy were made which had a more profound effect (Hendy 2000b).

First, there was a dramatic turnover in presenters, which saw established 'personality' DJs leaving and specialist musical experts being brought in. They were invited to 'playlist' meetings and asked to nominate records they regarded as suitable for playlisting – 'jungle', rap or indie tracks, for example, that could be put before a large daytime audience. Their shows were also soon moved wholesale to daytime slots. The music they played was modified to take account of the larger mainstream audience, but *within limits the presenters appeared to find acceptable* – largely because the playlist they now had to observe was in itself becoming a closer reflection of their specialist tastes.

Secondly, a subtle blurring of the chronological dividing line between the daytime and evening schedules was effected. The start of evening programmes at about 6 pm had traditionally been characterized by a sudden and jarring change of musical direction, from a tightly formatted mainstream pop-sound to an entirely unplaylisted free-form sound. It was the classic opportunity for large numbers of listeners to be frightened off. Now there was to be a much more gradual and controlled change, with evening programmes playing a higher proportion of playlisted records in their first hours, and only gradually moving to a majority of unplaylisted records.

In one sense, this process of 'master' scheduling was doing little more than what most commercial radio stations would also normally attempt: to minimize the number of points on the clock when listeners would instinctively turn-off. Hennion and Meadel showed how the music-radio station depends for a unity of tone and for its hold over listeners on the scheduling of music organized *externally* to each programme, by a central 'mapping' department sensitive to the daily and weekly rhythms of broadcasting. But the effect of powerful scheduling they observed at RTL-Radio Luxembourg was to 'banish' musical genres which were regarded as too specialized, or aggressive or marginal to the evenings (1986: 296). The same tool was evidently being used by Radio 1 after 1995, but to effect very much the *reverse* trend: to ensure the removal of familiar and apparently popular artists, to insert a controlled amount of specialized music content into the mainstream output, and to soften the boundaries of the specialist-mainstream divide (see box 5.2).

Box 5.2   BBC Radio 1 re-invents itself

Extract from a speech by the Controller of BBC Radio 1, Matthew Bannister, 1996:

> A combination of demographics and economics is driving commercial radio towards the middle-aged middle-class. And, in a sweeping generalization, what those middle-aged middle-class listeners want is comfort – music they already know or that sounds like something they already know . . . [commercial FM stations] are moving towards the middle ground, playing more established classic hits and taking fewer and fewer risks with new music and artists. But amidst all this . . . something is happening in music. New music in the UK has never been more exciting and is beginning to find a renewed foothold in that notoriously difficult market – the USA. It is here that we see the vital importance of a station whose only aim is to take risks with new talent and new music, a station which will ignore the bottom line in favour of a major cultural public service. In short, Radio 1.

Source: Matthew Bannister, quoted in Garfield (1998: 92–3)

Extract from a news report in The *Guardian*, March 1996:

ROCKERS ISSUE WRIT TO REGAIN STATUS
Michael Ellison on an image problem

Francis Rossi has come a long way in 30 years. Back when rock was young and dangerous it was a season at Butlins, Minehead. Yesterday, 110 million record sales later, it was the five-star Langham Hilton Hotel, across the road from the new orthodoxy, Broadcasting House, central London.

The leader of Status Quo leaned forward, eyes narrowed below creased brow, and announced: 'We're not having it.' No one could deny it. Rossi's band is not having its latest record played on Radio 1.

Neither are lots of others, but only Quo, the denim-encrusted custodians of the 12-bar boogie, issued a writ for breach of contract yesterday demanding £250,000 in damages. Their case is simple: Radio 1 is a top 40 station and Quo's records get in the charts, so they should be played. The BBC's case is even more simple: it is not a top 40 station.

Only a few years ago they were all the best of friends. Quo even headlined the Party in the Park, Birmingham, to celebrate Radio 1's 25th anniversary in 1992.

'Maybe Radio 1 doesn't like our music or the image of the band or maybe they think we're too old,' said singer and guitarist Rossi (aged 46). 'But these people aren't paid to be taste-makers or trend setters but to reflect tastes.'

These people are Radio 1's controller, young Matthew Bannister (37) and his head of production, young Trevor Dann (44). Each week Dann and a panel of producers select the records which will be played on the station. Those on the A-list will be heard up to 30 times in seven days, the B-list 20 times and the C-list 10 to 15 times. Status Quo, 50 hits down the line and new in the charts this week with Fun Fun Fun at number 24, do not figure on any of these.

David Walker (51), the band's manager, said: 'It has been brought to our attention that Mr Dann has, on behalf of Radio 1 FM, instigated a policy banning any producer from playing our new recordings other than the one play it would be necessary to give on their Sunday afternoon top 40 chart show.'

Mr Dann was 'abusing his power by unilaterally declaring that Status Quo do not suit the demographic of Radio 1's audience.' Three years ago, when keyboard player Andrew Bown was only 46, Mr Bannister took over the station charged with producing 'distinctive' broadcasting and lowering the audience's age profile. He promptly lost 5 million listeners, though the station has recovered slightly to retain 11.2 million.

Bass player John Edwards, with the band for 10 years, said: 'I still listen to Radio 1; just because I'm 42 doesn't mean I'm not allowed to listen to it any more, but there should be more of a mix.'

But the hugely successful 'senior statesmen of the rock and roll industry' are not going to court just to help themselves said Parfitt (47).

Radio 1 named some of the other victims as Mr Blobby, Michael Barrymore, Michael Ball, Robson and Jerome and Cliff Richard. 'Unlike everyone else, Status Quo don't seem to have noticed that there have been quite a few changes at Radio 1 in the last couple of years,' said a spokeswoman. 'We do not slavishly follow the Top 40. Records are chosen on merit.'

This did not satisfy Edwards. 'We're very popular. It's not as if we're The Thargs from Transylvania.'

Sources: Matthew Bannister, quoted in Garfield 1998: 92–3, and The *Guardian*, March 1 1996 © The Observer

These changes had the crucial effect of ending what one manager at the station called 'the isolation of success': records emerging from the margins of the music industry were being identified by knowledgeable presenters and producers and, instead of being restricted to the 'ghetto' of specialist shows, *were being scheduled before large daytime audiences*. This propelled many singles by new and unfamiliar artists into the sales charts. And this was chart success almost entirely dependent on the airplay provided by Radio 1. Commercial stations by and large continued to ignore many of the newer bands then loosely described as part of the 'Britpop' wave, and relied as usual on the familiar sounds provided by established artists. Even by the middle of 1996, when commercial radio had begun to play a little more 'indie' music, most of it was still selected from the 1990–5 back-catalogue of *proven* successes, whereas Radio 1 was programming a much higher proportion of unproven 'pre'-releases.

So far, of course, this change in music policy suggests merely that what we are seeing is the rather unexceptional phenomenon of a radio station seeking simply to distinguish itself from its rivals by identifying a new market niche: in Radio 1's case by carving out a 'New Music First' format. To some extent this is true. At the time, the station faced the threat of privatization as part of a review of the BBC by the Conservative government, and the Corporation was fighting off the threat primarily by trying to represent the station as providing something truly *different* to the array of commercial pop stations. Radio 1 would, as a matter of stated BBC policy, *have to* have more speech content, more live performances, 'new work' and ideas, and a presentation style that was 'clearly informative and intelligent'; music programming would have to emphasize 'range, diversity and innovation' (BBC 1992). The changes at Radio 1, then, were largely motivated by the BBC's immediate political concerns.

Even so, the wider cultural significance of this internal change came, not with the immediate issue of facing-down privatization, but with the ripples it created in the British radio and music industry in the following years. Through 1996 and 1997, commercial stations in the UK slowly began to play records by new and unfamiliar artists at something approaching the same level as Radio 1 – though only once they were in the charts. By 1998, commercial radio stations were consistently playing records by new, unfamiliar artists *in advance* of release, just as Radio 1 had done for some two or three years. The impression overall, then, is not just that Radio 1 was more inclined than its commercial rivals to play less-familiar material by less-well-known artists: it is also that *over time*, its music policy appears to have been followed by a sea-change in the music policy of British pop radio as a whole. It is significant that when interviewed in April 1998, Radio 1's Head of Music Policy, Jeff Smith, offered a subtle shift in emphasis in describing Radio 1, not so much as a 'new music first' station, but as 'modern mainstream':

The music we play is by modern artists, but the music is becoming more of the mainstream. Its the new mainstream. What Blur and Pulp and the Prodigy have done since they've become core [Radio 1] artists is they've gone into the mainstream. You go into HMV, Woolies or ASDA and you can buy all your records there. A few years ago you wouldn't have been able to buy their records in a supermarket. They are part of the new mainstream – things have changed. . . . We've even led by the nose commercial radio, who've realised they can't get away with playing the next Phil Collins, Joe Cocker and Tina Turner record automatically any more. . . . A lot of their audience has gone beyond that now . . . they want to hear Oasis. (Quoted in Moy 1998)

There is other circumstantial evidence of expanded activity within the British music industry at about this stage. The sales charts steadily showed a higher proportion of entries by newer, alternative artists through the mid and late 1990s, and turnover as a whole jumped (BPI 1998: 17). Sales of *singles* are more significant here than sales of *albums*, because they are the primary site of new artistic activity. It is perhaps significant, then, that while the period from late 1993 has witnessed a long-term decline in the rate of growth in album sales in the UK, there has been, beginning from precisely the same time, a significant reversal in the decline of sales in singles – indeed the steepest and steadiest reversal since the punk and 'new-wave' era of the late 1970s (1998: 9). Radio 1 did not, of course, single-handedly create the mid 1990s renaissance in British pop music. Even so, it appears to have been influential in 'breaking' the careers of many newer artists at the time. One of the record-company pluggers who dealt regularly with Radio 1 in 1995 described the impact of the new playlist policy introduced by the station: 'it championed Britpop. It was no coincidence that all the major record companies then ran around trying to sign up all the Britpop bands they could find' (Garfield 1998: 202–3).

But Radio 1's cultural power was not just based purely on its decision to pursue an unusual project to broadcast 'new' music. It was because it combined this with a nationwide *mass* audience which no other station possessed. By exposing its large audience – some 6–11 million listeners – to unfamiliar musical genres, it became in effect the primary force for 'crossover' within Britain, by mediating between the sub-genres and the mainstream of pop-music tastes. This ability to have a mass impact is clearly jeopardized if audiences fall below a certain level, and the need to retain large audiences will always set a limit to the amount of musical experimentation which a radio station allows itself. Nevertheless, Radio 1's musical re-engineering of the mid/late 1990s, offered an attempt to mediate between the two different but overlapping categories of 'record buyers' – invariably cutting-edge in taste – and the inherently more conservative mass of 'radio listeners'. Scannell and Cardiff have shown how the BBC's classical Music Department of the 1930s was invariably more in tune with the aficionados of the record-buying public than with the broader swathe of listeners. Then, there was a sincere but awkward attempt to 'educate' the public towards a taste for more 'serious' music, with significant prestige accruing to the BBC as a cultural patron – though invariably pitiful audience sizes on the ground (1991: 181–223; 277–303). The parallels with Radio 1 after 1995 are striking. But one difference is that Radio 1 appeared to succeed in narrowing, at least for a while, the gap between the 'serious' and the 'popular', the 'specialist' and the 'mainstream'; and it did so in a way that spread through the wider radio and music industry. It had found a way of breaking through some of radio's traditional fencing-off of musical genres into Douglas's 'mutually exclusive auditory niches'.

Of course, in claiming the ability to make a cultural impact, Radio 1 exposes itself to a serious counter argument: that in establishing its own standards of musical taste as the cultural norm, it exercises an unhealthy form of hegemony in the music industry. Alan McGee, who ran Creation Records and managed Britpop's best-known artists, Oasis, believes that there is indeed 'a certain sound that you need to adhere to to get on Radio 1' (Moy 1998). Taken at face value, this would suggest that, in neglecting some nascent musical styles, a national radio station with a mass audience is in danger of creating just one more musical orthodoxy, unintentionally homogenizing and narrowing musical output just as effectively as its commercial rivals. Twenty years ago, Frith argued that, 'the BBC is contemptuously certain that Radio 1 satisfies its listeners, but it can only be so certain because its argument is circular . . . the BBC molds as well as responds to public taste (1978: 91). In this view, a 're-ordering' of the repertoires of popular music is no less malignant because it is done in the name of public service than if it is effected through purely commercial forces. And there is some truth in the suggestion. The station, for example, generally plays a much higher proportion of *British* artists than any commercial rival: typically some 70 per cent of its output, compared with about 58 per cent for commercial stations (Hendy 2000b). Even so, 'Britpop' remains rather more a term of convenience than a definable musical category. Press coverage tended to lump together a very much wider range of sounds under the term in order to explain the collective success of British bands during the period, and airplay figures show that in this period Radio 1 played, not just quintessentially Britpop guitar bands like Oasis, but also 'trip-hop', 'drum'n'bass', 'Big Beat' and a new generation of

R'n'B bands. By most accounts, this was a repertoire inclusive of *many* sub-genres, not just one. The 'new mainstream' which Radio 1 helped create was, although perhaps more narrowly British, at least more broadly framed *stylistically* than that existing in the early 1990s.

Conclusion

Where has this extended discussion on the music programming habits of radio brought us? Looking at BBC Radio 1 suggests that radio need not everywhere be defined as a medium *intrinsically* hostile to musical diversity and change: that it is not *always* so highly for-matted and so completely segmented – either between stations or within schedules – that it becomes impossible for different musics to meet in fruitful collision. Radio *can* be the site of the 'hybridization' that Pickering and Shuker believe is precisely what makes musical culture *dynamic*.

The question here, though, is how typical a station like Radio 1 might be in effecting musical change. The *New York Times* observed in 1999 that the American FM dial was showing signs of becoming a rich 'ecosystem': a new wave of legalised micro-radio stations, college radio, a prospering NPR, all conspiring to translate a 'once parched territory' into a blooming landscape where, for example, 'accidental listeners' are 'serendipitously exposed to the pleasures of Brazilian samba or Indian pop' through programmes like *Morning Becomes Eclectic* on Santa Monica's KCRW 89.9 FM – a free-form programme 'closely monitored' by Los Angeles record executives – or almost any of the shows on New Jersey's WFMU (*New York Times*, 11 April 1999: 69, 73–6). When and where record industry execu-tives *do* take notice of such shows, radio has at least some claim to be a medium through which eclecticism can soon translate into cultural dynamism in the wider music industry: the range of music ultimately available at the record shops might evolve, perhaps even widen, at least in part because of exposure on the radio.

Yet programming like this needs to be put into perspective. New York's WNEW-FM, often described as America's 'first free-form pro-gressive rock station' – and a mirror for the city's cultural, musical and sexual vitality – captured only 1.4 per cent of the city's available audience in 1999, a situation which helped propel its owners into abandoning thirty-two years of history and reformatting it as a laddish all-talk station (Ellison 1999). This example helps illustrate what, in the end, makes BBC Radio 1's musical reprogramming the *exception* rather than the rule in contemporary radio: it was, we should recall, pursuing what could loosely be described as a 'progressive' cultural agenda by exposing new music to a *mass* national audience of several million listeners. Most 'free-form' stations – those that allow commentators to remark upon a 'blooming' radio ecology at the turn of the century – have very small (though admittedly devoted) audiences – too small, indeed, to have very much impact on the *mainstream* of culture in the way that perhaps Radio 1 did in the mid 1990s. They are, in other words, probably more important in nurturing *sub*-cultures than in feeding and shaping the musical centreground.

Indeed, for most radio, most of the time, cultural 'hybridization' is simply out of the question. Different musical cultures remain overwhelmingly fenced-off from each other. We saw in chapter 1 how the radio landscape has become increasingly segmented into niches, and in chapters 2 and 3 we noted how the patterns of daily production ensure the steady delivery of familiar and tightly targeted output to particular sections of the audience – listeners who are perceived to want more than anything else a diet of familiar and reassuring aural experiences.

But there is another limitation to radio's cultural impact, too. If any change in the relationship between various musical genres does occur through radio, it is certainly not necessarily accompanied by *wider* changes which breach boundaries of class, ethnicity or gender. Goodlad, in her recent survey of American 'alternative' radio, noticed how the potentially invigorating appearance of new-wave British music in the 1980s and 1990s was marketed mostly at 'white, usually college-bound or college-educated youth': the stations 'remained aloof' from the hip-hop culture of urban African-Americans (1999: 5–7). Similarly, although much of the new-wave music of the 1980s and 1990s was itself determinedly 'non-gendered', it was played on alternative stations which carried advertising aimed overwhelmingly at adolescent men. Alternative records that exhibited musical 'softness' were, on the other hand, favoured by those stations seeking female listeners. Radio, Goodlad suggests, is now actively *gendering* music in the same way that it has for a long time segmented listeners by *age*, and she concludes that 'the more sexual difference is emphasized, the more segregation occurs, thus justifying further amplifications of gendered norms' (1990: 12).

Is there *any* prospect of a radio environment which may be less, rather than more segregated – an environment, in other words, which offers the prospect of a less formulaic, more eclectic listening experience? To offer some sort of tentative answer to that question, I would like to return to the work of Pickering and Shuker, and their concern with the dynamic *balance* of forces needed to help protect indigenous New Zealand music against the perceived onslaught of Anglo-American imports:

> It is a rather bizarre situation where the music which constitutes an unknown quantity for radio programmers in New Zealand is locally produced, and that which they feel is already widely familiar in its general 'feel' is foreign. In a more healthy cultural environment this situation would be reversed. This is not some nostalgic harking-back to the relatively restricted intercultural trafficking of earlier times. When such trafficking is absent, cultural innovation is at the very least slowed down. Yet when a local culture is swamped by material from outside, the possibilities for indigenous development are also diminished. It is a question of creating a dynamic balance of forces. For the point remains that while cultural parochialism is to be discouraged, a large dimension of that protean phenomenon we call 'culture' is for many people about belonging, about feeling a sense of identity rooted in various ways in a geographical area or group which is quite different to that strategically constructed, mythic community of the nation. Popular cultural creativity is enhanced or even given purpose and point by association with this symbolic belonging, and music, perhaps more than any other art-form, should contribute to it by developing its own localized content or its own variations upon more broadly pervasive features. (1993: 53–4)

Radio's precise role within Pickering and Shuker's cultural landscape is as a key *mediator* between different cultures. Its international reach breaks the link between culture and place, enabling communities of interest to be built across large spaces. Through the very process of exposing each culture to other influences, radio can also ensure a constant evolution, through creative collision, of symbolic forms and processes. In the case of BBC Radio 1, such mediation took the form of 'intercultural trafficking' between 'minority' and 'majority' musical tastes within a single national area. The station is similarly placed to breach some of the recently erected boundaries between male and female listeners because, unlike the 'alternative' stations which Goodlad observed, it also seeks a broad balance of the sexes in its audience (BBC 1998).

My essential point is this, though: that such a model of cultural mediation – one which is capable of breaching radio's habitual desire to segregate us – could, theoretically at least, hold true for similar processes of 'intercultural trafficking' between local and distant cultures, between various ethnic identities, and – recalling our earlier discussion of talk-radio's role in democratic life – between various political beliefs and ideas. This perspective gives radio, at least potentially, a more productive cultural role than McLuhan once assigned. He, remember, was profoundly distrustful of the medium:

> The message of radio is one of violent, unified implosion and reso-
> nance. For Africa, India, China, and even Russia, radio is a profound
> archaic force, a time bond with the most ancient past and long-
> forgotten experience . . . literacy had fostered an extreme individual-
> ism, and radio had done just the opposite in reviving the ancient expe-
> rience of kinship webs. . . . It is really a subliminal echo chamber of
> magical powers to touch remote and forgotten chords. (1994: 301–2)

In McLuhan's view, the 'kinship webs' radio wove were not sup-
portive communities, but violently tribal and *separatist*. Given what
we now know about the highly segmented nature of contemporary
radio, this description clearly contains a kernel of truth. But his vision
of a society in which radio 'contracts the world to village size', yet
doesn't homogenize the 'village quarters', is slightly wide of the mark:
radio can and does erode the unique identity of 'the village quarter'
– we have seen that in the way that many of the same formats have
spread throughout the world. And where the 'balance of dynamic
forces' which Pickering and Shuker so desire can be found, radio can
sometimes make the world a more *open* and vibrant place to live too
– a world where the contradictory forces swirling around the medium
are kept in some sort of check: neither full-scale cultural separatism,
which may protect cultural identities but brings with it the prospect of an ever-more fragmented human experience, nor untamed
globalization, which may expose cultures to new and enriching
experiences but also threatens to bring the extinction of regional
differences.

In the end, though, the fact that the ability to create such a delicate balance is most easily identified with a *public-service* radio station
is significant. Despite the pressures which even public-service broadcasters face to maximize their audiences, many are still relatively free
to risk audience size for the sake of *cultural* enterprise. Commercial
radio is, by its very nature, in the business of minimizing risk: it
cannot afford to lead, rather than simply follow, public taste, and a
certain degree of cultural stasis is the inevitable by-product of its
caution. And it is precisely this – the highly formatted, fully automated, thoroughly market-researched commercial radio station – that
is now *the* defining identity for the radio medium. It is not *all* like
this, of course. Radio, as I tried to argue near the beginning of this
book, is infinitely diverse in form and always impermeable to new
participants. It can open up much of the world to us, connect us –
enfold us even – in ways that are useful, enjoyable and sometimes
inspiring, genuinely culture-*changing* if you like. But, there are considerable pressures within the medium – technical, social, political
and perhaps above all economic – that make much of what it offers

us less than inspiring, less than what it *could be*. Surveying what she saw at the close of the twentieth century, Douglas asked, 'are we excited by what we hear?' (1999: 348). If radio is to be a medium that achieves its potential, it is a question we undoubtedly need to keep putting to those who control it.

Bibliography

Abercrombie, N. 1996: *Television and Society*. Cambridge: Polity Press.

Adorno, T. W. 1990: On Popular Music. In S. Frith and A. Goodwin (eds), *On Record: Rock, Pop and the Written Word*. London: Routledge, 301–14.

Adorno, T. W. 1991: On the Fetish Character in Music and the Regression of Listening. In J. M. Bernstein (ed.), *The Culture Industry: Selected Essays on Mass Culture by Theodor Adorno*. London: Routledge, 26–52.

Albrow, M. 1996: *The Global Age*. Cambridge: Polity Press.

Anderson, B. 1991: *Imagined Communities: Reflections on the Origins and Spread of Nationalism*. New York: Verso.

Arbitron 1999: *The Arbitron Internet Listening Study: Radio in the New Media World*. http://www.arbitron.com/studies/20nmw.htm

Armstrong, C. B. and Rubin, A. M. 1989: Talk Radio as Interpersonal Communication. *Journal of Communication*, 39 (2), 84–94.

Arrow-FM 1999: *Rates*. http://www.arrowfm.co.uk/rates.html

Attali, J. 1985: *Noise: The Political Economy of Music*. Minneapolis and London: University of Minnesota Press.

Barboutis, C. 1997: Digital Audio Broadcasting: The Tangled Webs of Technological Warfare. *Media, Culture & Society*, 19, 687–90.

Barnard, S. 1989: *On the Radio: Music Radio in Britain*. Milton Keynes: Open University Press.

Barnes, K. 1990: Top 40 Radio: A Fragment of the Imagination. In S. Frith (ed.), *Facing the Music*, London: Mandarin, 8–50.

Barnett, S. and Morrison, D. 1989: *The Listener Speaks: The Radio Audience and the Future of Radio*. London: HMSO.

Barnett, S. and Curry, A. 1994: *The Battle for the BBC: A British Broadcasting Conspiracy*. London: Aurum Press.

Barrie, C. 1999: News report in *The Guardian*, 3 February 1999.

Barthes, R. 1973: *Mythologies*. London: Vintage.

Barthes, R. 1975: *S/Z*. London: Jonathan Cape.

Barthes, R. 1977: *Image-Music-Text*. London: Fontana.

Bauman, Z. 1992: *Intimations of Postmodernity*. London: Routledge.

Bauman, Z. 1998: *Globalization: The Human Consequences*. Cambridge: Polity Press.

BBC 1992: *Extending Choice: The BBC's Role in the New Broadcasting Age*. London: BBC.

BBC 1998: *Annual Report and Accounts 97/98*. London: BBC.

BBC CDR 1997: *BBC Digital Radio: clearing the way for radio's future*. CD-Rom. London: BBC.

BBC DRRF 1998: *BBC Digital Radio Research Findings*. London: BBC.

BBC ENPSN 1997: *BBC ENPS Newsletter*, April 1997. London: BBC.

BBC NRRA 1996: *BBC Network Radio Research and Analysis: Tomorrow's Listener*. Data presented to Radio Academy Conference, Birmingham, July 1996.

BBC Radio 1 1997: *BBC Radio 1 Commissioning Strategy 1997/8*. London: BBC.

BBC Radio 4 1998: *BBC Radio 4 Commissioning Guidelines 1998/9*, 2nd edn. London: BBC.

Beck, A. 1998: Rezoning Radio Theory (A draft book in electronic form), *Sound Journal*, http://speke.ukc.ac.uk/sais/sound-journal/index.html

Bennett, A. 1997: 'Village greens and terraced streets: Britpop and representations of Britishness'. *Young: Nordic Journal of Youth Research*, 5 (4), 20–33.

Bennett, T., Frith, S., Grossberg, L., Shephard, J. and Turner, G. (eds) 1993: *Rock and Popular Music: Politics, Policies, Institutions*. London and New York: Routledge.

Bensman, J. and Lilienfeld, R. 1979: *Between Public and Private*. New York: Free Press.

Berland, J. 1993a: Radio Space and Industrial Time: The Case of Music Formats. In S. Frith et al. (eds), *Rock and Popular Music: Politics, Policies, Institutions*. London: Routledge, 104–18.

Berland, J. 1993b: Contradicting Media: Toward a Political Phenomenology of Listening. In N. Strauss (ed.), *Radiotext(e)/Semiotext(e)*. 6 (1), 209–17.

Blumler, J. 1991: The New Television Marketplace: Imperatives, Implications, Issues. In J. Curran and M. Gurevitch (eds), *Mass Media & Society*, 1st edn. London: Edward Arnold, 194–215.

Blumler, J. and Gurevitch, M. 1982: The Political Effects of Mass Communication. In M. Gurevitch, T. Bennett, J. Curran and J. Woollacott (eds), *Culture, Society and the Media*. London: Methuen, 236–67.

Bourgault, L. M. 1995: *Mass Media and Sub-Saharan Africa*. Bloomington: Indiana University Press.

BPI 1998: *Statistical Handbook*. London: British Phonographic Industry Limited.

Brand, G. and Scannell, P. 1991: Talk, Identity and Performance: The Tony Blackburn Show. In P. Scannell (ed.), *Broadcast Talk*. London: Sage, 201–26.

Brecht, B. 1932: Der Rundfunk als Kommunikationsapparat. In *Blattaer der Hessischen Landestheaters*, Darmstadt 16. Reprinted and translated in N. Strauss (ed.), *Radiotext(e)/Semiotext(e)*. 6 (1) (1993), 15–17.

Briggs, A. 1995: *The History of Broadcasting in the United Kingdom*, (5 volumes). Oxford: Oxford University Press.

Browne, D. R. 1990: Aboriginal Radio in Australia: From Dreamtime to Prime Time? *Journal of Communication*, 40 (1), 111–20.

Browne, D. R. 1992: *International Radio Broadcasting: The Limits of a Limitless Medium*. New York: Praeger.

Cairncross, F. 1997: *The Death of Distance: How the Communications Revolution will Change our Lives*. London: Orion Business Books.

Cantril, H. 1940: *The Invasion from Mars: A Study in the Psychology of Panic*. Princeton, NJ: Princeton University Press.

Carlton 1998: *Annual Report and Accounts 1998*. London: Carlton Communications PLC.

Carroll, R. L., Silbergleid, M. I., Beachum, C. M., Perry, S. D., Pluscht, P. J. and Pescatore, M. J. 1993: Meanings of Radio to Teenagers in a Niche-Programming Era. *Journal of Broadcasting & Electronic Media*, 37 (2), 159–76.

Cashmore, E. and Rojek, C. 1999: *Dictionary of Cultural Theorists*. London: Arnold.

CIN 1998: *Presspack*. London: Chart Information Network.

Chapple, S. and Garofalo, R. 1977: *Rock 'n' Roll is Here to Pay: The History and Politics of the Music Industry*. Chicago: Nelson Hall.

Chrétien, J., Dupaquier, J., Kabanda, M., Ngarambe, J. and Reporters Sans Frontières 1995: *Rwanda: Les médias du génocide*. Paris: Karthala.

Classen, C. 1993: *Worlds of Sense: Exploring the Senses in the History and Across Cultures*. London: Routledge.

Collins, J. 1992: Some Anti-Hegemonic Aspects of African Popular Music. In R. Garofalo (ed.), *Rockin' the Boat: Mass Music and Mass Movements*. Boston: South End Press, 185–94.

Coward, R. 1984: *Female Desire*. London: Paladin, Grafton Books.

Crisell, A. 1994: *Understanding Radio*, 2nd edn. London: Routledge.

Crisell, A. 1997: *An Introductory History of British Broadcasting*. London and New York: Routledge.

Croteau, D. and Hoynes, W. 2000: *Media/Society: Industries, Images, and Audiences*, 2nd edn. Thousand Oaks, CA: Pine Forge Press.

Curran, J. and Seaton, J. 1997: *Power Without Responsibility: The Press and Broadcasting in Britain*, 5th edn. London and New York: Routledge.

de Mateo, R. 1997: Spain. In B. S. Østergaard (ed.), *The Media in Western Europe: The Euromedia Handbook*, 2nd edn. London: Sage, 194–209.

Digital One 1998: *Press Release: Digital One Gets the Go Ahead to take Radio into the Digital Age*, 12 October 1998.

Digital One 1999: *Press Release: Digital One begins Test Transmissions*, 16 April 1999.

Donovan, P. 1997: *All Our Todays: Forty Years of Radio 4's 'Today' Programme*. London: Jonathan Cape.

Douglas, S. J. 1999: *Listening In: Radio and the American Imagination, from Amos 'n' Andy and Edward R. Murrow to Wolfman Jack and Howard Stern.* New York and Toronto: Random House.

Drew, R. 1996: Narration Can be a Killer. In K. MacDonald and M. Cousins (eds), *Imagining Reality: The Faber Book of Documentary.* London and Boston: Faber and Faber, 271–3.

Dunnett, P. J. S. 1990: *The World Television Industry.* London: Routledge.

Dyson, F. 1994: The Genealogy of the Radio Voice. In D. Augaitis and D. Lander (eds), *Radio Rethink: Art, Sound and Transmission.* Canada: Walter Phillips Gallery, 167–86.

Elliott, P. 1974: Uses and Gratifications Research: A Critique and a Sociological Alternative. In J. Blumler and E. Katz (eds), *The Uses of Mass Communications.* London: Sage, 249–68.

Ellis, J. 1982: *Visible Fictions.* London: Routledge.

Ellison, M. 1999: Post-rock Radio Daze. In the *Guardian*, 18 October 1999, G2 16.

Fairchild, C. 1999: Deterritorializing Radio: Deregulation and the Continuing Triumph of the Corporatist Perspective in the USA. *Media, Culture & Society*, 21, 549–61.

Fathi, A. and Heath, C. L. 1974: Group Influence, Mass Media and Musical Taste among Canadian Students. *Journalism Quarterly*, 51, 705–9.

FCC 1999: *Federal Communications Commission Audio Services Division: Broadcast Stations Total*, 31 March 1999. http://www.fcc.gov/mmb/asd/totals/bt990331.html

Feld, S. 1994: *Sound and Sentiment: Birds, Weeping, Poetics, and Song in Kaluli Expression*, 2nd edn. Philadelphia: University of Pennsylvania Press.

Fiske, J. 1987: *Television Culture.* London: Methuen.

Fiske, J. 1989: Moments of Television: Neither the Text nor the Audience. In E. Seiter, H. Borchers, G. Kreutzner and E.-M. Warth (eds), *Remote Control: Television, Audiences, and Cultural Power.* London: Routledge, 56–78.

Fiske, J. 1990: *An Introduction to Communication Studies*, 2nd edn. London: Routledge.

Fiske, J. and Hartley, J. 1978: *Reading Television.* London: Methuen.

Fornatale, P. and Mills, J. E. 1980: *Radio in the Television Age.* Woodstock, NY: Overlook Press.

Frith, S. 1978: *The Sociology of Rock.* London: Constable.

Frith, S. 1987: Towards an Aesthetic of Popular Music. In R. Leppert and S. McLary (eds), *Music and Society: the Politics of Composition, Performance and Reception.* Cambridge: Cambridge University Press, 133–49.

Frith, S. 1996: *Performing Rites: On the Value of Popular Music.* Oxford: Oxford University Press.

Gallagher, M. 1982: Negotiations of Control in Media Organizations and Occupations. In M. Gurevitch, T. Bennett, J. Curran and J. Woollacott (eds), *Culture, Society and the Media.* London: Methuen, 151–73.

Garfield, S. 1998: *The Nation's Favourite: The True Adventures of Radio 1.* London: Faber and Faber.

Garfinkel, H. 1984: *Studies in Ethnomethodology.* Cambridge: Polity Press.

Garner, K. 1990: New Gold Dawn: The Traditional English Breakfast Show in 1989. *Popular Music*, 9 (2), 193–202.

Garnham, N. 1986: Contribution to a Political Economy of Mass-Communication. In R. Collins, J. Curran, N. Garnham, P. Scannell, P. Schlesinger and C. Sparks (eds), *Media, Culture & Society: A Critical Reader*. London, Beverly Hills, Newbury Park and New Delhi: Sage, 9–32.

Garnham, N. 1992: The Media and the Public Sphere. In C. Calhoun (ed.), *Habermas and the Public Sphere*. Cambridge, MA: MIT Press, 359–76.

Garnham, N. 1994: The Broadcasting Market and the Future of the BBC. *Political Quarterly*, 65 (1), 11–19.

Garofalo, R. 1992: Introduction. In R. Garofalo (ed.), *Rockin' the Boat: Mass Music and Mass Movements*. Boston: South End Press, 1–13.

Gell, A. 1995: The Language of the Forest: Landscape and Phonological Iconism in Umeda. In E. Hirsch and M. O'Hanlon (eds), *The Anthropology of Landscape: Perspectives on Place and Space*. Oxford: Clarendon Press, 232–54.

Giddens, A. 1984: *The Constitution of Society*. Cambridge: Polity Press.

Giddens, A. 1991: *Modernity and Self-Identity: Self and Society in the Late Modern Age*. Cambridge: Polity Press.

Gillet, C. 1988: *Making Tracks: the Story of Atlantic Records*. London: Souvenir.

Glasser, T. L. 1984: Competition and Diversity among Radio Formats: Legal and Structural Issues. *Journal of Broadcasting*, 28 (2), 127–44.

Goffman, E. 1980: The Radio Drama Frame. In J. Corner and J. Hawthorn (eds), *Communication Studies*. London: Edward Arnold.

Goffman, E. 1981: *Forms of Talk*. Philadelphia: University of Pennsylvania Press.

Goodlad, L. M. E. 1999: Packaged Alternatives: the Incorporation and Gendering of 'Alternative' Radio. Unpublished paper, University of Washington.

Goodwin, P. 1998: *Television Under the Tories: Broadcasting Policy 1979–1997*. London: BFI.

Gough, D. 1999: Soaps in Front Line of Battle against Aids. News report in *The Guardian*, 4 January 1999.

Graham, A. 1998: Broadcasting Policy and the Digital Revolution. In J. Seaton (ed.), *Politics and the Media: Harlots and Prerogatives at the Turn of the Millennium*. Oxford: Blackwell Publishers, 30–42.

Graham, J. 1999: Personal interview with Jefferson Graham, Independent Radio Group, 28 May 1999.

Green, L. 1998: Constructing Community through Broadcasting Communications in Remote Western Australia. Paper delivered to Radio Studies Network, Third Annual Association of Media, Cultural and Communication Studies Conference, Sheffield, 11–12 December 1998.

Green Paper 1998: *Regulating Communications – Approaching Convergence in the Information Age*. London: Department of Culture, Media and Sport, July 1998.

Grice, P. 1989: *Studies in the Way of Words*. Cambridge, MA: Harvard University Press.

Grierson, J. c.1934–6, 1996: First Principles of Documentary. In K. MacDonald and M. Cousins (eds), *Imagining Reality: The Faber Book of Documentary*. London and Boston: Faber and Faber, 97–102.

Guralnick, P. 1991: *Sweet Soul Music: Rhythm and Blues and the Southern Dream of Freedom*. London: Penguin.

Gurevitch, M. 1996: The Globalization of Electronic Journalism. In J. Curran and M. Gurevitch (eds), *Mass Media and Society*, 2nd edn. London: Methuen, 204–24.

Gustafsson, K. E. and Hultén, O. 1997: Sweden. In B. S. Østergaard (ed.), *The Media in Western Europe: The Euromedia Handbook*, 2nd edn. London: Sage, 210–28.

GWR 1998: *Annual Report and Accounts 1997/98*. http://www.gwrgroup.musicradio.com

Habermas, J. 1989: *The Structural Transformation of the Public Sphere*. Cambridge: Polity Press.

Hachten, W. A. 1974: Broadcasting and political crisis. In S. W. Head (ed.), *Broadcasting in Africa: A Continental Survey of Radio and Television*. Philadelphia: Temple University Press, 395–8.

Hamm, C. 1991: 'The constant companion of man': Separate Development, Radio Bantu and Music. In *Popular Music*, 10 (2), 147–73.

Hamm, C. 1995a: Privileging the Moment of Reception: Music and Radio in South Africa. In C. Hamm (ed.), *Putting Popular Music in its Place*. Cambridge: Cambridge University Press, 249–69.

Hamm, C. 1995b: Music and Radio in the People's Republic of China. In C. Hamm (ed.), *Putting Popular Music in its Place*. Cambridge: Cambridge University Press, 270–305.

Handel, S. 1989: *Listening: An Introduction to the Perception of Auditory Events*. Cambridge, MA: MIT Press.

Hardy, J. 1997: Julian Hardy of Capital Interactive, speech to 'Radio Meets the Web' Radio Academy Conference, London, November 1997.

Harris, R. 1997: Dick Harris, speech to 'News Radio' Radio Academy Conference, London, 1997.

Hartley, J. 1982: *Understanding News*. London: Methuen.

Harvey, D. 1989: *The Condition of Postmodernity*. Oxford: Blackwell Publishers.

Head, S. W. and Sterling, C. H. 1990: *Broadcasting in America: A Survey of Electronic Media*, 6th edn. Boston: Houghton Mifflin.

Held, D., McGrew, A., Goldblatt, D. and Perraton, J. 1999: *Global Transformations: Politics, Economics and Culture*. Cambridge: Polity Press.

Hendy, D. 1994: Radio Five Live – Is it Too Fast for its Own Good? *British Journalism Review*, 5 (2), 15–17.

Hendy, D. 2000a: A Political Economy of Radio in the Digital Era. *Journal of Radio Studies*, 7 (1) 213–34.

Hendy, D. 2000b: Pop Music in the Public Service: BBC Radio 1 and New Music in the 1990s. *Media, Culture & Society* 22 (6) November 2000.

Hennion, A. and Meadel, C. 1986: Programming Music: Radio as Mediator. *Media, Culture & Society*, 8 (3), 281–303.

Hesmondhalgh, D. 1996: Flexibility, Post-Fordism and the Music Industry. *Media, Culture & Society*, 18 (3), 469–88.

Higgins, C. S. and Moss, P. D. 1982: *Sounds Real: Radio in Everyday Life*. St Lucia, London and Sydney: University of Queensland Press.

Higgins, C. S. and Moss, P. D. 1984: Radio Voices. *Media, Culture & Society*, 6 (4), 353–75.

Hirsch, P. 1990: Processing Fads and Fashions: An Organization-Set Analysis of Cultural Industry Systems. In S. Frith and A. Goodwin (eds), *On Record: Rock, Pop and the Written Word*. London: Routledge, 127–39.

Hobson, D. 1980: Housewives and the Mass Media. In S. Hall, D. Hobson, A. Lowe and P. Willis (eds), *Culture, Media, Language*. London: Routledge, 105–14.

Hochheimer, J. L. 1993: Organizing Democratic Radio: Issues in Praxis. *Media, Culture & Society*, 15, 473–86.

Hutchby, I. 1991: The Organization of Talk on Talk Radio. In P. Scannell (ed.), *Broadcast Talk*. London: Sage, 119–37.

Kaplan, E. A. 1987: *Rock Around the Clock*. London: Methuen.

Katz, E., Gurevitch, M. and Haas, H. 1973: On the Use of Mass Media for Important Things. *American Sociological Review*, 38 (2), 164–81.

Katz, E. and Wedell, G. 1978: *Broadcasting in the Third World: Promise and Performance*. London: Macmillan.

Keith, M. C. 1997: *The Radio Station*, 4th edn. Boston: Focal Press.

Kellow, C. L. and Steeves, H. L. 1998: The Role of Radio in the Rwandan Genocide. *Journal of Communication*, 48 (3), 107–28.

Lazarsfeld, P. and Field, H. H. 1946: *The People Look at Radio*. Chapel Hill: University of North Carolina Press.

Ledbetter, J. 1997: *Made Possible By . . . : The Death of Public Broadcasting in the United States*. London and New York: Verso.

Levin, M. 1987: *Talk Radio and the American Dream*. New York: Lexington Books.

Lewis, P. M. and Booth, J. 1989: *The Invisible Medium: Public, Commercial and Community Radio*. London: Macmillan.

Lewis, T. 1993: Triumph of the Idol – Rush Limbaugh and a Hot Medium. *Media Studies Journal*, 7 (3), 51–62.

Lloréns, J. A. 1991: Andean Voices on Lima Airwaves: Highland Migrants and Radio Broadcasting in Peru. *Studies in Latin American Popular Culture*, 10, 177–89.

Longhurst, B. 1995: *Popular Music & Society*. Cambridge: Polity Press.

Lowery, S. and De Fleur, M. L. 1983: *Milestones in Mass Communication Research: Media Effects*. New York and London: Longman.

McChesney, R. 1997: *Corporate Media and the Threat to Democracy*. New York: Seven Stories Press.

McCourt, T. and Rothenbuhler, E. 1987: Commercial Radio and Popular Music: Processes of Selection and Factors of Influence. In J. Lull (ed.), *Popular Music and Communication*. Beverly Hills: Sage, 101–15.

McCourt, T. and Rothenbuhler, E. 1997: Soundscan and the Consolidation of Control in the Popular Music Industry. *Media, Culture & Society*, 19, 201–18.

McLeish, R. 1994: *Radio Production*, 3rd edn. Oxford: Focal Press.

McLuhan, M. 1994: *Understanding Media: The Extensions of Man*. Boston: MIT Press.

McQuail, D. 1983: *Mass Communication Theory*. London: Sage.

MacDonald, K. and Cousins, M. (eds) 1996: *Imagining Reality: The Faber Book of Documentary*. London and Boston: Faber and Faber.

Manaev, O. 1991: The Influence of Western Radio on the Democratization of Soviet Youth. *Journal of Communication*, 41 (2), 72–91.

Mann, R. (ed.) 1999: *The Blue Book of British Broadcasting*, 25th edn. London: Tellex Monitors.

Marr, W. 1999: *An Investigation into the Role of Music Radio Producers*. Unpublished BA Media Studies dissertation, University of Westminster, London.

Matic, V. 1999a: Letter from Belgrade. News report in the *Guardian*, 5 April 1999.

Matic, V. 1999b: Will the real Radio B92 please stand up! Email received from Belgrade, 13 April 1999, via B92 support group in the Netherlands. http://helpb92.xs4all.nl

Media Research Limited 1998: *Credentials: Broadcast Analysis Examples*, mimeograph press-release, Radio Academy Conference, London.

Mendelsohn, H. 1964: Listening to Radio. In L. A. Dexter and D. M. White (eds), *People, Society, and Mass Communications*, New York: Free Press of Glencoe, 239–49.

Montgomery, M. 1986: DJ Talk. *Media, Culture & Society*, 8, 421–40.

Montgomery, M. 1991: Our Tune: a study of a discourse genre. In P. Scannell (ed.), *Broadcast Talk*. London: Sage, 138–77.

Mosco, V. 1996: *The Political Economy of Communication*. London: Sage.

Moy, S. 1998: *The Renaissance of Radio 1 and British Music*. Unpublished BA Media Studies dissertation, University of Westminster, London.

Mulholland, S. 1998: Stephen Mulholland, BBC Digital Radio, speech reported in *Radio Academy Festival Report 1998*. London: Radio Academy.

Murdock, G. 1981: Organising the Imagination: Sociological Perspectives on Radio Drama. In P. Lewis (ed.), *Radio Drama*. London and New York: Longman, 143–63.

Murroni, C., Irvine, N. and King, R. 1998: *future.radio.uk: public policy on the future of radio*. London: IPPR.

Music Week: various editions. Published weekly, London: Miller Freeman / United News and Media.

Negus, K. 1992: *Producing Pop: Culture and Conflict in the Popular Music Industry*. London: Edward Arnold.

Negus, K. 1993: Plugging and Programming: Pop Radio and Record Promotion in Britain and the United States. *Popular Music*, 12 (1), 57–68.

Negus, K. 1996: *Popular Music in Theory*. Cambridge: Polity Press.

Negus, K. 1998: Cultural Production and the Corporation: Musical Genres and the Strategic Management of Creativity in the US Recording Industry. *Media, Culture & Society*, 20, 359–79.

NERA 1998: *Report on UK Commercial Radio's Future: Final Report*. London: National Economic Research Associates.

New York Times 1999: The Glow at the End of the Dial. In *New York Times Magazine*, 11 April 1999, 68–77.

O'Connor, A. 1990: The Miners' Radio Stations in Bolivia: A Culture of Resistance. *Journal of Communication*, 40 (1), 102–110.

Østergaard, B. S. (ed.) 1997: *The Media in Western Europe: The Euromedia Handbook*, 2nd edn. London: Sage.

Page, B. I. and Tannenbaum, J. 1996: Populistic Deliberation and Talk Radio. *Journal of Communication*, 46 (2), 33–54.

Page, T. (ed.) 1990: *The Glenn Gould Reader*. New York: Vintage.

Parker, M. 1991: Reading the Charts – Making Sense with the Hit Parade. *Popular Music*, 10 (2), 205–17.

Pease, E. C. and Dennis, E. E. 1993: Radio the Forgotten Medium: Preface. *Media Studies Journal*, 7 (3), xi–xix.

Performing Rights Society 1999: *Welcome to Radio: Payment Comparison*. Mimeograph. London.

Pickering, M. and Shuker, R. 1993: Radio Gaga: Popular Music and the Radio Quota Debate in New Zealand. *New Zealand Sociology*, 8 (1), 21–59.

Plowright, P. 1999: Interview with Piers Plowright, former Chief Producer, BBC Radio Features, 24 June 1999.

Poulantzas, N. 1978: *State, Power and Socialism*. London: New Left Books.

Powell, Adam Clayton, III 1993: You Are What You Hear. *Media Studies Journal*, 7 (3), 71–6.

Powell, M. 1997: Is it Live? Does it Matter? Mike Powell, Chief Executive UKRD, 28 July 1997. http://www.vru.co.uk/Live.htm

RAB 1998a: *Effective Radio Weights: A Guide to What Constitutes an Effective Weight of Radio Advertising*. London: Radio Advertising Bureau.

RAB 1998b: *Media Planning on Radio: A Guide to Best Practice in Radio Media Planning*. London: Radio Advertising Bureau.

RAB (US) 1999: Radio Ad Sales Surpass $15 Billion in 1998. Press Release, US Radio Advertising Bureau 8 February 1999. http://www.rab.com/pr/dec98rev.html

Radio and Records Online 1999: *Arbitron Ratings: New York, June 1999*. http://www.rronline.com/Subscribers/Ratings/Homepage.htm

Radio and Records 1999: Radio & Records Directory: Ratings, Industry Directory & Program Supplier Guide, vol. 2. Los Angeles: Radio and Records.

Radio Academy 1998: *Radio Festival Report*. London: Radio Academy.

Radio Authority 1998: *Radio Authority Pocket Book, June 1998*. London: Radio Authority.

Radio Authority 1999: *Radio Authority Pocket Book, June 1999*. London: Radio Authority.

RAJAR 1999a: *Rajar 99*. London: Radio Joint Audience Research Limited.

RAJAR 1999b: *Quarterly Summary of Radio Listening: Survey Period Ending 28th March 1999*. London: RAJAR-Ipsos-RSL.

Rehm, D. 1993: Talking Over America's Electronic Backyard Fence. *Media Studies Journal*, 7 (3), 63–9.

Ross, S. 1993: Music Radio – The Fickleness of Fragmentation. *Media Studies Journal*, 7 (3), 93–104.

Rothenbuhler, E. 1996: Commercial Radio as Communication, *Journal of Comunication*, 46 (1), 125–43.

Rothschild-Whitt, J. 1979: The Collectivist Organization: An Alternative to Rational-Bureaucratic Models. *American Sociological Review*, 44, 509–27.

Sakolsky, R. and Dunifer, S. (eds) 1998: *Seizing the Airwaves: a Free Radio Handbook*. San Francisco and Edinburgh: AK Press.

Scannell, P. 1988a: The Communicative Ethos of Broadcasting. Paper presented to the International Television Studies Conference, British Film Institute, London.

Scannell, P. 1988b: Radio Times: The Temporal Arrangements of Broadcasting in the Modern World. In P. Drummond and R. Paterson (eds), *Television and its Audience*. London: BFI, 15–31.

Scannell, P. 1991: The Relevance of Talk. In P. Scannell (ed.), *Broadcast Talk*. London: Sage, 1–13.

Scannell, P. 1996: *Radio, Television and Modern Life*. Oxford: Blackwell.

Scannell, P. 1997: Radio and the music industry in Zimbabwe. Unpublished paper, Centre for Communication and Information Studies, University of Westminster, London.

Scannell, P. and Cardiff, D. 1991: *A Social History of British Broadcasting, volume 1: 1922–1939*. Oxford: Blackwell Publishers.

Schlesinger, P. 1978: *Putting 'Reality' Together: BBC News*. London and New York: Routledge.

Schulman, M. 1988: Radio and Cultural Identity: Community and Communication in Harlem, USA. *RTV Theory and Practice*, Special Issue 3, 185–214.

Seymour-Ure, C. 1991: *The British Press and Broadcasting since 1945*. Oxford: Blackwell Publishers.

Shapley, O. 1996: *Broadcasting A Life*. London: Scarlet Press.

Shingler, M. and Wieringa, C. 1998: *On Air: Methods and Meanings in Radio*. London: Arnold.

Sieveking, L. 1934: *The Stuff of Radio*. London: Cassell.

Silverstone, R. 1985: *Framing Science: The Making of a BBC Documentary*. London: BFI.

Silvey, R. 1974: *Who's Listening?* London: George Allen and Unwin.

Smith, R. B. 1998: Absolute Talk on the Radio. *Media Studies Journal*, 12 (2), 72–9.

Smythe, D. 1977: Communications: Blindspot of Western Marxism. *Canadian Journal of Political and Social Theory*, 1 (3), 1–27.

Soley, L. 1993: Clandestine Radio and the End of the Cold War. *Media Studies Journal*, 7 (3), 129–38.

Soley, L. and Nichols, J. S. 1987: *Clandestine Radio Broadcasting: A Study of Revolutionary and Counterrevolutionary Electronic Communication*. New York: Praeger.

Sparks, C. 1998: *Communism, Capitalism, and the Mass Media*. London: Sage.

Stavitsky, A. 1993: Ear on America. *Media Studies Journal*, 7 (3), 77–92.

Stokes, M. 1994. Introduction: Ethnicity, Identity and Music. In M. Stokes (ed.), *Ethnicity, Identity and Music: The Musical Construction of Place.* Oxford: Berg, 1–27.

Stoller, P. 1989: *The Taste of Ethnographic Things.* Philadelphia: University of Pennsylvania Press.

Storr, A. 1992: *Music and the Mind.* New York: Free Press.

Synott, A. 1993: *The Body Social: Symbolism, Self and Society.* London: Routledge.

Thompson, J. B. 1995: *The Media and Modernity: A Social Theory of the Media.* Cambridge: Polity Press.

Thompson, M. 1999: Interview with Matt Thompson, Producer, Loftus Productions, 26 October 1999.

Thorn, R. 1997: Hearing is Believing: the evidence. *Sound Journal.* http://speke.ukc.ac.uk/sais/sound-journal/index.html

Tolson, A. 1991: Televised Chat and the Synthetic Personality. In P. Scannell (ed.), *Broadcast Talk.* London: Sage, 178–200.

Tran, M. 1999: Yahoo nets broadcast.com in $5.7bn multi-media deal. News report in The *Guardian,* 2 April 1999.

Trappel, J. 1997: Austria. In B. S. Østergaard (ed.), *The Media in Western Europe: The Euromedia Handbook,* 2nd edn. London: Sage, 1–16.

Troldahl, V. C. and Skolnik, R. 1968: The Meanings People have for Radio Today. *Journal of Broadcasting,* 12, 57–67.

Tusa, J. 1993: Live Broadcasting: The keynote address. In N. Miller and R. Allen (eds), *It's Live But is it Real? Proceedings of the 23rd University of Manchester Broadcasting Symposium,* London: John Libbey, 6–14.

Tyler, B. and Laing, D. 1998: *The European Radio Industry: Markets and Players,* 2nd edn. London: Financial Times.

UKDRFN 1998: *UK Digital Radio Forum Newsletter,* Issue no. 4, July 1998.

Valentine, C. A. and Saint Damian, B. 1988: Gender and culture as determinants of the 'ideal voice'. *Semiotica* 71, 3 (4), 285–303.

Wall, T. 1999: The Meanings of Black and Dance Music in Contemporary Music Radio. Paper delivered to Third Triennial British Musicological Societies' Conference, University of Surrey, Guildford, July 1999.

Wallis, R. and Malm, K. 1990: Patterns of Change. In S. Frith and A. Goodwin (eds), *On Record: Rock, Pop, and the Written Word.* London and New York: Routledge, 160–80.

Wallis, R. and Malm, K. 1993: From State Monopoly to Commercial Oligopoly. European Broadcasting Policies and Popular Music Output Over the Airwaves. In T. Bennett, S. Frith, L. Grossberg, J. Shephard and G. Turner (eds), *Rock and Popular Music: Politics, Policies, Institutions.* London and New York: Routledge, 156–68.

Weintraub, N. T. 1971: Some Meanings Radio has for Teenagers. *Journal of Broadcasting,* 15, 147–52.

White, I. 1998: Auntie Catches Up with the Net. News report in *Broadcast,* 20 February 1998.

Wilby, P. and Conroy, A. 1994: *The Radio Handbook.* London and New York: Routledge.

Williams, R. 1974: *Television: Technology and Cultural Form.* London: Fontana.

Williams, R. 1983: *Towards 2000*. London: Hogarth Press.

Winston, B. 1998: *Media Technology and Society: A History, from the Telegraph to the Internet*. London and New York: Routledge.

Wolfe, K. 1984: *The Churches and the British Broadcasting Corporation, 1922–1956*. London: SCM Press.

Woolf, M. and Holly, S. 1994: *Radio Survey: Employment Patterns and Training Needs 1993/4*. London: Skillset.

World DAB Forum 1998: *Country Progress Reports, July 1998*. London: World DAB Forum.

Index